MW00399043

one
and
one
make
three

To Doris, our long
(but not old) friend,
Joseph Fabry

April 16, 1989

one and one make three

STORY OF A FRIENDSHIP

PETER FABRIZIUS

(MAX KNIGHT
JOSEPH FABRY)

• BENMIR •

בּ

Book Design by Wolfgang Lederer
Editorial Consultant: Carol Talpers
Technical Consultant: Marla Wilson
Printed in the United States by Braun-Brumfield, Inc.

ISBN 0-917883-03-9

For Wendy and Otto

Contents

The
Old World

The
New World

Foreword

This is a multi-layered book—an adventure story of two survivors in a killer world; the saga of what friendship can accomplish; and an account of how one's potentials can develop under the blows of cruel reality.

The richness of this "duography" should not have surprised me. "Peter Fabrizius" has been a living legend to me most of my life. When I grew up in Vienna in the 1930s, one of the two newspapers I read daily was the *Telegraf*, whose short-story page frequently printed the yarns of Peter Fabrizius, with their many settings and colorful subjects. I learned only much later that these entertaining stories were written by two persons. Peter Fabrizius was the joint pseudonym of two doctors of law, Max Eugen Kühnel and Josef Epstein, later Max Knight and Joe Fabry. I was delighted with the whimsy, wit, and unexpected twists at the end, which often contained or implied a moral that even young people could appreciate.

Two decades later, in the 1950s, I had the pleasure of reading some Peter Fabrizius stories with my students in Clair Hayden Bell's editions (which first revealed to me the meaning of the authors' motto One and One Make Three). The canny Professor Bell described Peter as "one of those rare authors who walk on four legs." Having enjoyed also their edition of three comedies of the inimitable Johann Nepomuk Nestroy ("translated and fondly tampered with" by Joe and Max, according to the title page), I invited them to contribute their version of a more tragic play to a Karl Kraus reader I edited a dozen years ago.

For many years now I have carried on a lively correspondence with Max and a more sporadic one with Joe, but I have never met either man—an absurd and untenable situation that will, I hope, be remedied by the time these remarks appear in print.

Joseph Fabry and Max Knight have chosen to tell the life story of "Peter Fabrizius," with first-person chapters by each, Max and Joe, alternating with third-person accounts by their joint *alter ego* Peter; this makes for an uncommonly lively stereoscopic presentation with a unique shifting perspective that brings out the author's (or authors') "multility" (a term that has been coined for the mercurial Heinrich Heine). The account of the authors' youth in Vienna is a worthy companion to the autobiographies of such other former Viennese as Joseph Wechsberg, Richard Berczeller, George Clare, Edmund Schechter, and Robert Starer. But this book properly gives pride of place to their life in America, which makes it a heart-warming and inspiring American success story. Those people who had to flee from Nazi Austria after the Anschluss became known as "thirty-eighters," a term created in analogy to the "forty-eighters" who came to America after the abortive 1848 revolutions in Germany and Austria (and in some cases became "forty-niners" when they heard that there was gold in California). Well, what do two spirited thirty-eighters add up to? The spirit of seventy-six, of course.

W. H. Auden diagnosed our century as the "age of anxiety." I would be more specific and call it the century of the (physically and psychologically) displaced person, because in our time upheaval, uprooting, exile, and worse have been the lot of millions. In this sense the lives of Joe and Max are truly exemplary. Before they were privileged to enjoy the freedom and opportunities of this country, the authors were fated to experience the uncertainties and face the perils of an emigration that separated them for the first time since their meeting in law school. Even before the Anschluss, the two men had succeeded in having their stories published in England. Max became the "first swallow" to reach England and, unlike Joe, was able to help his parents reach a safe haven. After Joe's release from a Belgian detention camp, the friends were reunited in London and continued their unique mutual-support system, each developing an "ability to become a successful refugee who saw shipwreck as a challenge to build a new life." The two men repeatedly displayed true grit as well as true wit, and in their attempts to "survive chaos, uprooting, and loss of values" their *chutzpah* often stood them in good stead. In an effort to obtain the guarantees for his parents required by the British government as a condition for admission to England, Max left no stone unturned in London, finding a way of approaching such unapproachable men as the Baron de Rothschild and Lord Winterton—although with very uneven results. Ignoring their own ignorance and playing an "as if" game, Max obtained a job on the Manchurian and Chinese desks of the U.S. Office of War Information, and Joe parlayed minimal experience as a California gardener into work as an agricultural expert that ultimately led to a twenty-five-year editorship of agricultural publications for the University of California. Time and time again the friends charmed Dame Fortune (or Lady Luck) into smiling on them—eventually, anyway. In all vicissitudes Peter Fabrizius was their good fairy or guardian angel. This *nom de plume* became a *nom de guerre* when the authors' pens, singly and jointly, had to be tools for survival.

Joe arrived in Boston in the spring of 1940 (a few months before I did), but Max, obliged to wait until his immigration quota "matured," had to undertake a long voyage, from England via Canada and Japan, to Shanghai (where he became an English teacher and found his beginning students at Downtown University clamoring for Shakespeare!). Readers will not soon forget Max's account of his torment of Tantalus (or *crise de conscience*) when he found himself, en route to the Far East, on the Canadian side of Niagara Falls, and entry into the United States with the holiday crowds seemed to be his for the faking. But the Peter Fabrizius "duography" is, among other things, the eminently ethical story of how emigrants become immigrants, and Max preferred not to become too quiet an invader (*The Quiet Invaders: The Story of the Austrian Impact Upon America* being the title of a book by E. Wilder Spaulding in which he and Joe are listed).

As a small child I heard the United States described as "*das Land der unbegrenzten Möglichkeiten.*" Peter Fabrizius must have thought of it that way, too, for in this book we read that "America truly was the land of unlimited opportunities." After Max had reached this country, and before and after he and Joe were sworn in as American citizens (together, of course), the friends engaged in various "ladder-building" activities and did not allow a number of temporary occupations ("beam boy," janitor, shipfitter, etc.) to deflect them from their literary aspirations. They have written an uplifting chapter in the generally sad saga of refugee writers in the United States. Thomas Mann, Bertolt Brecht, Erich Maria Remarque, and Lion Feuchtwanger already had a sizable American readership when they came to these shores, but the lot of most others was frustrating hack work at best and destitution and desperation at worst. Even though the "short short story" had been originated by an American (W. S. Porter, known as O. Henry), Joe and Max discovered that there no longer was much interest in their literary specialty—their kind of finely spun, lighthearted tale with a surprise ending that they had published in fourteen languages in thirty-nine countries—and that "Peter Fabrizius could not be naturalized." Still, at least half his name was preserved in Joe's new American name, and his initials lived on in Pacific Features, the feature story and news agency through which the friends presented the peaceful face of the American West to the world. Their multifarious and wide-ranging freelancing activities as factfinders, feature writers, broadcasters, and translators are detailed in this book, as is their long tenures on the editorial staffs of the University of California at Berkeley. When they retired from these positions, Max took the University Press home, as it were, continuing to write, edit, translate, and run writing workshops. It must have given him great satisfaction to translate a seminal work work by his former Viennese legal mentor, Hans Kelsen (*The Pure Theory of Law*) and to publish (first in private printing, then commercially) *The Original Blue Danube Cookbook*, containing the treasured recipes of his mother. Joe, having revisited Vienna in 1965 as a sort of Ripp von Winkel (whereas Max preferred a "return to the Alps," the title of his mountain book), started a new career as the chief American spokesman of Viktor Frankl and the interpreter of his logotherapy ("health through meaning"), writing and lecturing widely on existential psychology and presiding over an institute and even a press. When Joe published his book *The Pursuit of Meaning* in 1968, he realized that "for the first time in our lives, Max and I were writing in different fields."

Despite having been on the same wavelength and having sustained a friendship for more than a half-century, Joe and Max are no Tweedledum and Tweedledee, no tandem talkers like Koby and Loby in Dürrenmatt's *The Visit*. When Joe and his wife ("a female Max") decided to transcend the faith of their fathers and become active members of the Unitarian Church (in contrast to Max's "religion of nature"), "Peter Fabrizius passed the test" and the friends continued on their "long and battle- tested path," ultimately a "duoquest" rather than a "uniquest" (the title of Joe's magazine). Their lifelong loyalty reminds one of Schiller's ballad *Die Bürgschaft,* which assures us that "friendship is not an empty delusion."

Today each author is a late-septuagenarian patriarch, each presiding over a colorful clan, following his own "retirement" interest, separate but equally rooted in the soil of their life-long friendship that made Peter live on long after Joe and Max helped each other discover their individual uniqueness.

Brandeis University   Harry Zohn
Waltham, Massachusetts
September 1987

Preface

When we decided to write a shared autobiography—Joe and Max using a shared pen name, Peter Fabrizius—our chosen title *One and One Make Three* was a measurable fact: the sum of what we jointly accomplished was more than the sum of what each of us would have accomplished alone.

When we discussed the book we discovered that this mathematically unsound formula had sound human applications for any twosome. Max had discovered gifts in Joe that Joe didn't know he had, and vice versa, and we have helped each other come closer to our potentials than each of us would have been able by himself. That this occurred in the pressure-cooker atmosphere of flight from Hitlerism and of war may have brought the result into sharper focus, but it could happen between any two people living in this brutal century. Each reader will have to decide what the ingredients of this cooperation are for each relationship.

Although Max and Joe come from the same background, we have different personalities. Max sees reality as presenting problems that must be addressed and, if possible, solved before they get out of hand. Joe sees reality as benevolent; problems exist but have positive elements on which to focus. This combination of world views worked well in our flight (it is doubtful that each of us would have survived without the other), but in the secure haven of Berkeley our individual personalities surfaced. As we put the pieces of our lives together, we grew in different directions. This did not impair but test our friendship. Each of us leads his own life, but we continue to have common interests and memories. Joe and Max still make Peter.

Because this is a story of friendship, rather than a comprehensive biographical statement, we have discussed our families and friends only to the extent that they related to the Peter Fabrizius part of ourselves. The stories of Max and Joe as husbands, fathers, and grandfathers would be material for two other unequal equations.

P. F.

The
Old World

———

* 1 *

Peaks, Abysses, and "Ahas"

1909–1931

JOE

When I was almost sixty and thought I knew myself pretty well, I participated in an encounter group. Each of us was given a large piece of paper and a set of color crayons, and told to "draw your life." Dutifully I started at the lower left corner with a rising line, indicating a happy childhood surrounded by parents, family, friends. The line kept rising during my years of college and the start of my writing career, and came to an abrupt stop when Hitler annexed my native Austria in 1938. I marked the Nazi invasion with a large orange bolt of lightning, sending my lifeline tumbling down to the bottom of the sheet. My line began to recover when I met my future wife in New York, we married, had children, and I found work to support my new family. In 1948 we discovered the First Unitarian Church of Berkeley, a marvelously supportive group of people who helped me come to grips with my shattered past. My lifeline took a steep upturn—raising our children, growing roots in California, working as an editor for the University of California. In the early sixties, the line flattened again—the children had grown, the job was stale, the midlife crisis had struck. Then, in 1963, another turning point: my daughter Wendy gave me Viktor Frankl's *Man's Search for Meaning*, which focused my attention on a meaningful future and led to a retirement career.

I

When I looked at my drawing, I was puzzled that I had drawn the Nazi blitz, the Unitarian Church, and the book by Dr. Frankl the same orange color. What could this abyss and the two peaks have in common? Then I had an "aha" flash: all three had been decisive growth experiences. The Nazi invasion pushed me out of the nest, the Unitarian Church encouraged me to venture beyond the treetops, and Frankl's meaning-oriented logotherapy challenged me to soar.

I took my drawing home to study it further. The three "orange events" were three new beginnings, but others, too, showed up along my zigzagging lifeline. You don't have to be a cat to have nine lives, nor be born a Hindu to experience reincarnation. I was born November 6, 1909, and my physical birthday meant much to me when I was a child; it means little now. I remember the annual birthday celebrations when some twenty members of the family gathered for cake and coffee, gifts, and love. I was born again on September 9, 1938, when I left the womb of my home in Vienna, my family, my country, my tradition and security. It was a violent birth, Hitler as midwife. I remember the train pulling out of the railroad station, my parents standing on the platform. When the train started moving, my father's face shattered like a window pane, and I knew that a life had ended, though not that another had begun.

A third birth took place February 12, 1943, when my first child, Wendy, was born. I remember my first glimpse through the nursery window, her face pink and wrinkled, her eyes closed. Suddenly one of her eyes opened and she looked straight at me, and I knew, not in my head but in my gut, that I was in charge, of my life and that of this helpless infant. This little creature pushed me into a new life of responsibility. The umbilical cord for both of us had been severed.

My fourth birth, also orange in the drawing, was in September of 1948. My wife and I heard about an inspiring minister, J. Raymond Cope, and we were looking for inspiration. My life-shattering experience had made me a skeptic. What could religion do? It was my Jewishness that had caused my troubles. I remember my discomfort in church, a term I associated with "the others," the anti-Semites, the threat. The minister's robe, the hymns, made me

2

feel even more uncomfortable. Then the minister spoke and my life connected. He spoke of the Judeo-Christian tradition, of the word *religio* meaning "I bind together," which I should have known after eight years of highschool Latin. But my discovery was not intellectual—I knew that here was a way to overcome the past. For the first time since losing my family I felt part of the web of life. I came to be accepted in the church family, and gained a glimpse of a larger family outside.

My fifth birth took place in November, 1963, when I heard Dr. Viktor Frankl speak in San Francisco. I had read his book, and I remember the small man wildly gesturing as he spoke—another peak. Here was a psychiatrist and philosopher from my own University of Vienna, who stated clearly what I had groped for so painfully: that life has meaning and that it is up to us to find it. It was a challenge, and I wanted to know more. He promised to send me his untranslated writings, and did—twenty books.

My sixth birth came March, 1968, when my own book, *The Pursuit of Meaning*, was published. It was my declaration of personal and literary independence. I remember sitting behind a microphone of a call-in radio show and being introduced as an "expert" in helping people find meaning in life. I might have panicked, but didn't. I know now that I drew strength from all my other lives— having outlived the Nazi experience, the groping, skepticism, meaninglessness. I answered the incoming calls, wondering all the time: Is that *me* encouraging others? I acted *as if* I were the expert people thought I was and, deep within, I knew I could be.

My seventh birth was retirement from university work in May, 1972: I entered the delightful world of mastery over my own time. I explored, with a child's thrill of discovery, new areas of adventures—presenting lectures and workshops, creating an institute of logotherapy, editing its journal, teaching, training, sponsoring international congresses and, what I find most gratifying, helping people in crises. It was the birth of a new, self-confident person, yet I was aware that within I was still shy and groping.

If I can do as well as a cat I still have two lives left, and I am curious where they will lead.

In review, I see my life has gaps—stretches for which I have no recollections or only hazy ones. I do not believe the gaps represent

3

repressed traumas that have to be dug up and reexamined. I believe that one of nature's greatest gifts is our ability to forget.

But another of nature's gifts is memory. What we remember is significant, even if it concerns seemingly insignificant events. My earliest memories are three little fragments. I see them clearly although I was only four and five when they happened. More important than the visual recollection, however, is the revival of feeling that comes with them.

I see myself walking with my father down the street where I was to live for twenty-five years. We had moved from the apartment where I was born to a new place only a few blocks away. My mother went with the moving van and our furniture. My father and I walked. It's just a vignette—holding his hand, trying to keep up my steps. I clearly remember my feelings: a little sadness at having lost my old home but, much more, curiosity about what the new home would be like. Here was the first expression of a character trait that kept me going through all the migrations as a refugee and immigrant, from country to country, place to place, until I grew new roots in California.

My second memory is also of my father. His mother had died, and I see us walking down the staircase in our apartment building to go to the funeral. (I have no recollection of the funeral itself.) He was ahead, and again I was trying to keep up. His father had died before I was born. I hear myself say: "Now you don't have a daddy or a mommy." He answered: "Yes, but I have you. You must be a good boy." What a declaration of love—to be able to replace both a daddy and a mommy! But what responsibility! I felt proud and a bit scared.

The third memory is related to the second, although quite different. I had a personal nursemaid, Mina, a woman in her seventies. At first Mina had been hired by various family members to take care of newborn babies until their mothers recovered. My parents decided to keep Mina, although no more babies were expected in our family, because she was too old to look for new employment. (She stayed with us until her death, when I was sixteen, and greatly spoiled me; my wife still complains that I expect her to find buttons to be sewed on and suits to be checked for spots.) During my preschool days Mina walked with me to the park,

4

carrying a little folding seat on which she sat while I played. One day she fainted. When she recovered, *I* took *her* home, carrying the folding chair. I remember my feeling of achievement. Looking back I see again the values of love and responsibility. Love enveloped me from childhood on, sustaining me during periods of trial. The feeling of responsibility lay dormant until wakened by baby Wendy looking at me with her first glance. Responsibility has been a guiding value ever since.

Our Vienna family was tightly knit, some thirty people living within easy reach by streetcar. An inner circle of about a dozen met twice a week in homes and coffeehouses to chat and play cards. The entire family met on birthdays and holidays, especially on New Year's Eve, a major festivity. At that time family events of the year were reviewed through songs, sketches, and satirical poetry. We wrote, composed, practiced for weeks, made costumes and simple scenery. My mother had a knack for making costumes out of discarded clothing; my part, when I was a teenager, was writing and performing. Little incidents, achievements, misunderstandings, mistakes became material for our annual performances. Some sayings, wise (intentionally or not) or funny, became part of the family folklore, told and retold like Greek myths or Bible stories. I remember Aunt Helen's phrase, "Bad luck isn't sent by God," and my mother's innocent remark when the talk was about snoring: "I sleep quietly—they all say so."

My parents' generation was the first in our family to rise from merchants to become officials and academics. My father, Ernst Epstein, was director of the municipal storehouses of the city of Vienna, my uncle an official in the Ministry of Justice. There was a short time of opportunity for Jews in Vienna. One generation later—my own—and, even in pre-Hitler fascist Austria, government careers were closed.

My mother was thirty-eight when I was born; she had tried for seven years to have a child. My cousin Arthur told me only a few years ago of an episode that illustrates the affection with which my entire family surrounded me. He had received his first suit with long pants on his thirteenth birthday. He was to wear that suit for his bar mitzvah ceremony, the traditional Jewish ritual of admission to adulthood. He proudly presented himself to the family gathered

5

at the occasion of my birth. No one paid attention to him and his suit. Everybody admired the new baby. It took him years to forgive me, if he ever did. He was eighty when he told me, and he remembered it vividly.

My parents' love carried me through childhood and adolescence into adulthood. I still float securely in it. When I first visited Israel and floated in the Dead Sea, a warm feeling of happiness flooded through me. It reminded me of my parents' support. It was impossible to sink.

Of the many instances of my parents' love and wisdom, two examples stand out in my memory. When I was ten we visited Kuttenplan, the village in Czechoslovakia where my father was born. The Jews of the village had all moved to Vienna, Prague, and other cities. The Jewish cemetery had been closed for years, and we had to get a key to open the wrought-iron gate. The gravestones were overgrown with brambles. Eventually we found the grave of my great-grandparents. Big, juicy strawberries grew on it, and I eagerly sampled them. My parents did not stop me. Only much later did I marvel at their good sense, letting a little boy eat fruit nourished by the dust of his ancestors. Much of my attitude toward death, and of my security, my feeling of being part of a web of life, came from that experience.

The second example occurred much later. I was twenty, still living at home and financially dependent on my parents. Into my life came Myra and my first sexual encounter. I told my mother that Myra and I wanted to go away for an Easter weekend; she understood, and gave me money for the trip.

Actually my parents appreciated Myra's introducing me to the mysteries they were not prepared to discuss. They went to the coffeehouse on Sunday afternoons, knowing well that our apartment became a trysting place during that time. Later on things became "official." Myra waited until they came home, and we all had dinner and chatted. This was unusual in prudish Freudian Vienna, and in a family with traditional values. But, in more than one way, "love conquered all."

My parents' caring also had negative consequences. I was overprotected. My father's brother had died of pneumonia. His illness and death were blamed on the fact that he had cooled off after a

6

dance by taking a cold drink. I never was allowed to drink anything when I was the least bit warm, and had to hold a handkerchief against my nose when stepping out on the street on a cold night. In spite of such coddlings I did survive when pushed from my warm surroundings into the cold world.

My eight high-school years were uneventful. I did what was expected but no more. I see myself as inconspicuous. Our Latin teacher divided the class into "good students" who prepared the translation of the Latin texts, and "bad students" who were tested by being asked to repeat what others had translated. I was the only student in a class of twenty-two in neither group. I slipped by unnoticed. I could sit in a streetcar and the conductor hardly ever checked my ticket. I went to a dancing school, and few girls noticed me when it came to ladies' choice. I had no interest in joining a sports club or political youth movement. Several of my classmates were members of (illegal) Nazi youth groups. One classmate was a member of the Socialist youth movement; we once had a serious talk, and he wanted me to join. I said, "What does my life have to do with politics?" He replied, "How do you imagine your life *without* politics?" I didn't know what he was talking about until much later, after 1938.

My great passion was the theater. I went to a play at least once a week. I read plays, reviews of plays, books about plays. I still recall many productions and can name their casts. To me the most unforgettable production was *Cyrano de Bergerac*. I identified with that man whose big nose ruined his amorous chances, so that he had to find vicarious fulfillment through a handsome and stupid rival. I look at old photos and know that my "big nose" was in my mind— but its effect on me was real.

My preoccupation with the theater resulted in my hobby of collecting autographs. It began in an odd way. At fifteen, I was too shy to walk up to famous people and ask for their signatures. My cousin Arthur, a reporter, went to press conferences, including one held by Pietro Mascagni, who was in Vienna to conduct a giant outdoor performance of Aida in the city's largest soccer stadium. I asked Arthur to get me Mascagni's autograph. He later gave me a slip of paper bearing Mascagni's signature. Thus began a happy and long-lasting hunting trip. Several years later Mascagni came to

7

Vienna again, and I got a second autograph. It looked completely different. I confronted my cousin, who confessed he had faked the signature, perhaps to get even with me for distracting attention from his new suit when I was born. In the meantime I had become an enthusiastic autograph hunter, shyness thrown to the winds when it came to haunting strangers in their homes, on the streets, in hotels, at railroad stations, and of course at stage doors. My fondest memory is of sneaking upstairs in the Hotel Bristol, one of Vienna's most elegant, after eavesdropping at the reception desk to learn the room number of Rabindranath Tagore. The door of his room was wide open and Tagore, serene and white-bearded, sat on the floor watching intently a bouquet of flowers in a vase beside him. I didn't have the heart to disturb him, and waited a few minutes while he observed a little worm on one of the flowers. He finally noticed me, waved me in, and signed my autograph book in Bengali. This episode came back fifty years later when I saw my two-year-old granddaughter watch an insect in the grass with the same concentration. The wisdom of poets and children!

The second consequence of my preoccupation with the theater opened a world of fantasy to me. In my imagination I was everything I was not in real life: Romeo the lover, Peer Gynt the adventurer, Cyrano the dashing swordsman, Faust the bargainer with the devil. I had always read avidly, and now my heroes were flesh and blood on stage. My favorite books were *Robinson Crusoe* and Jules Verne's *Mysterious Island*. These two books seem to have foreshadowed my ability to become a successful refugee who saw shipwreck as a challenge to build a new life.

My interest in books and plays kindled my wish to write, and that was stimulated further by my German teacher, Josef Lesowski, the only high-school teacher who left an imprint on me. We had to write an essay about Schiller's drama *Don Carlos*. I wrote a playlet in which Schiller, Goethe, and characters from *Don Carlos* met in heaven and discussed their ideas. It was my first attempt at playwriting, and teacher Lesowski read it to the class. Although I was embarrassed I felt encouraged to go on with writing.

Mostly I wrote poems, all lost and forgotten, except one. We read Horace in Latin, and I translated one ode into German. The boy who sat next to me snatched it from me and read it aloud in class

8

during our Latin lesson. There was good-natured kidding by my classmates, but at least they noticed me. They dated girls, won prizes in tennis and skiing, and participated in political demonstrations, but I was a "poet" (always in quotation marks)—naive, impractical, odd, unsuccessful in the things that counted. I proved them right by writing a novel and a play, neither ever published or performed.

I had one classmate, Fritz Fleischer, with whom I shared my secret ambitions, and who in fact was co-author of my early play. Together with another classmate, Harry Freud (Sigmund Freud's nephew), we formed a threesome that lasted through college and emigration. The Freud family met every Sunday in the home of the Freud matriarch, Harry's grandmother, Sigmund's mother. Every Monday, Harry came to school with a selection of jokes that his uncle had told. When I was fifteen, I knew Sigmund Freud only as Harry's uncle who seemed to have an unlimited supply of good jokes. I didn't know that Freud had written a famous book on the psychology of wit. Later Harry took me to his uncle's house for hot chocolate and cake. Several of Harry's aunts were present, Mrs. Freud was hostess, and the professor made a brief appearance, for coffee and cake. Then he made a formal little bow toward us and said, "If the young gentlemen will excuse me, I have some work to do," and disappeared through a door that led to his consultation room. I knew by then that he was some kind of doctor, and that patients, including princesses and even kings, came to Vienna to see him, but I didn't know what psychoanalysis was. His consultation room was off limits to me except on one unforgettable occasion, which I have not seen described in the Freud literature.

Freud took daily walks with his dog Jofi in Vienna's large park, the Prater. He would hire a *fiaker* (a two-horse carriage) to go to the park, take his walk, and then take another *fiaker* back home. One day Jofi chased a rabbit, and Freud spent an hour looking for the dog. He eventually gave up and came home, just as Harry and I arrived for a snack. There was a great commotion, and Freud was told that Jofi had returned by himself. Jofi knew where Freud hired a *fiaker*, the drivers recognized the dog, and one of them had brought him home. When Freud arrived, we paced through the whole apartment, including Freud's consultation and waiting rooms, looking for the "bad dog." This is when I saw the famous couch (but only realized its significance years later). As Harry reported, with the humor characteristic of the Freud family: now Jofi was the dog "you don't walk—he takes a *fiaker.*"

Our threesome went on to study law. Fritz Fleischer was a brilliant student, and without Hitler's intervention would no doubt have become a successful lawyer. Harry was to take over his father's *Tarif-Anzeiger*, a renowned journal on tariff questions, for which a legal background was desirable. I was to enter my uncle's practice as a tax consultant. This prospect had little appeal, but it never occurred to me to protest seriously. I always did what my parents decided, always "for my own good." My ambition to become a writer only elicited smiles. I had been living in a dream world; it was time to enter reality.

I met reality right after high-school graduation when I became a part-time apprentice to my uncle Hugo Benedikt, while I was attending the university. Austria's tax system demanded that taxpayers submit a detailed statement of income to the Ministry of Justice. One of its officials reviewed the statement and automatically doubled the estimated income. Since the taxpayer knew that this would happen, he sent in an estimate of about half his real income, and in the end all came out about even. Usually a certain amount of haggling occurred during an auditing session. When I accompanied my uncle to learn how this was done, I was witness to a humiliating spectacle. The officials were self-important, arrogant bureaucrats who treated my uncle as if he were a cheat representing cheaters (which was true, because cheating was built into the Austrian tax system). My uncle was one of my unachievable role models—tall, handsome, a ladies' man, successful, self-confident. But during the audit I saw him cajole and grovel, trying to get some concessions out of these pre-Hitler anti-Semites who didn't yet kill, only humiliated. This was the reality I was about to enter.

Attendance at the university was at best boring, and often dangerous. The professors read their lectures in a monotonous voice, from a script. They never looked up—certainly not when, occasionally, a Nazi student beat up one of his Jewish colleagues. Under the abused privilege of academic freedom, the Vienna University was off limits to the police. The Nazi students took advantage of this. I escaped injury because of my ability to remain unnoticed, but my friend Fritz Fleischer was severely beaten up. This, too, was reality.

One day, in a class on German law, a number of students wearing armbands with the illegal swastika entered the classroom shouting: *Juden raus!* (Jews out!). Professor Voltelini stopped his lecture and silently, probably approvingly, watched the Jewish students leave. In the hallway a crowd of Nazi students formed a narrow path through which we had to run the gauntlet. They pushed and kicked us from one side to the other, enjoying themselves loudly. They achieved their goal, at least so far as Fleischer, Freud, and I were concerned. After that day, instead of going to class we went to cram courses. Some enterprising go-getters had been taking notes and used them to teach courses privately—for a juicy fee, of course—in a more interesting way than that of the professors. They also knew what questions were asked and what answers expected at the orals. This was important because on some subjects professors held different views, and one could flunk you for answers his colleague would praise. One professor, Othmar Spann, invented new words and incomprehensible definitions. The cram class was so efficient that I passed his exam without understanding what I was saying.

In one of these cram classes I first saw Max, but I don't think we spoke to each other there.

In the summer of 1932, Uncle Hugo took me to Semmering, a spa near Vienna, and we stayed in one of the large hotels. Max was staying in the same hotel as tutor to the owner's two boys. We recognized each other. One evening after dinner, we went up to the hotel's roof terrace, and talked for a long time. It was the beginning of a lifelong friendship.

* 2 *

Romantic Lad
and Stupid Idiot

1909–1931

MAX

When I was born as Max Kühnel in the benign Austria of Francis Joseph, the cherries were ripe, and cherry time has ever since been birthday time for me. The peace that blessed the world then was reflected in our serene and secure home in Vienna. My father had a permanent position—ironic in view of what happened in the thirties—as vice-president in the *Wiener Bankverein*, later merged with the *Credit-Anstalt*. Later he worked at the Stock Exchange as a stockbroker (an official position in Vienna, assumed under oath).

He married my mother, Margarethe Hoffer, daughter of a grain dealer, on September 20, 1908. I was born on June 8, 1909.

When I was old enough to figure it out, I was delighted that I was a wedding-night child. Years later I passed by Venice in a cruise ship and saw the Hotel Royal Danieli in the piazza, where my parents spent their honeymoon, the place where I was conceived.

I was a wanted child. Throughout my protected childhood the feeling of being wanted and loved was pervasive. I took my security for granted and it formed a firm basis for my life.

My parents came from small villages in the German-speaking part of what is now Czechoslovakia. My maternal grandfather was well off, my paternal grandfather a very poor trader who died early and left my teenage father to help support his mother. To establish historical perspective: When my father was born, one hundred years after the Declaration of Independence, Queen Victoria ruled in England and Ulysses S. Grant was president of the United States, then thirty-seven states. Airplanes, automobiles, electric lights were dreams of science-fiction, not to mention radio and television.

My father told me that his family was so poor that when he was a child, an egg would be a birthday gift for him. But when I was seven or eight years old and my mother asked me on one occasion just before dinner whether I was hungry, I did not know what she was talking about. I was never hungry.

My father made good, and, although we did not live in luxury, I never lacked anything I needed. As was customary in middle-class families in Vienna in the opening years of the century, we had a live-in maid and also a cook in our apartment. The maid looked after me when my mother was busy, and was like a second mother to me.

My earliest recollection dates back to when I was three and a half years old. I see myself in my crib in my dark bedroom in the evening, standing up against the bars that protected me from falling out, and being restless because nobody was paying me any attention although I was not yet asleep. That was most unusual. The next room was my parents' bedroom. The door was closed but I could see some light through the crack at the base of the door and I heard a lot of bustle inside. It was 10 P.M., as I later learned when the door opened, and I was told that I had a little brother, Otto. My mother was in bed because the stork had bitten her on the leg.

At a very tender age I learned from my father to appreciate nature. He took me regularly on Sunday hikes in the Vienna Woods, usually with my mother and relatives and friends. I rejoiced in anticipation when I saw him on Sunday morning getting into his hiking outfit, and knew we soon would be strolling in the woods or relaxing on a meadow. I was not yet five when I was initiated into the wonders of Vienna's "house mountain," Rax, and my father patiently told me the names of the beautiful Alpine flowers. These trips made a lasting impression, foreshadowing many experiences in later life.

At age six I started grade school in the place where Franz Schubert was once a schoolteacher. When I was seven, the maid came into my parents' bedroom with tears in her eyes and the morning paper in her hand; it had a black border: Francis Joseph was dead. The "peace emperor" had died in the middle of World War I, in 1916.

Friends of the family, who owned a store in the street through which the funeral was scheduled to pass, invited us to watch. I felt no particular sorrow about the emperor's demise, but felt the solemnity of the occasion when the horse-drawn hearse passed, followed on foot by kings walking in shiny plumed helmets.

Later in that year, near Christmas, with snow in the streets, an episode occurred that in retrospect I realize was a personal milestone. The maid was taking me on my daily evening walk, holding my hand. Suddenly I tore loose and insisted on going home in a hurry. I said I had something in my head that I had to write down. Puzzled, the maid complied. At home, lying on my stomach over a red-velvet rug on a couch, I penciled tall, careful Gothic letters into a lined school notebook. This was a poem about soldiers who were freezing and dying on the battlefield. When the poem was finished, I was no longer interested and left the sheet where it was. It was my first literary production.

Years later I found that sheet in my mother's desk, together with a clipping from a Viennese women's magazine, *Die Frau und Mutter*. The poem had been printed in that magazine next to an announcement that it had won the first prize in a contest, "How Does the Child See the War?" My mother had entered the poem which, the clipping said, was the only one that showed compassion for the soldiers and awareness of the misery, while the others glorified uniforms, marching military bands, waving flags, and generals on horseback. I still have the original.

There was nothing surprising about my writing a poem. It was a tradition in the family for Father to put together some verses on my mother's birthday and have me and my brother memorize and, flowers in hand, recite them. He produced poems on other family occasions—no masterpieces, but they jingled neatly in the *Herz/Schmerz* manner. Since my mother's birthday was in late November (the same day as my brother's), perhaps the idea of doing a poem was with me on that winter evening.

I remember the last year of the First World War. Food was

scarce. The bread tasted terrible and crumbled because it contained sawdust.

Our maid took my little brother and me to the countryside to fatten us up on her parents' farm in Moravia. They had such treasures as milk, butter, and eggs. I remember soldiers coming by our house and collecting household objects made of copper, needed for the war. Patriotic citizens gave up their golden wedding bands in exchange for iron rings inscribed: I Gave Gold for Iron. I saw lines of Russian war prisoners in long heavy cloaks and fur hats emerging from trains at a railroad station in mid-town. My mother's brother, Uncle Siegfried, a private in the Austrian army who lived in Prague, visited us on leave and impressed me with his rifle. (After the war he hung up this rifle in his living room as a souvenir. Twenty years later, when the Nazis occupied Czechoslovakia and their security head in Prague, Reinhard Heydrich, was assassinated by Czech patriots, the Nazis found that rifle. The penalty for the possession of weapons was death. Uncle Siegfried was put against the wall of Pankrac Prison in Prague and shot.)

Shortly after the war, we children were taken from school to a nearby barracks for "official" feeding—the same barracks in which, twenty years later, my father would be imprisoned by the Nazis. We were fed large mugs of cocoa, mush, and a large dumpling, courtesy of President Hoover of the United States of America. The food was nourishing but we did not like the hard and tasteless dumplings, and many children stuffed them secretly in their backpacks (we were not supposed to leave anything on our plates). Soon the relief workers found out and checked the packs as the children were leaving. I did not care for the dumpling either, and so I stuck it between my pack and my back, the backpack holding the hard ball in place for the short moment of backpack inspection.

One day we were called to the school gym, which served as an auditorium, and were told that the war was over, that we no longer had a kaiser but were a republic. The director of the school talked a lot more but it made little impression on me.

It was at about that time that a short episode occurred whose impact I did not grasp until years later. A schoolmate had visited me for an hour's play and left. An uncle, just coming in as the boy left, asked me:

"Was that a Jewish boy?"

It seemed a fatuous question to me. "I don't know," I said. "What's the difference? That's not important."

I'll never forget the expression on my uncle's face, as he lowered his head and said: "It is very important, my child."

The way he said it made me look up. I felt the gravity of the brief exchange, though I did not understand why. "Jewish" didn't mean anything to me. I did not have a religious upbringing; my parents did not observe the traditions. They chose their friends—as I indeed chose mine—with no thought of their affiliations.

I did not realize that, regardless of how I defined myself, the world had placed me in a particular camp. I would find out.

In 1919, at age ten, I entered high school. One morning, my brother Otto, who was still in grade school, jumped up from the breakfast table. He had just remembered that a homework composition was due that morning. When he told me that his assignment was to describe a policeman, I said I would dictate the whole piece to him because I had been given the same assignment when in grade school and I remembered pretty well what I had written. "You'll get a good grade," I said. I had received an A.

He came home angry. He had received an F and was the subject of ridicule, besides. I had described the uniform of our Viennese policemen at the time of the monarchy—peaked helmets, dark-blue frocks, tasseled sabers—whereas in the republic the police wore flat caps and an entirely different uniform. I hadn't thought of that, only remembered my former homework. This was my first literary disaster affecting my brother.

The high school I had entered was the eight-year, classics-oriented *gymnasium*. We were taught Latin from the first year, Greek from the third, and by the last year had read all major classics in the original, after formal instruction in grammar and the structure of language. The study of these languages was a character-shaping experience. It guided my thinking in terms of categories—the distinction of tenses, cases, active and passive modes, different parts of speech, different clauses. Organizing principles of thought were established and logically developed. We learned how to think clearly. Acquaintance with Latin grammar provided a fundamental lattice of reasoning to which the experiences in later life could be connected, even after grammar rules were forgotten.

I was also introduced to history, to the ancient world and its values, to the roots of Western culture. I could not have acquired a facility for expressing myself in English in a professional way had I not had grounding in classical languages. Since English is based on a combination of Teutonic and Romance (Latin) roots which I could recognize, it was easy for me to learn. The value of foreign languages was acknowledged in the Viennese educational system. Some high schools taught classical languages, others English and French. Modern languages were not taught in my school, and so my parents arranged for me to be privately tutored in English and French. In addition, I had private tutoring in piano, gymnastics, fencing, dancing, literature, and art history. Piano lessons I found unpleasant, probably because I had a pedantic, humorless teacher, unable to arouse appreciation for music. I rejected her and hence music in general, and regret to this day that I remain unappreciative of this precious aspect of life's beauty.

Things were different with literature and art history. We had an inspired teacher in Greek. He opened up the Hellenic world and the splendor of Homer, and made us aware that many of our contemporary institutions were rooted in the classics. He introduced us to our literary and artistic heritage in classes given after regular school hours. We were not obligated to take these classes but many of us did, and they enriched and refined our lives. This teacher, on his own time, paying his own way, took us to Italy and Greece during summer vacation and showed us what he had talked about in class. Antiquity and the Renaissance became real to us.

How important teachers are! One day in German class I wrote my composition in verse. When the teacher was about to return our graded notebooks, he placed his hand on the stack before him and in mock-grave tones said: "Ladies and gentlemen, I have an announcement to make. We have a Poet in our midst!" Then he pointed to me. Red in the face, ready to sink into the earth, there I stood while the class roared in amusement. Well, yes, I had been writing verses all along at home, and I had thought it nothing special to write this composition in verse. But teachers can be stupid and children cruel. This ridicule left a deep scar. For years I concealed my hobby and did not show my poems to anyone.

In my high school days I did well in what are now called humanities and social sciences, but was terrible in the natural sciences—physics, chemistry, and especially mathematics. I limped along in these, barely passing, and was desperate in the last three years of high school when we studied calculus. (Yes, we studied calculus in high school.) My more practical schoolmates used logarithm tables and employed other mechanisms to solve calculus problems. But I wanted to know why these mechanisms were used and how they operated, and I never got over this. Without knowing the why, I could not get to the how. The logical connection was broken and I did not have the down-to-earth flexibility needed to bridge the gap.

When, after eight years of high school, we took our grand final examination in all major subjects—we were even required to write a dissertation—I squeaked by in math. Without passing this final examination (*Matura* in Austria, *Abitur* in Germany) no student could attend the university. The *Matura* was the equivalent of college entrance examinations in the United States.

At age eighteen, when I had finished high school, I was a young lad filled with romantic ideals of beauty and harmony, about life in general and girls in particular. About girls I learned nothing from my parents. Not until I was twenty—much later than most of my classmates—was I initiated in the mysteries of love. For years I had fantasies about a beautiful first experience born of "love" (all of the crude alternative phrases used by my friends were forbidden in my thoughts). When it finally happened—with a girl I met at a carnival dance—I convinced myself that this was indeed the beautiful fulfillment of my noble dreams. There was a glow about the relationship that compensated for waiting until the "right" young woman came along. I romanticized encounters with other girls in later relationships: sexual encounters had to be "clean," perhaps in tune with the "good-and-beautiful" ideal of the ancients imbued in me by my teacher.

But I am ahead of myself. When I finished high school, my parents asked me what I would choose as a career. I said I wanted to become a writer. My parents did not take this choice seriously but were sensitive enough not to ridicule it. We had quite a talk. Becoming a writer, they said, was desirable but chancy. Yes, I was talented, but I shouldn't stake my whole future on such a "volatile" occupation. They advised me to continue writing but at the same time to take up some "sensible study," just in case I did not become a best-selling author. They talked so kindly and convincingly that I accepted their reasoning. In the fall of 1928 I enrolled in law school at Vienna University.

I had, indeed, continued with my poetry even after I was pilloried by my German teacher. But contrary to the image of me he may have elicited among my merciless classmates, that of a long-haired, moon-gazing "poet" writing verses about nature and the woes of love, I was attracted by "the lighter muse" that played with the whimsies of the small objects of daily life—a lump of sugar, a candle, a cobblestone, a telephone dial. I also wrote short prose in a similar vein. I still concealed my masterpieces from the outside world, except my family.

Then, an announcement in the influential *Neue Freie Presse* triggered a soul-searching revolution in this budding poet. The paper would print a weekly youth section, that would give young authors a chance to place their efforts before the public. The best contributions would be awarded cash prizes. It seemed a wonderful break, but I still did not dare come out of my shell. The first few youth sections appeared, and it was agony for me to see others in print while I was hiding out.

Finally I took a couple of poems—one about a bat, one about a telephone—to the older brother of one of my schoolmates. The brother was a successful author and movie script writer. It was like a confession when I told him about the youth section and my poems. I asked him whether I should send them to the newspaper. Were they good enough? "Show them to me," he said.

He read them carefully—taking more time than my patience could stand.

"Well?"

He handed them back to me. Then he said gravely: "You are a stupid idiot."

The insult was music to my ears. It meant that I was silly to doubt. Of course I was to submit them.

I went home, put the verses in an envelope—and still hesitated. I could not bring myself to type my name under them as author. Yet—how sweet it would be, if the paper accepted them, with my name beneath them . . . As a last-ditch compromise, I wrote my brother's name—Otto Heinz Kühnel—under the poems and mailed them.

On November 21, 1929, our telephone rang at 7 o'clock in the morning. My mother answered. It was a neighbor. "Congratulations, Frau Kühnel! I did not know that you had *two* poets in the family!" She had opened the morning paper and found the two poems printed in the youth section!

The storm broke at once. As I ran to our own, as yet unopened, copy of the paper and found the poems, my triumph was muted by my furious brother Otto. How did I dare use his name under false pretenses? And I hadn't even asked him!

I could not see the problem. It was an enormous honor, was it not?

No! Perhaps I could crow but I surely made him look silly.

Again, my literary success was a disaster for my brother.

But the ice was broken. I was out of my shell, the telephone rang all day, and I basked in the sunshine.

Two more poems appeared shortly under my own name—and one of them won a prize.

This was the beginning. In 1930, one after another of my store of "secret" poems appeared in the youth section of the *Neue Freie Presse*, followed by a number of prose pieces.

Still, there was a fly in the ointment. I was patronizingly acknowledged in the *youth* section, but I had tasted printer's ink. Now I wanted to "graduate" into the main part of this or any other paper. I made some efforts and indeed had some minor successes— acceptance in two obscure newspapers—but I had not really attained my goal.

Life at the university was very different from life at high school. There was no daily routine of organized teaching. We could go to lectures or ignore them—all we had to do was pass our examinations. The lectures were pedantic, boring, uninspired. There was a musty atmosphere in the hallowed, old-fashioned classrooms of Vienna University, the *Alma Mater Rudolfina* founded in the fourteenth century, the second-oldest (after Prague) German-language university.

In the beginning I attended lectures. But after a while I discovered, as everyone else did, that they were a waste of time. We could learn what we needed from notes carefully taken by "professionals" who prepared students for the examinations in privately run seminars. There were about twenty-five students in the series of seminars I attended. Among them was one student I noticed because he always seemed to have the right answer. The tutor would ask a student a question—we were sitting around a large table—and when that student did not know the answer, turn to the next one, and so on down the line. No matter how complex the question was, the line consistently would stop with Joe. This fellow, it seemed, always had the answer. And he did not proclaim it in triumph, but just quietly, almost shyly, said his piece—and he was always correct. I made a mental note of this remarkable character, who was knowledgeable yet modest. But these were not social meetings. We assembled to learn, were coached, crammed the stuff into our heads, and went home again. We hardly talked to each other at these impersonal get-togethers.

During the summer I was hired by the director of a hotel near Vienna as a live-in private teacher of his two young sons (ages 11 and 12). The hotel was in a beautiful place, three thousand feet up in the mountainous resort area of Semmering. The structure had a flat roof with a view onto the picturesque peaks around. Many visitors from Vienna came for weekends or longer.

One of those weekend visitors was that secretly admired fellow student, Joe.

* 3 *

Birth of
a Four-Legged Author

1931–1938

PETER

We recognized each other at dinner, and later went up to the hotel roof terrace to chat. It was a beautiful, warm evening, and we discovered that we had more in common than the cram course in law. Max told about his contributions to the youth section of the *Neue Freie Presse* and Joe about movie reviews he wrote for his cousin Arthur Steiner, who was on the staff of another Viennese newspaper, *Kronenzeitung*. Joe considered these reviews more as expressions of love for the theater than of literary ambition. We talked until two in the morning. It was instant understanding with no need for explanations—friendship at first sight. We decided then and there to write something together—we didn't know what or how. We only knew that our writings were to be published not in a youth section or a movie column but in the main part of a serious newspaper.

Vienna had more than a dozen daily papers that published stories other than news in every issue, and in their Sunday supplement. Those papers used first-person adventure reports, love stories, and short short stories.

Instinctively we liked the short short that fits into one column. We thought a story of no more than one thousand words would be easy to write. When Max came back to Vienna from Semmering in the fall, we sat down at the typewriter. How do two people write one story? We actually tried to write alternate sentences. This was ridiculous. Then one wrote a whole paragraph and turned the typewriter over to the other. The story went in an unexpected direction. We wanted a surprise ending, but not one surprising to us. Also, the story was too long. We learned the hard way what every writer knows: that nothing is more difficult than to write tersely.

About this time one of Joe's distant relatives came back from a business trip to New Mexico and told him about oil discovered on an Indian reservation. Joe wrote the article and showed it to Max. Max sat down and rewrote it as if he himself had just spoken to the Indian chief. Joe did some improving, and we called our cooperative effort "Indians as Oil Millionaires." We knew exactly which paper would be interested in this "firsthand" piece of journalism, put it in an envelope, addressed it, and were about to take it to the post office to mail it when we remembered we had not chosen a by-line. What name should we use as author?

Joe was Josef Epstein, Max was Max Kühnel. We wanted one common pen name. The first name was easy. Max's girl friends called him "Peter," a name popular among young men in Vienna. The "family" name proved a problem. We were intrigued by the Latinized sound of many pseudonyms used during that period— Veramicus, Sagittarius, Ironymus. We considered similar ones but none seemed right. So we did not mail the article immediately. Later that evening Max called Joe on the telephone: How would Fabrizius be? Max, a museum buff, may have had a seventeenth-century Dutch painter (Barent Fabritius) vaguely in the back of his mind—he just liked the sound. Joe liked it too. The next morning, "Indians as Oil Millionaires" went out under the by-line of Peter Fabrizius, and it was published three weeks later in the weekend supplement of the respectable *Neues Wiener Tagblatt*. A writer was born.

Twenty years later, when a selection of our short stories was published in New York for use in German classes at American universities, its editor, Professor Clair Hayden Bell, in his foreword, identified Peter Fabrizius as "one of those rare authors who walk on four legs." He might have added that this writer also had two heads and twenty fingers used simultaneously on two typewriters.

Our "double features" paid off during the following months and indeed years. We soon discovered, and gradually ˙ refined, the mechanics of working together. It was a collaboration of minds, not fingers. We concentrated on the short short with a final twist. The topics often literally lay on the streets of Vienna, like the button that became our first success in fiction.

To illustrate how a Fabrizius story came to be written, here is our first short story followed by an explanation:

The Button

When Thomas, the master sleuth, and his friend George boarded the bus, Thomas found a button on the seat he was about to take. With a flick of his trained fingers he picked it up and examined it carefully through his magnifying glass, silently absorbed in his scrutiny. George knew better than to disturb the master and paid both fares. A smile flitted across the detective's lips which over the years had been worn thin from smile-flitting. Putting the magnifying glass aside he said:

"The person who lost this button is a high-ranking Navy officer. He lives at Hander Street, Number 14 in the fourth district, is about fifty-eight years old, not married. He pays little attention to appearances. Tonight at 8 P.M. you can meet him at Central Plaza, Number 38."

George was well aware of his famous friend's incredible feats of logical deduction. He merely needed to remember Series 1 to 8 of *Detective Classics* which preserved Thomas' exploits for posterity. Still, he was intrigued and asked his friend for explanations.

After allowing another smile to flit across his lips, Thomas leaned back, placed his fingertips together, and said:

"This button shows the anchor of our Imperial Navy. Hence the wearer belongs to it because uniforms may be worn only by those entitled to wear them. The button is gold-colored, hence the wearer is a high officer—lower ranks wear silver- or brass-colored buttons. Three years ago

24

Navy uniforms were changed. This button shows the design of the old uniform, hence the officer is retired—otherwise regulations would have required his wearing the new uniform. Earliest retirement age is fifty-five, so the man must be at least fifty-eight. He is probably unmarried, because this button, judging from the needle scratches on its back, has been clumsily sewed on by a man, presumably himself; to miss the button's holes with the needle is a typically male ineptitude. Now his address: Our subject must have left the bus at the stop where we got on because the button, lying at the edge of the seat would have been brushed off in this crowded bus before this. Why did the man get off? Next to the stop is the home for retired Navy personnel, Hander Street, Number 14.

"You may have noticed the bulletin boards announcing a special performance tonight at 8 P.M. for retired military personnel at the Central Plaza Theatre; that's at number 38. This is a rare occasion, and I presume that you can find him there at eight. As for appearances—in the military, metal buttons are always highly polished, but this button has not been shined for quite a while; no longer in service, the wearer did not care."

George was so enthralled and Thomas so deep in thought that they missed the station to get off.

*

The man who really lost the button was a woman, seventeen-year-old, charming Tilly, who had been asked by the cloak-room attendant of the Central Plaza Theatre to pick up a Navy coat from a costume rental place for tonight's special performance. Tilly had taken the coat to the theatre on foot, not using the bus. She lost the button in the street. A boy picked it up and played with it, depriving it of its polish. He later dropped the button in the bus where Thomas found it. The scratches on the back of the button stemmed from the boy's unsuccessful attempt to spear the button. Tilly, the loser of the button, lived not in the fourth district but the twelfth. She would have scratched out the eyes of anyone who on the basis of sleuthy-sleazy deductions would have made her fifty-eight years old.

And at 8 P.M. that night? She did not sit among the white-bearded veterans in the Central Plaza Theatre, but on a bench in Schiller Park with a handsome young fellow.

It so happened that Thomas and George walked by in the darkness. As they passed, the detective said to his friend: "From the osculatory sounds, I draw the conclusion . . ."

This time he was right.

We actually did find a button in a bus. Max picked it up and wondered who might have lost it. Joe chimed in, playing Sherlock Holmes, who was popular at that time. There was not much to go by—the insignia, the gold color, the scratches. What would Conan Doyle do with these clues? It could have been a straight Sherlock Holmes story.

But now came the "step." How about turning the story around and providing *two* explanations for each clue, showing that this sleuth-genius had made a fool of himself? The Sherlock Holmes imitation became a Sherlock Holmes parody. We had fun finding second explanations and tossing the ball back and forth. The second step would have been impossible without the first. Now it was—or could be—a complete story.

But there came a third step. In the final sentence, the story is turned around again: this time, when the situation is obvious, the great detective is right.

We had no illusion of having created immortal literature. All we meant to produce was a smile on the lips of readers who looked at the newspaper at breakfast, before they went on to the daily murder or sex scandal.

The stories grew from tiny seeds. Joe's dog picked a woman's glove from the gutter. How would it be if we let a dog lead his young master to a romantic adventure by sniffing out the owner of the glove? How could it end in a surprise? Or we went the other way. We saw a magician pull flowers, flags, and rabbits out of a suitcase. How would it be if a thief stole a suitcase, believing it contained money, and was caught by a policeman who asked him to

open the valise? Anything we saw, heard, or imagined triggered a
chain of ideas. We were young, observant, interested in the world
around us. Everything aroused our curiosity and set the wheels in
motion. We called the steps (when one of us built on the idea of
the other) "spinning the story." We walked up and down the streets
of Vienna, spinning. We might meet at Max's, talk about a story,
not come to a satisfying conclusion, and continue while Max
accompanied Joe to his home, a walk of about half an hour. If the
story seemed not quite right, Joe would accompany Max back to his
place. We often walked back and forth several times. The stories
were whimsical, the dialogue breezy, the situations bizarre, popu-
lated by mischievous young men, hats askew, ready for anything,
and dimpled blonde girls with stunning figures. The twist had to
come in the last sentence, possibly the last word. The stories were
an escape for the Austrians, living through a depression and under
a political cloud from neighboring Germany, and the papers
gobbled them up. Peter Fabrizius produced about two hundred
stories between 1931 and 1938.

We also wrote two other types of stories: love tales and
first-person adventures. We shunned mushy love stories; ours were
tongue-in-cheek and often take-offs on stock-in-trade romances. We
had fun with the adventure stories. Since we lived bourgeois lives,
we were looking for people who had been in exotic countries and had
had unusual, possibly cliffhanger experiences. The editors insisted
on first-person accounts. And so the readers learned about Peter
Fabrizius being shipwrecked in the Atlantic, miraculously saved
from an avalanche in the Alps, interned in a leper colony in the
Pacific, and escaping from the First World War prisoner-of-war
camp Ahmednagar in India (in five sensational installments).

Eventually one editor began to wonder about our indestructi-
bility. Reluctantly we used other pen names. This was also necessary
for another reason. Vienna newspapers paid scandalously little for
freelance contributions—the equivalent of two to five dollars per
story. We lived at home, did not need to make a living from
writing, and had no intention of getting married or being on our
own. But we wanted to prove to our parents that a writing career
held promise, that it provided at least pocket money to pay for our
entertainment budget. Although we turned out a continuous stream

of stories, and most of them were printed, the income was modest, and we did what most other freelance writers did: we sold one story, with different titles and under different by-lines, over the years to several publications. We invented names or used those of friends and relatives (Max carefully excluded his brother), our maids, and even Joe's pedigreed fox terrier, Brandy von Brandenburg.

The multiple selling of stories was quietly tolerated by newspaper editors, who did not expect exclusive rights for the equivalent of two dollars. But we had to be careful to sell the same story to papers with different readerships and to space out submissions so that at least a few months would have passed between publications.

This practice of selling stories under different names did get us into trouble once. An afternoon paper, the *Telegraf*, a frequent outlet for short stories, had a new editor who did not like our stories; he insisted we didn't know how to write. But when we submitted stories under a different name, he blandly printed them. In November 1936 the *Telegraf* announced a big short-story contest, with cash prizes. We entered two dozen stories under various names. The top five winners were published in descending order on consecutive days. The fifth-prize winner was published on a Tuesday, the fourth-prize entry on Wednesday, and so on. No prize for us. On Saturday we received a furious call from a distant relative of Joe. She had received a congratulatory telephone call from the editor, who told her that she had won first prize and that her story was just being set in type to hit the newsstand within the hour. The relative denied her authorship but suspected Joe and called him. When the editor found out that we were the true authors and that he had been duped, he wanted to pull out the story, but it was too late—the pages were already made up. All he could still do was scratch the name. And so the story that won the first prize appeared with a blur as a by-line.

How naive we were! On Monday we thought we had proved our point and proudly presented ourselves to confirm our true authorship. We actually thought the editor would see his "error" and from then on would publish our stories under our name. Instead, he threw us out and never gave us the cash prize. Brandy von Brandenburg, however, had many stories published in the *Telegraf* after that.

People kept asking us how we wrote these stories together, whether a specific story was written by Max or Joe, and "who was Fabri and who was Zius." We could not answer these questions. While spinning the story, one of us would have a brainstorm, which would inspire the other, spark another twist, and so on. We tossed ideas between us and it didn't matter who scored. One would type the first draft, the other go over it, pass it back, until we were satisfied. Sometimes one had the lion's share of a story, and it even happened, especially during the summer when we were on separate vacations with our parents, that one wrote an entire story, sent it to the paper under the joint pen name, and the first time the other knew about it was when he saw it in print. Over the years, if one of us went through a stale period, the other would keep Peter Fabrizius going, pulling the partnership along. Together we accomplished more than the sum of what each of us would have accomplished individually. One and one made three—this was mathematics that even Max with his mathematical inferiority complex understood.

Neither of us has ever been able to duplicate this partnership with anyone else. Our working relationship was and still is based on complete trust and cooperation, never on competition. We have never haggled over royalties or credits.

Our companionship spread to other common interests—hikes in the Vienna Woods, skiing trips with friends, visits to the theater, carnival dances, and hour-long "nonprofessional" chats.

Oddly, perhaps fortunately, we had different tastes concerning the opposite sex. Our remarkable affinity in writing and in daily life was paralleled by mutual indifference to the women in each other's lives. Joe was attracted by flashy, highly made-up, experienced (sometimes older) females in colorful dresses and wide-brimmed hats (Max called them movie-star types), Max by more "soulful," nature-loving, plainly dressed, homey girls (Joe called them cleaning-woman types). We rarely went out as a foursome. We never disagreed on how to describe desirable women in our short stories. But in real life our ideals were poles apart, and we never competed for the same girl. Perhaps this was part of the secret of our friendship.

In 1933 we completed our studies, passed our final examinations and won our doctor-of-law hats. To become an attorney it was necessary to serve one year as a law clerk at a Vienna court, then apprentice for seven years with a licensed attorney before taking the bar examination. We both served our year in court, disliking the bureaucracy, the indifference of the judges, the merciless judicial system. But it was only after that year that we faced a real problem. It was almost impossible to become an apprentice with an attorney; there were no vacancies. It was not unusual for an apprentice to receive no salary, at least for the first year or two, or even to pay the attorney—either in cash or by bringing in clients—for the privilege of working in his office.

Here fate seemed to split us apart. A pattern became apparent that followed us throughout life. Jobs fell into Joe's lap, while Max had to struggle to find them. But Max did not acknowledge that his situation was hopeless. Slowly he built his ladder.

Although we blended our efforts in spinning our stories, we divided the territories of our contacts with newspaper and magazine editors. Joe visited some offices, Max others, and some editors identified Peter Fabrizius with Max, others with Joe. We tailored our contributions to the needs of the publications, and we had no literary ambitions—until Max got to know the feuilleton editor of the *Neues Wiener Tagblatt*, Dr. Moriz Scheyer.

A feuilleton was an elite contribution. A special front-page space was assigned for it, separated by a horizontal black line from the journalistic part of the newspaper. This space was reserved for "name" authors. To be printed "under the black line" was the goal of a literary author, and became Max's ambition.

Max spent the summer of 1934 crossing Europe from north to south by a method commonplace in the United States but then a novelty in Europe: hitchhiking. He had various adventures as a backpacking "tramp" and proposed to write about them from the viewpoint of a middle-class "intellectual" developing a "vagabond philosophy."

He suggested the subject to Dr. Scheyer who, with a smile and a shrug, and without promising acceptance, agreed to consider the manuscript for a feuilleton if the piece met the paper's standards.

This was an enormously important opportunity for Max in his ladder-building efforts. No persuasion was necessary to convince Joe that this piece would have to be written under Max's own by-line, a leap to make himself a name with the *Tagblatt*.

Max made a special effort in a carefully written essay, which he submitted under the title *Landstrasse* ("On the Highway"). He received a congratulatory telephone call from Dr. Scheyer the following day, and before long the contribution appeared under the black line. The by-line was Max, but the triumph was unstintingly Peter. It was the first test of our friendship.

The countertest came shortly afterward, and was more severe. One of Joe's hunting grounds was the Rob Publishing Company, which published three magazines: *Die Muskete*, a satirical weekly; *Mocca*, a belletristic monthly; and *Wiener Mode*, a fashion magazine. All three used the kind of stories we wrote. Joe went there every second week, left some stories with a receptionist, and picked up the acceptance or rejection slip of the previous submission. One day, when Joe delivered new stories, the receptionist said Mr. Karl Rob wished to see him. This could only mean trouble—perhaps Rob had found out that one of our stories had been published elsewhere. Joe entered the inner sanctum with trepidation but Rob, behind his huge desk, was friendly. He had read the Peter Fabrizius stories (which he assumed were Joe's alone) and had published several of them. His short-story editor had suffered a nervous breakdown— would Joe temporarily take his place? Rob made it clear that he intended to take the editor back after he recovered.

Rob gave Joe one day to think it over. The offer was a miracle. Neither of us had ever heard of an editing position being offered out of the blue. But what would Max think of Joe getting a dream job on the strength of stories they both had written? And what would Joe's parents say of his giving up his precious position as an attorney's apprentice for a job that would be over as soon as the other editor recovered? But Max was happy, as if he himself had been offered the job. And Joe's parents knew that Joe was unhappy at the attorney's office. They also saw that Joe's writing was good enough to have stories published in the Viennese newspapers, and to get him a job offer.

So Joe became short-story editor of three of Vienna's major magazines. It truly was a dream job. It allowed him time to collaborate with Max on stories that Joe himself was able to accept for publication! He read other writers' submissions. It was he who now wrote acceptance and rejection slips. And there were other

31

assignments. Rob, in addition to being a publisher, was an art dealer. He bought paintings, reproduced them in his magazines, then sold the originals. Part of the editorial offices was an art gallery. Joe had to write little mood pieces, in prose or poetry, to go with the reproductions. Rob also bought cartoons and published them in the *Muskete*. Then, a year later, he reprinted them, with different legends, in another of his magazines. Every two or three weeks he brought Joe a handful of cartoons, with their legends cut off. He would dump them on Joe's desk and say: "Here, Herr Doktor, write me new jokes for these."

These were great challenges. Sometimes Max was called in to help: "Can you think of something funny a man would say while hanging upside down from a crane on a construction site?" Actually this was what we liked. We expanded from the printed page to the cabaret stage where gags and one-liners were in demand. Vienna, in the thirties, sprouted several cabarets in the basements of coffee-houses where young, often unemployed actors, writers, and com-posers performed before audiences who sat at little tables and consumed snacks. The programs were political and literary satire. Some of the songs and short sketches were takeoffs on political figures and events, and often these caused problems with the censor. We concentrated on harmless parodies of current plays, actors, and singers. It was a small additional income, and Joe, in particular, savored being part of the theater scene.

Max, meanwhile, had his own minor miracle. He answered an advertisement of a trade paper looking for a "dig-up man" and got his first full-time job. It consisted of reading the regular papers for clues of "relevant" (trade-related) stories, then interviewing traders in coffee, tea, grains, fruit, or spices. A far cry from Peter Fabrizius stories, but another rung up Max's ladder.

While we were proving—to our parents and ourselves—that we could build our lives as writers, we were living on a powder keg. Hitler became chancellor of Germany and defied the Allies by ordering troops into the Rhineland, which, by the Treaty of Versailles, was demilitarized. Had Hitler been stopped then, when still weak and bluffing, World War II might never have taken place.

In Austria a three-cornered political fight was going on among the Catholic clerical right-wing party, the left-wing Social Democrats, and the Austrian Nazis. Engelbert Dollfuss, head of the Catholic party and chancellor of Austria, fought the Social Democrats on the left and the Nazis on the extreme right. On February 12, 1934, he dissolved parliament, and smashed the Social Democrats in a bloody civil war. In May he abolished the democratic republic, declaring a "Christian Estate" with a fascist militia. The competing Nazis in Austria he declared illegal.

Five months later, on July 25, 1934, two Nazis murdered Dollfuss. He was succeeded by Kurt Schuschnigg, who continued to fight a two-front war against the illegal Socialists and the illegal Nazis. But the Nazis increased their power because they were supported by neighboring Germany. They terrorized Austria with bomb throwing, murders, Jew baiting, and other provocations.

As we dealt with the political reality of the thirties, a basic character difference between Joe and Max became apparent. Joe was an optimist; he saw the best in others and they usually turned out to be friendly; he expected breaks and got them. Max was a "realist," with a streak of pessimism. He looked at others with caution. If we had remained in our law careers, as we sometimes speculated, Joe would probably have become a public defender, Max a district attorney. This disparity did not separate us, rather it drew us closer. In many situations during the ensuing fifty years, Joe's optimism was balanced by Max's warning, and Max's caution was superseded by Joe's confidence.

This difference first and decisively surfaced in regard to the political situation. Neither Max nor Joe was politically active, although some of our friends were. But Max monitored the Nazi excesses in neighboring Germany with increasing alarm. For years he read warning reports and forecasts of things to come, especially in Leopold Schwarzschild's weekly *Das Neue Tagebuch*, and he passed them on to Joe. Joe read the material but found reasons to rationalize. It couldn't happen in Austria. And if it did, the jolly old Austrians wouldn't do those terrible things the Germans were reported to be doing. And such things certainly wouldn't happen to him because he had kept himself aloof from political activities. In hindsight, Joe's optimism ("sticking your head in the sand," Max called it) is hard to understand, in view of daily bloody brawls in the streets of Vienna between supporters of the Austrian government and the still illegal Nazis, our experiences at the university, and Joe's position as editor of magazines that published cartoons ridiculing Hitler.

The political realities should have been obvious to Joe for another reason. In the editorial offices of a Viennese newspaper he met Valinka, who also wrote and tried to publish stories. She was a refugee from the Russian revolution, a whimsical creature with the widest-brimmed hats and the most sophisticated makeup. She had a wild imagination, put to good use in her stories, written in a quaint German that Joe helped her improve. (He was repaid for his good deed years later in New York, when his American wife did the same for his English.) Valinka told Joe weird tales. One was about her mother fleeing Russia across frozen lakes, chased by wolves, and clad in the three fur coats that were all she could take along. Joe took these as products of her fertile brain, like her article about the room servant in a high-class Paris hotel who collected toothbrushes stolen from famous people. Not until he himself was a refugee did he realize that those fantastic stories about people fleeing for their lives had been true.

Joe lived in a world of security, protected by parents, maids, family, and a faith that "it couldn't happen here." Max's assessment about the coming political storm pointed in the opposite direction. He was supported in his attitude by his "steady," Gerda, the daughter of Ernst Benedikt, publisher of the influential *Neue Freie Presse* (the paper that in its youth section had printed Max's pre-Fabrizius poems). Gerda, also a reader of *Das Neue Tagebuch*, shared Max's political concerns. Through her father's connections with political circles she heard many alarming stories not printed in the Austrian press, stories that confirmed forebodings expressed in *Das Neue Tagebuch*. The Benedikts lived in a sumptuous villa in an elegant suburb of Vienna, a meeting place not only for leading politicians but also for the literary greats of the time, such as Stefan Zweig and Herman Broch. The Benedikts were unenthusiastic about their daughter's involvement with one half of the obscure Peter Fabrizius. Although Max occasionally went to their villa, Peter Fabrizius received no preferential treatment in the *Presse*; our stories were handled strictly on merit by the paper's features editor.

Max continued to cultivate his ties with the *Neues Wiener Tag-*

blatt, the main rival of the *Neue Freie Presse*. After that first success with the hitchhike feuilleton, Dr. Scheyer published several more essays under Max's name and gave him reporting assignments. Max's dream was coming closer to reality. He began to consider himself a member of the outer orbit of the paper's contributors. Sometimes, when we passed the lit-up editorial offices of the *Tagblatt* building at the Fleischmarkt at night, he would point to the upper floors and say: "Up there—that's where I hope to be some day."

Peter Fabrizius expanded too. We began "to conquer Europe." First the German-speaking parts: the Austrian provinces, Switzerland, and German-language papers in Czechoslovakia, Hungary, Rumania. A special triumph was an occasional publication in Germany where Jewish authors were banned—but who knew the ancestry of Brandy von Brandenburg? Sales were arranged through an agent. Agents also helped us get our stories translated and placed in most of central and northern Europe—in fourteen languages including Esperanto. Every time a new country was approached the agent was doubtful—each country had a different taste—but love and light humor seemed universal.

In 1937 Joe received a setback when Rob rehired the former editor, now recovered from his illness, and Joe was again reduced to freelancing. At this time, Peter Fabrizius developed a new area. We were approached by a playwright, Ernst Friese, to collaborate on a play. Friese had lived with the theater all his life. He was the son of a well-known actor, had traveled with his father from stage to stage, and had played small parts. His ambition was to write a comedy, and he thought that our short stories had the right tone. He was an ideal partner for us. He knew the ins and outs of playwriting but had no ideas. We had ideas but didn't know how to put them into dramatic form. We concocted a plot, and Friese shaped our characters into types that would be effective on stage. We thought up the dialogue, and Friese directed it. "Here we need a joke," he ordered, and we produced it. "Here we have to get Didi off the stage, and the cook has to come in through the middle, and something funny has to happen," he said, and we found a reason to get Didi off and the cook on.

We doubt that many plays have been written in this manner, but it worked and was fun. Friese had another asset for us in the German orbit of the thirties: he could prove his "Aryan" ancestry through several generations. The control for plays was rigorous. Playwrights had to prove that their grandmothers had "pure" (non-Jewish) blood. And for a new play to be successful, the German market was indispensable. We agreed to credit Friese as the sole author—at least for the time being. Our day, we hoped, would come.

We wrote two more plays together. Friese made the necessary arrangements to document his genetic credentials, and he found an agent. In the midst of our playwriting activity we read in the paper that the editor of the Rob magazines had taken his own life. Rob called next morning and asked Joe to resume work.

This was the first time that tragedy touched Peter Fabrizius. Life's surprise endings were not always as happy as in our stories. It was difficult to accept that one man's dream job depended on another's death. And there was another drawback to Joe's resumption of his work. The *Muskete* for years had been struggling with the censor about risqué jokes and illustrations that revealed too much female charm. The imprint of every publication in Austria had to list the name of a "responsible editor." Rob had been that person for many years, the fines had grown heavier with every violation, and jail terms were now a possibility. He asked Joe to be named as responsible editor—"a formality." Joe had no criminal record, therefore the fines would start at a lower level, and jail terms were unlikely, according to Rob. He would pay the fines on Joe's behalf. Joe was so glad to be back at his job that he agreed.

Max, at that time, went through one of those conflicts of conscience that are always painful but can prove productive. Peter Fabrizius was successful in many areas, Max had built his ladder at the Tagblatt, and he still was digging up stories for his trade sheet. But the tone of the political news in *Das Neue Tagebuch* grew more urgent. He felt lonely in his assessment of the political situation. This was an area where there was no collaboration with Joe. None of Max's friends would take his fears seriously. Even in Germany few emigrated; the Nazis, while pressing for emigration of Jews, defeated their purpose by barring them from taking their savings to start new lives abroad. Rather than emigrating as beggars, most German Jews thought they could sit out the storm. Austrian Jews felt even more secure: "it couldn't happen here."

Max had many sleepless nights. Finally, in late summer of 1937 he thought he saw a way out.

He made a formal visit to the *Tagblatt* and told the managing editor he wanted to become their London correspondent. He would go at his own expense and send in articles. Max had decided that in this way he would establish a foothold in England, in case life in Austria became intolerable. At the same time he would maintain the connection with the *Tagblatt*, a valuable tie if his fears proved unfounded. He intended to ride two horses in London: write for the *Tagblatt* and also try to find English outlets for our Peter Fabrizius stories.

Dr. Scheyer and his colleagues listened to Max with polite surprise. Well, if he really wanted to go to England just when they were getting more interested in him—all right. They gave him a to-whom-it-may-concern letter, which turned out to be useless.

Max scraped together his savings and went to London. He rented an attic with a slanted ceiling and a tiny balcony, just large enough for a typewriter table and a chair. To her parents' dismay, Gerda also packed her things and, in a gesture of youthful revolt and enthusiasm, joined him in London where she found a room nearby. She also had a portable typewriter and helped him type the stories he sent to the *Tagblatt*.

To win an English audience for Peter Fabrizius stories seemed almost hopeless. The first problem was to find a competent translator who was willing to work "on spec," sharing the expected payments. Not a very tempting proposition, especially from an author who had never published in England.

Eventually Max came across Akiba Schonfeld, an outgoing, intelligent Oxford student. While Akiba translated some of our short shorts, Max tried to establish links with the editors of newspapers on Fleet Street. Occasionally he managed to outflank the secretaries and leave sample stories. They came back with printed rejection slips. But he was possessed by missionary zeal. He was convinced Peter Fabrizius was good for the English reading public.

Finally there came the day when Max was face to face with Horace White, fiction editor of the gigantic (circulation five million) *Daily Herald*. White listened with an ironic expression as Max told him that Peter Fabrizius had as many as thirty stories a month printed on the

Continent, and that these stories had been translated and published in a dozen countries. White picked up a few samples Max had brought along, and shook his head before he read a word. "Even if the content of these stories were suitable for our readers," he said, "they are entirely unsuitable in length. We have strict requirements for our short stories. Each story has to fill exactly one page. Yours are only half that long. I cannot print such a short short."

In his youthful enthusiasm Max said: "Why don't you print two of my stories on one page?" White shook his head in comical desperation and said nothing, but he was wavering. Max suggested leaving some stories: if White liked them he could run a couple as a trial balloon. Let the readers decide. "If your readers don't like my stories," Max said confidently, "I'll never bother you again."

To print two stories on one page must have appeared to White like wearing a green tie with tails. It was unorthodox, un-British. But he was amused, perhaps sorry for the young man fighting a lost cause. He agreed to look at some stories.

A few days later a letter from the *Daily Herald* informed Max that two stories, "The Anonymous Letter" and "Courage," were accepted, and was the fee of four-and-a-half guineas acceptable?

For Max this was the crowning glory of months of effort, the justification for risking his savings for a trip into uncertainty. He sent a telegram to Joe, and Joe danced in the streets of Vienna as Max danced in the streets of London. It was a triumph—sweet, dizzying, and glowing.

On October 30, 1937, Max got up at dawn to catch the newspaper vendor as he arrived at his newsstand at the nearest tube station. It was a drizzly, overcast day, but as Max, shaking all over, opened the *Daily Herald*, the sun shone on the two stories, nicely illustrated by-line drawings, filling the whole page. He bought twelve copies.

Four-and-a-half guineas was many times more than we had received for any story in any country. And it was only the beginning.

Publication in the *Daily Herald* seemed to have broken the ice. Two weeks later, the *Daily Sketch* bought one story for six-and-a-half guineas, and the *Herald* raised its price to seven guineas for a pair. Reader reaction was favorable, and in December the paper announced that stories by Peter Fabrizius, the "well-known Austrian writer," would be run for a full week, two every day! The money for this series paid for Max's entire trip to England.

He returned to Vienna before Christmas and we had a jubilant reunion. He felt that he had prepared a mouse hole into which he (we) could run if things turned out as badly as *Das Neue Tagebuch* prophesied. Joe, meanwhile, had kept Peter Fabrizius running in Vienna, and Friese had placed our "Aryanized" play with an agent who submitted it to theatres. Dr. Scheyer received Max warmly at the *Tagblatt*. He had liked Max's reporting from London and had heard about his "cracking the British market." He gave Max several assignments, including a series of articles about a quack country doctor who attracted thousands of patients. The series was advertised in sensational manner on large posters on motor vehicles cruising the streets of Vienna.

In February 1938 Max received the most far-reaching assignment yet. He was sent to the fashionable ski resorts of Austria: Kitzbühel, St. Anton, Zell am See, to write about the social life of VIPs: the Duke of Kent, Queen Wilhelmina of the Netherlands, Prince Nicholas of Rumania, Prince Bernhard and Juliana (on their honeymoon), and Prince Ferdinand of Liechtenstein. Max's stories appeared in the *Tagblatt* almost daily. He was approaching the top of the ladder to a permanent job.

But the illegal Austrian Nazis had become increasingly strong and vocal, demanding Austria's union with Germany. In 1936 Hitler and Schuschnigg had signed an agreement confirming Austria's independence. But early in February of 1938 Hitler summoned Schuschnigg to Berchtesgaden and ordered him to hand over all political power. Schuschnigg agreed for the moment, but on returning to Austria defied Hitler and announced a plebiscite for March 15, to give the Austrians a chance to vote for or against union with Germany.

During those early March days political strife reached a climax. Thousands of people roamed the streets, singing, shouting, tossing election leaflets, and painting political slogans and symbols on pavements and walls—the rake cross of Schuschnigg's Austro-fascist party, the swastika of the Nazis, and the three arrows of the Socialists who, in their dilemma, supported Schuschnigg as the lesser evil. Max did not trust Schuschnigg to stand up to an irate

Hitler if the plebiscite should favor Austria's independence. He was ready to leave for England before the plebiscite.

But first he wanted to do his own little power play. He went to the publisher of the *Tagblatt*: he was going back to London, unless he was given a permanent position with the paper—now!

On March 10 his dream of many years came true. He received a contract as an editor of the *Tagblatt*, with a fixed salary. No longer would he have to walk by the building and wistfully look up at the illuminated offices where other people sat.

The dream lasted twenty-four hours. Throughout March 10 the street demonstrations became frightening. Joe visited Max in his home in the afternoon of historic March 11, a Friday. Max was ready to leave the next day, to wait in London for the result and consequences of the plebiscite. He tried to persuade Joe to come with him. As a correspondent of the *Tagblatt* and with the earnings of our short stories we both could survive until things became clearer. Joe was tempted but decided against leaving. It was a fateful decision.

At 7 P.M. of that day Chancellor Schuschnigg went on the air and announced that, in order to avoid bloodshed, he was calling off the plebiscite. Nothing stood in the way of Hitler's annexation of Austria.

* 4 *

The First Swallow

1938–1939

MAX

When Schuschnigg announced on the radio his resignation as chancellor, our family was having dinner. He concluded with the words, "May God save Austria." I dropped my spoon without finishing the food. I said, "This is the end," walked into my room where my suitcase was packed but not closed, and called to my mother to telephone the Western Railroad and ask when the next train was leaving for London. I heard her say on the phone: "Nine thirty-five? That's too soon, when is the next one?"

"It isn't," I called back. "I'll catch it." I closed the suitcase.

I hurriedly kissed my mother. I was getting out. Unattached and unencumbered, I was the one in the family best qualified to try and get them all out eventually. My father called for a taxi and drove with me to the railroad station. The streets were crammed with shouting people and we had trouble getting through. My father promised the taxi driver a reward if he reached the station in time. At one crossroad the way was blocked by a long column of Nazi motorcyclists preceded by an open automobile with two men in it, one driving, the other holding aloft a large red banner with a glaring swastika. Up to a few minutes ago all Nazi symbols had been illegal; that was the only "official" Nazi flag I ever saw.

My heart was feverish with impatience as we waited for the

cyclists to pass. Every moment counted. At a break between two sections in the procession our driver shot through.

We got to the station minutes before the train was to depart. Only three people were in line at the ticket window, but even they seemed too many. I had my eyes glued on my wrist watch. "Plenty of time," I said to my ashen-faced father, and pretended to be calm.

My hands trembled as I received the ticket. We rushed to the train and I got on. Mercifully, the leave-taking was short. The train pulled out almost immediately. As we began to move I heard ear-splitting yells from the plaza next to the station: "Heil Hit-ler! Sieg Heil!" There must have been thousands shouting. It seemed like the howling of wolves. The yelling, reverberating, was the last sound I heard as I left my home town, my country, forever.

But, of course, I was still eight hours from the Swiss border. Every station was patrolled by Swastika-bearing guards. Illegal and underground only hours ago, they had been prepared for the takeover.

I shared the compartment with three silent men who tried to appear calm. One was visibly shaking, the second, sitting by the window, gave the Nazi salute whenever a guard passed on the platform in the stations—a primitive attempt at a camouflage; I had no doubt he was a refugee. The third huddled in his corner.

In Salzburg we stopped for an uncomfortably long time. I did not know it then but as we were crossing Austria from east to west, the first Nazi troops were on their way from Germany in the north and would reach Salzburg during the night. We must have missed them by a few hours. That was the closest shave I had with the Nazis.

Well, not quite. The hours crept by slowly as we approached the border, and the temperature in the compartment seemed to be rising.

At dawn we stopped close to the border. A man with a swastika armband stepped into our compartment.

He collected our passports and asked each of us where we were going. The saluting man said London, and so did I; the other two said Paris. The Nazi returned the passports and left. We breathed a sigh of relief. Was it that easy?

It wasn't. He came back within minutes, this time with a man in a leather jacket. The new man pointed at the two going to Paris. "Come with me." The shaky man could hardly stand up, but they both followed the leather jacket, and I saw them being marched to the station building. The leather jacket returned and pointed his finger at the saluting man.

"Out," he said gruffly. The two disappeared in the same direction as the others.

My turn was next. I was sitting on hot coals but no one came. After what seemed like an endless time, the train started on the last kilometers to the border. I was alone in the compartment.

Then the door opened again. This time it was the shaky man who entered. I was glad to see him, but asked nothing and he said nothing. He sat down and smoked furiously. The door opened again, and the saluting man entered. He too was silent. But the door did not open a third time.

We were not checked at the border itself. We rolled over it. Nobody spoke until we reached the station of Buchs on the Swiss side of the border.

Railroad officials in Swiss uniforms walked the platform. It is impossible to describe our relief at the sight of those uniforms after eight hours of tension.

Now the two men came alive and gushed out their stories. The shaky one, an artist, had been taken to the stationmaster and briefly interrogated. The other man, who was beside himself with elation, told us that all his life savings had been hidden in his shoe in large-denomination bills. He had pretended to tie his laces as he was being taken to the stationmaster, rested his shoe at the base of a pillar of the building, and hid the money behind the pillar. When they searched him for money, they found nothing.

"I got rid of it, I got rid of it," rejoiced the man, who had just lost all his earthly fortune, the money he had hoped to use to build a new life abroad. I fantasized a cleaning woman, wielding a broom in routinely tidying up the yard of the station, finding this treasure . . .

Two obvious questions remained: What happened to the third man, and why was I spared? There was no one to ask. The third man had vanished; he was not allowed back on the train.

And I? As I later tried to understand it, the Nazis at borders

43

close to Vienna—at Hungary and Czechoslovakia—were trying to catch political refugees, those with the most to fear, those who had been closest to an exit. The guards at the Swiss border primarily looked for refugees smuggling money out of Austria. I was a young student, less likely than the others to be a plutocrat. In those very first hours of the takeover, the Nazis had their hands full, and perhaps concentrated on the most likely targets. Besides, the three others were visibly seething with fear. Although I was just as scared, I may have shown it less. These are, of course, guesses.

Actually, the Nazis were right. I carried no more cash than allowed under the stringent currency regulations of the Austrian government—they became much more severe a few days later. I had the equivalent of fifty dollars, in British pound notes. With that amount I was to start my new life.

The train stopped in Basel, long enough for me to make a telephone call from the rail station to the editorial office of the *Basler National-Zeitung* to which Joe and I had contributed short stories. I was lucky to catch "our" editor—the man with whom we had corresponded. Though in safe Switzerland, he was shaken by the events in Austria and was receptive to my plea to accept as many contributions as possible from now on. He understood that fifty dollars would not last long.

In Paris the passenger who had said he was going to Paris got off. The other traveler continued on with me. We reached the coast and took the Channel boat to Folkestone.

There we were grilled by an immigration officer. British policy required foreign travelers to stay no longer than three months, to have enough money to maintain themselves during that time, and not to take jobs. A specific permit or visa was not required in early 1938.

I had to play the role of a visitor. I was not "immigrating."

The officer asked how long I intended to stay, and I said three months. Did I have money? I showed him my pathetic amount, in English currency (it was part of my preparation for leaving Austria), and that seemed to make a good impression. But these paltry pounds would certainly not last for three months. What was I to do when they were spent?

I said I was a journalist. I would write articles for British

44

newspapers and live on the fees. I showed him some Fabrizius manuscripts I had brought with me.

It was the wrong thing to say. The officer, up to now coolly correct, turned tense. No, I was not to do any such thing. In writing for British newspapers I would be taking away space from British journalists. He was not going to admit me into England on that basis.

The world seemed to fall apart. I had caught the first train leaving Vienna after the Nazi takeover, slipped through Nazi border control, and now, at the gate, the door slammed shut.

I said I had done the same thing only three months ago—I had been in England, sold stories, and returned to Austria. I planned to do the same now. I showed him my passport with the entry and exit stamps and thought this should be convincing.

But that was three months ago. Something had happened yesterday that alerted the immigration officers to be especially careful with "visitors" who could become a burden to the already precarious British employment situation.

While he inspected my passport, I had a few precious moments to think of a better answer. It is not melodramatic to say that life and death depended on it. The answer had to be convincing and given in a calm, self-assured way—not by a frantic refugee, but by a working journalist, already a contributor to the British press, traveling between England and the Continent.

And so I said, and tried to be almost ironical without being offensive that, as a freelance writer, I could write stories anywhere— for example in France, if he chose to send me back—but that I would be free to mail my articles to England from there or anywhere else; the payment I would receive from the British newspapers I would then spend in France, instead of in England where the country at large would benefit from it.

It was an inspiration. The man bought the story. He did not discover the big hole in it—namely that I could *not* send stories from France. If the British sent me back to France, the French would also refuse to admit me and either ship me back to Austria or lock me up in a refugee camp.

The officer waved me on. As I walked through the gate, I could just make out another officer refusing admission to my remaining companion. I never saw him again and know nothing about his fate.

Gerda had remained in London when I returned to Vienna the previous December. Now she received me with open arms. She had expected me and had taken a tiny room for me at Swiss Cottage, around the corner from where she lived. It was a miserable attic but it looked glorious. Exhausted, I dumped my suitcase and opened it. On top lay a spoon. I had dropped it there inadvertently in closing the suitcase when I rushed from our last family dinner.

*

The next morning I sat opposite a distinguished-looking, mild-mannered gentleman, Leonard Montefiore, head of a committee that had been established five years earlier to assist refugees from Germany. I assumed that this committee would be the right group to approach now, although I was from Austria.

"Do you realize," he said, "that you are the first swallow?"

Indeed, of the four on that first train out of Vienna, one was taken off at the border, one left in Paris, and one was turned back at Folkestone. I was the first refugee from Austria in England—the first of thousands.

He gave me a ticket that entitled me to one free meal a day in the basement of Woburn House, the headquarters of the German-Jewish Refugee Committee.

It was noon and I went downstairs to try out my ticket.

Many people, mostly young, sat on benches at long tables, eating. Several women ladled out food—not to the refugees but to other women, well-dressed, in white aprons, who served the ticket holders. I remembered the free food I had received as a child after the First World War, a mass handout in a military barracks.

Here now, at Woburn House, a nice-looking woman with a few friendly words brought me my dish. This "waitress" was a society lady. She wore her jewelry and treated me and the others as guests and social equals. As she placed the plate before me, I was so overwhelmed with gratitude to these Jewish women who showed so much tact that I had a lump in my throat and could hardly mumble thanks. I preserved that meal ticket—it is a treasured memento.

The meal ticket was only a small part of the enormous effort, in England and later throughout the world, by private Jewish charity to help refugees; no government money was asked for or given.

After the meal the ladies would sit down beside their "guests," chat with them, and in thoughtful ways ask about their circumstances. In the days that followed many of us received private invitations to their homes. These women arranged social gatherings so that we could meet English people who might help us earn a living. This was a delicate business in view of the government's strict regulations against employing "aliens," who were rarely granted labor permits.

I attended some of those gatherings. I was accompanied by Kurt, a close friend and schoolmate from Vienna who, to my great joy, arrived in London before entry to England was severely restricted. He stayed in the same rooming house as I did and we formed a close alliance. In a way this was an echo of my relationship with Joe, although Kurt and I did not share the writers' bond. Kurt was a rare-book dealer, an art historian and scholar. He had brought with him as much cash as I had, but also a few rare books which he hoped to sell, just as I had brought my sheaf of Peter Fabrizius stories.

Ours was an eerie situation. Our means were sufficient for six weeks rent and food if we had our main meal at Woburn House. We could not afford to panic. This was the short story of life: two friends, dumped as from a parachute into an unfamiliar environment, a new language, a different lifestyle, no friends, and told: "Live!" It was sink or swim, and we were determined to swim. We raced against those six weeks—sell a story or a book, stretch our "life expectancy." We tried to look at this enterprise as a game.

I revived my connection with the *Daily Herald,* but Horace White did not want to satiate his readers with Peter Fabrizius. I had to break new ground.

I went from editor to editor, and Kurt from book dealer to book dealer; in the evening we compared notes and counted the days left.

When we were down to one week, I hit the jackpot. The *Daily Mirror* commissioned me to write a sob story, presumably done by a lonely woman who "in a desperate letter to the editor" explained that she had lost her husband and was on her own with a child. The story was to have the title "Won't Any Man Marry Me?" I was to describe in credible detail the problems of the English woman. The story should have been done by one of the paper's own hacks, but the editor gave me this break. I had no knowledge of daily life in England, yet I concocted something after many talks with women at Woburn House. The article appeared under a woman's by-line, and I walked home with four guineas—enough for two weeks' living expenses. I was back at three weeks' breathing space.

Three weeks! Life was wonderful. Kurt shared my happiness. He sold his first book the next day. We felt we had it made.

The *Daily Mirror* was the beginning of a lucky chain. Other acceptances followed and our "life span" gradually increased. We graduated from Woburn House meals to self-bought spaghetti dinners or pancakes we prepared on a gas ring in one of our rooms.

It was a happy though precarious existence, and I began to speculate about a real job, instead of this hand-to-mouth living.

"Happy existence" may sound frivolous. The happiness came from winning the race against our resources. We were of course deeply preoccupied with events on the Continent. Nobody in England seemed much concerned. It was exasperating to see how little the non-Jewish British knew or cared about what was going on across the Channel. They were apparently unaware of the danger that threatened the mighty British Empire. The treatment of the Jews in Germany and Austria (and soon Czechoslovakia) affected them about as much as might the treatment of the Glug-glug tribe by the ruling class in Afghanistan—to be read about at breakfast and dismissed with a not quite genuine "Oh, my." The newspaper reports of events in Austria were utterly inadequate, and rarely on the front page. It was at that time that I first came across a periodical that carried accurate, mature news and interpretations of the events that had brought me, Kurt, and a steady trickle of others to England. This was an old, venerable, conservative weekly, the *Jewish Chronicle*, often referred to as the Jewish London Times. I sometimes borrowed copies from subscribers, because I could not afford to buy my own copies. We were worried about family and friends. My father had been dismissed from his position. Kurt's rare-book business had been usurped by one of his employees. Joe had lost his job and had tried, unsuccessfully, to escape.

"My" *Tagblatt*, the day after I left, had dropped the line "A Democratic Newspaper" from its masthead and sported a swastika.

It was now a purely Nazi paper, indistinguishable from the *Völkischer Beobachter*.

The *Neue Freie Presse* also was Nazified. Gerda's parents had succeeded in escaping to Sweden. Gerda, meanwhile, became a secretary to Stefan Zweig, who was then living in London, and she also did secretarial work for other writers, earning just enough for her basic living expenses.

Several additional publications in London, and later outside London, started printing Peter Fabrizius stories: those that I had brought with me, others that Joe sent, and some that I wrote independently. I began to write feature stories, like an accredited correspondent, for newspapers on the Continent—primarily in Switzerland, the Scandinavian countries, and the Netherlands. Horace White relented and accepted stories again. I made an interesting deal with him, whereby the *Daily Herald* acquired so-called empire rights for our stories: the *Daily Herald* paid extra for the right to resell them to other publications in the empire. Our stories were reprinted in Australia, South Africa, India, and Ceylon.

Yet, each such success was an individual transaction, dependent on whether an editor happened to like a specific story. I dreamed of a monthly paycheck.

Suitable employment is difficult to find even in normal circumstances, but my situation was far below normal. Permits for employment for noncitizens were granted only to those who had skills not found in England. My law degree was useless here, and my English only good enough to buy groceries.

Language was the key to the future. I had to learn English to free myself from dependence on translators. I knew I would never get rid of my Austrian accent; at least I could try to get rid of it in my writing.

I read newspapers, listened to the radio, watched the mouths of the English speakers, and asked questions. I had a long way to go, and it was uphill.

But beyond the hurdle of the labor permit and the language, was my inability to determine what to aim for—what could I offer that anybody wanted?

I could not aim at anything requiring a good knowledge of English. Yet I wanted to find a niche in the world of publishing, where the word was the primary tool. I had to find something that was useful to an English newspaper but that did not require the ability to write in English.

I turned this over in my mind incessantly, stubbornly, for weeks. When I wandered past the newspaper palaces of Fleet Street, they seemed more out of reach than the glittering lights of the *Tagblatt* had been in Vienna. There did not seem to be anything a wretched refugee could offer to those giants in an empire that controlled a good part of the world.

The solution came suddenly and convincingly. It had been so close all the time: The *Jewish Chronicle*! Where did they get their well-informed articles? They must read the German press, of course! Somebody must monitor the daily Nazi press. Perhaps I could assist this person, point out important stories, and roughly translate them in my faltering but intelligible English—he could then polish them. Maybe first as a freelancer or part-time—while learning about the operations of the British press that might prepare me for . . . ah, the sky was the limit!

*

The chief of the staid, conservative *Jewish Chronicle*, Mr. David Kessler, was not an old, bearded rabbi as I had imagined, but a well-dressed, clean-shaven man in his thirties who quietly and sympathetically listened. It took only a few minutes for me to realize I had hit a bull's eye. Yes, one of his editors, Jack Spector, had been scanning the German press for years but the events of the past months had brought such an avalanche of Nazi material that indeed he needed help. If I could select items and do a rough translation of important news stories, Mr. Spector could go on from there.

And what about the labor permit from the Home Office?

When, in later years, I heard about the misery of unemployment during the Depression in the United States, nobody seemed to be aware that even the most miserable, hungry laborer had at least *the right* to work. We did not even have that.

Mr. Kessler thought there was a chance. He would apply for the permit. I would have to wait for a decision. Should it be positive, would three guineas a week be satisfactory?

In this day and age, forty-nine years later, in safe, affluent

America, how is it possible to convey my feeling of the immense good fortune that this potential job offer represented!

Shortly after the interview, I received a copy of the letter Mr. Kessler had written to the Home Office. In it he pointed out that I was "a specialist" who had "a rare combination of qualifications" that he had been unable to find on the British labor market. I was familiar with the Jewish situation in the German-speaking countries, I could monitor the German press and, as a former newspaperman, I had the judgment to sift essential material. Absurdly, here it was an *asset* that I was a refugee.

Not only did this letter encourage me—it convinced the Home Office. In July, four months after I had been admitted to England by that officer at Folkestone, my labor permit was issued.

July 19, 1938, was a milestone in my life. I started work—first part-time, soon full-time. After the first week, I received a small manila envelope with three crisp pound notes and three shiny shillings, my first salary. I read and clipped the hate sheets of the Nazis (received through a Swiss subscription agency). Later I also reported what I heard from newly arrived refugees. On one occasion I obtained a copy of the regulations of the concentration camp at Esterwegen. It was a major scoop and was printed by Spector in its entirety despite its length. In the editorial office everybody treated me as an equal; in fact, I was favored in subtle ways, the staff giving me credit for every small contribution. I was able to write to my parents and to Joe that I was "in."

At the end of each week I felt like a king when I received the little manila envelope, and was happy to pay my dues to the Union of British Journalists. I was a "British" journalist. My membership book looked to me like a passport to heaven.

But heaven was still a long way off. News from Vienna became daily more desperate. In September my father was jailed, falsely accused of trying to smuggle money to me. (I wished he had!) His securities and liquid assets were taken from him. He received an ultimatum: leave the country within two months or be shipped to a concentration camp. My mother wrote in anguished terms asking if I could get an entry permit to England for him—and soon. He was ill in jail and would not last long.

I received the letter in my shabby room in Swiss Cottage. This was a challenge far greater than getting a job. To receive permission to enter England, a British "subject" had to sign a guarantee that the "alien" would never become a public charge. The signer was financially responsible *for life*; the alien could not accept work in England.

I turned the letter this way and that. I well remember my feeling. Here was something impossible, and it *had* to be accomplished. I could not think of a single English subject to whom I could even *tell* my request, let alone ask to sign such a monstrous pledge. And yet, even at that darkest moment, I had no doubt I would get this pledge eventually.

I could not approach Mr. Kessler, that much was clear. He had gone out of his way to give me a job, more out of charity than because of my ability: I did not fool myself. He had gone to great trouble to convince the Home Office that I had "special skills not easily found in England." After so short a time it was impossible to ask a favor that meant a lifelong obligation.

In my mind I went over the people I knew—they were almost all Austrians. The few others, for one reason or another, were unsuitable.

I felt an irrepressible need to talk to someone, anyone. Kurt was out, Gerda was not home either. Upstairs lived my landlady, a nondescript, short woman who was generally friendly to me. I slowly walked up and knocked.

It was a darkish room, old-fashioned, lower middle class. I told her about the letter, about my father in jail, the British conditions for entry. I realized that she had no interest in the troubles of one of her many tenants. I told her that, of course, I did not expect her to give me a guarantee, but I wanted her to give me the names of two friends, British citizens, who would listen, although they might not give me guarantees themselves. In desperation I said I would not leave the room until she gave me the two names.

She was a complete stranger. The names she gave were of people of a different world who only vaguely knew from newspapers what went on in Austria. They lived far from Swiss Cottage. I went to see them the same afternoon—my work ended at 3 P.M.—and told my story.

They were polite enough to listen. I told them that the

guarantee was only a matter of form, to satisfy the Home Office. I would be financially responsible for my parents. At three guineas a week? We had relatives in Paris—my mother's uncle, a banker—who would help when the time came. I told them I did not expect them to sign themselves but would they please give me the names of two friends who would at least listen? They reluctantly passed the buck.

The following day immediately after work I pursued the four new addresses. I told my story four times. I tried to relieve the people at once by saying that I primarily wanted two names but in the course of the discussion told everything. I came home very late that evening—I had skipped dinner to be able to see all four—and was exhausted the next morning. But I had eight new addresses.

This way I discovered a system I used later in job hunting. To start with one person, any person, and widen the chances in a geometric chain. I drew a "family tree" of people I saw, to know who sent me where and who gave me what names. I took little time to eat, hardly saw my friends, traveled from one end of London to the other, often walking long distances to save fares. I had one purpose and husbanded every ounce of strength to carry it out. I got ever more tired and miserable. I was profoundly aware that the life of my parents depended on my ability to convince *someone* that signing would in fact be a formality.

I refined my story-telling techniques in various ways. I heard objections and arguments, and anticipated them in my next presentation. And I asked everyone for two more addresses.

I found out how enormously large London was. I traveled on buses, by underground, in a daze, often half asleep.

Twenty-nine days I traveled through London and told my story. On the thirtieth, in the longest month of my life, I found my man.

Captain B. H. Elliott of South Norwood Hill was a retired British officer. He asked few questions. He believed my story and trusted my promises. It was as simple as that. He was rather unemotional about the matter—he wanted to help. But he did not underestimate the responsibility. "If I am ever held to fulfill the pledge I am herewith signing," he said, "I, my wife, and my two daughters will be ruined. I am not a rich man."

I was so happy, so weary, so exhausted. But my belief in

humankind was confirmed. The solution did not come too soon. The deadline the Nazis had set for my father—to get out or be sent to Dachau—was close. Another deadline was approaching—one neither I nor anyone else knew of in advance: November 10, the "Night of Broken Glass," when synagogues throughout Germany and Austria were set afire, shops looted and destroyed, Jews picked up in the streets or dragged from their homes and sent to Dachau. On *that* day my parents left Vienna.

While my parents were on their way to the airport, the Nazis came to get Father. "They left," said the house caretaker. "The apartment is closed." We learned about this hair-breadth escape later through a relative who had talked with the caretaker.

While fires burned throughout the land, my parents were flying to Brussels, changing there to a British plane. At the Brussels airport, they were joyfully met by Joe, who by an ingenious scheme had obtained a temporary visa for Belgium as discussed in the next chapter. The meeting was just long enough to embrace and bring him loving greetings from his parents. "Joe is unchanged," my mother later wrote his parents, "and I happily transmitted your kisses to him—I enjoy kissing young men."

The same fateful day, November 10, 1938, they arrived at Croydon airport in London. I had taken a small room next to mine, and we celebrated with Viennese pastry which a friend had baked for that occasion.

When my mother arrived, she was wearing a hat decorated with a beautiful crystal butterfly with diamonds and emeralds, her most precious piece of jewelry, a gift from my father on their silver wedding anniversary. Smuggling jewelry out of Germany (Austria) was a crime under Nazi "law." She said, foolishly or bravely, that she did not smuggle it—she had flaunted it for all to see, giving the impression that it was a costume bauble. Although their baggage had been searched, no one paid attention to her hat, tossed casually, with her coat, in the corner of her plane seat. It was a dangerous gamble but she had won.

The day my parents arrived I telephoned Captain Elliott and told him they wanted to thank him. He invited us for tea.

We were welcomed by the captain and his wife. To relieve the tension, I immediately said what I felt the Elliotts wanted to have confirmed: that this meeting would be the first and last. The air cleared, a warm glow settled over these so very different couples. The thanks, haltingly expressed, were graciously accepted, and the meeting was mercifully short. As promised, the parties never saw each other again.

It was one thing to proudly refrain from asking for financial help, another to pay rent and groceries. My salary was barely enough for one person. Father was not allowed to work, and the guarantor was a fiction.

My solution would not be acceptable in any fiction; I decided to go to see—face to face—the wealthiest man in England, Baron Lionel de Rothschild, and ask for help.

Thereby hangs an unlikely tale.

I had been interested in family history since childhood and had drawn a crude family tree. My mother's uncle, the Paris banker, had told me that two brothers of the London branch of the Rothschild family, Lionel and Anthony, had married two sisters, Nelly and Marie Louise Beer, who had a great-grandmother in common with my mother. Years before, I had entered their names on our family tree as a curiosity.

During those excruciating weeks when I was scouring London for a guarantee signer, I wrote to my Paris uncle to substantiate the family connections, and this he had done by the time my parents arrived.

In the financial district of London is St. Swithin's Lane, the fortress of the Rothschild bank. I walked in with my parents and asked to see the baron.

Did I have an appointment?

I said I was a relative.

My English, my appearance, the cut of my Austrian suit did not help., "I see," said the receptionist; she disappeared into the next room and reappeared with receptionist number two. There were large oil paintings of the Rothschild ancestors on the wall. They and the new receptionist looked bored by the intruder. I said something about a common ancestor, clutching an excerpt of our family tree— it didn't sound convincing. They did not know what to do with me, and a long line of buck-passing ensued. I told the same story over and over, adding irritation to their boredom but, driven by desperation, I stood my ground. Finally I was asked to wait in a small room with heavy furniture.

After a while a large, hulking man with a lion's mane of graying hair rushed in, ebullient, loud . . . and friendly! Without sitting down, he summarized the situation, having apparently been briefed. I showed him my family chart and told him my parents were waiting in the first reception hall, under the oil paintings. Credibility was established when I mentioned the Paris uncle whom Rothschild knew.

"They are here?" said Lionel (how fitting the name was). "Show them in."

A minute later the legendary financial giant shook hands with the newly arrived Austrian refugees. Lionel said a few encouraging words, then introduced a distinguished-looking gentleman with a disabled leg, Captain Vivian Bulkeley-Johnson ("he will take care of things"), and rushed out with the same flourish he had entered. The encounter took less than three minutes. But three minutes with a Rothschild can have long consequences.

Captain Bulkeley, in a warm, quiet way, said my parents would be the beneficiaries of a special account, apparently established to support certain persons without humiliating them. The beneficiaries were treated like shareholders receiving dividends. Realizing the immediate financial precariousness of the new clients, Bulkeley, on the spot, gave them an envelope with their first "dividends." To begin with, the "pension" (as he charitably called the charity) was to last a year.

I promised myself right then that I would do everything possible to become independent of the pension within that year.

Just as my parents never saw Captain Elliott again, so they never again saw Lionel de Rothschild. But on one occasion, the thirteenth birthday of Lionel's and Nelly's son, my mother sent them one of her celebrated cakes and received a warm, handwritten thank-you from Nelly. This note, on Rothschild stationery, is another treasured memento.

Shortly after this encounter a big van arrived with our furnishings and other belongings from Vienna. My parents had shipped their possessions before the Night of Broken Glass—after that night the systematic dispossession of Jews made it impossible to transport property, even with payment of the extortionist tax the Nazis imposed.

While I was crisscrossing London to find a sponsor for my parents, Joe had managed to reach Belgium. He sent me short stories as if nothing had changed but his address, but then a letter from him arrived, written in a Brussels jail. His Belgian visa had expired, and he was in danger of being shipped back to Austria.

I had just received Captain Elliott's pledge for my parents, and it seemed hopeless to find a second guarantor. I had to try something unprecedented, cut through the red tape, reach those who controlled the immigration bureaucracy, and try for an exception.

I had to reach someone in power, somebody in the government of Great Britain. I used the "snowball system" again, now with experience. This time, my goal was to reach Lord Winterton, the High Commissioner for Refugees. I did it in three stages: In our boardinghouse was a middle-aged woman who had been secretary to the former Austrian ambassador to England, Baron Frankenstein— a man well liked in British government circles and now a refugee himself, though with connections. The woman asked Baron Frankenstein if he knew a member of Parliament who might intervene in Joe's behalf with Lord Winterton. Baron Frankenstein approached The Right Honourable J. O. Wedgwood, D.S.O., M.P., a member of the Liberal Party, who actually sent an appeal to Lord Winterton. Wedgwood received a cold reply on stationery imprinted "Home Office, Whitehall, S.W.1." In it, the man whose task it was to help refugees, wrote that "it appears that Dr. Kühnel is not in a position to support Dr. Epstein." Wedgwood was so incensed that he sent Joe a letter inviting him to be a guest in Wedgwood's home, but the British consul in Brussels was not impressed and did not permit Joe to go to England as Wedgwood's guest. Bureaucracies are not easily penetrated.

Fortunately, Joe's next letter did not come on jail stationery. He had been released in the custody of the Jewish Refugee Committee in Brussels, to be sent to a newly established refugee camp. For a few days he was free in Brussels, and it was during this time that he met my parents at the Brussels airport.

Joe's problem flared up two months later. The American consul in Antwerp made demands indicating that Joe, who meanwhile had received an affidavit from America, would not be granted his visa in Belgium even when his quota number came up. If he could wait for his quota number in England, his chances would be vastly improved. Besides, it was clear to me that the Nazis would overrun Belgium, as the Germans had done in the First World War. I asked high and low how I could get Joe to England, and eventually discovered that an "alien" who possessed an American affidavit and one hundred pounds would be granted an interim stay in England, to wait out his quota number.

We scraped together the hundred pounds. I had sold enough stories, including one of mine called "The First Swallow." (The prestigious *Cornhill Magazine* had published this account of my escape from Austria; the story was reprinted in *World Digest*, a British version of *Reader's Digest*.) I made the necessary applications to the Home Office, and Joe received its permission. The American consul in London, unlike the one in Antwerp, did not make additional demands. On March 22, 1939, I met Joe at Victoria Station. Peter Fabrizius was reunited. Forty-nine days later the Nazis overran Belgium.

* 5 *

Stranger than Fiction

1938–1939

J O E

When I left Max's home that fateful March 11, 1938, I felt threatened although I saw no violence. At home, the mood was subdued. After Schuschnigg's radio announcement, my parents phoned other family members, asking: "What do you think will happen?" No one knew.

Max phoned me that evening, saying good-bye. He was leaving immediately, hoping to reach London.

The next day, a Saturday, the streets were filled with swastikas, on flags, banners, arm bands. We stayed indoors and turned on the radio. The triumphant Nazi speeches were frightening.

The first indication of what was to come happened Monday morning on my way to the office. A brown-shirted, arm-banded young man stopped me: "Are you Jewish?" When I said yes, he pushed me into a car where four other Jews huddled together. We were taken to a public building. Another swastika-banded man wrote down my name and address, took my overcoat, gave me a pail of soapwater and a brush, and ordered me to clean the Schuschnigg slogans off street pavements and house walls. Men in business suits and well-dressed women were on their hands and knees, scrubbing. I joined them, keenly aware of the grotesque situation. Despite my apprehension, momentarily and perversely the thought flashed

59

through my mind what a story this experience would make! It would be anything but humorous. Passersby, those reputedly *gemütlich* Viennese, kicked my fellow street cleaners, shouted profanities, and spat at us. One man, in worker's clothes, thrust his fist in my face: "Look at my hands! A laborer's hands! And look at yours—never done a day's work. Now we'll teach you to sweat and labor!" He kicked me so my arm tipped into the bucket with the dirty water. He laughed, kicked me once more, and left. A Viennese policeman stood there, five feet away, and laughed, too.

After a few hours every bone in my body ached, but whenever I tried to rest, a brown-shirt shoved me to a wall and pointed to more graffiti. Once in a while a name was called out, and a man or a woman was led inside the building. Finally my name was called and I was taken to a room where a black-shirted SS-man looked over a list before him. Suddenly fear gripped me: I remembered that my name was printed in the *Muskete* as responsible for its anti-Nazi gibes and cartoons. But apparently the SS lists were not detailed enough on this first day, and the Nazi said, "Get lost." Naively I heard myself say: "Where is my overcoat?" The man pointed to the next room where I found my coat in a heap of others. How slowly values undergo change.

My parents were pale with worry. Karl Rob had called and told them that his publishing house had been taken over by one of the cartoonists whose work he had often bought and who turned out to be a high-ranking Nazi. I no longer needed to come to work. He also told my parents that I had not shown up. They were relieved when I came home, dirty and bleeding.

The same evening the family met. All were alarmed, but most thought things would blow over and "we ought to sit tight." But Uncle Hugo, who had spoken with many Jewish refugees from Germany during the past years, saw little future for us in Austria and urged us to emigrate.

This was inconceivable to most of us. Vienna was home. We didn't know people in other countries, or any other language. Many were in the same position as my father: they were retired, received pensions, had not been politically active—surely they would be allowed to live out their lives in peace. I was twenty-eight, and three cousins were in their late thirties; the rest of the family were in their fifties and older.

Despite the street-cleaning humiliation, the loss of my job, and the realization that no publication would any longer accept my contributions, I was not ready to leave the nest.

But soon enough, and reluctantly, when I saw all our friends applying for visas to other countries, I came to grips with reality. Where was I to go? The only country that had any appeal to me was England because Max was there. He had slipped through but now the borders were closed.

Worse, it turned out that the entire world was closed. It was not for me to have preferences. I stood in line at the Swiss, French, Swedish, and Danish consulates. Rumors flew through the city: someone had received a visa to Portugal, and a long line formed at the Portuguese consulate. The condition for receiving a visa was always the same: you had to have a "sound reason," usually business or family, to get even temporary permission to enter a country. Persecution was not a sound reason. One exception was the United States of America. It allowed limited immigration, the number dependent on country of birth. The Austrian quota was six thousand a year—sufficient in normal times but pitifully inadequate when fifty thousand or more wanted to leave Austria. I went to the American consulate without much enthusiasm. What would I do halfway around the world, trained in Austrian law, and able to write only in German? But I stood dutifully in line and secured a quota number just in case. It would take months, perhaps years, until my number would come up. And there was a second condition: an American citizen would have to send me an affidavit guaranteeing that for five years I would not become a financial burden on the United States. I did not know a single American citizen.

Here Max came to the rescue, in true Peter Fabrizius fashion. He drafted a letter describing my plight and my potentials as a writer, and had Akiba Schonfeld, who translated our short stories for the British press, put my plea into flawless English. Then Max went to the London Public Library and picked out two dozen Epsteins from telephone books of major American cities. He sent me the addresses and the draft, and I sat down and wrote two dozen appeals to namesakes all over the United States, hoping against hope that one of them would sign a guarantee for a total stranger.

The situation of the Jews in Vienna became more precarious. People were picked up at night and never seen again. Some returned with stories of imprisonment and mistreatment, which were passed on surreptitiously, and never quite believed. ("He must have done something illegal, this cannot happen to me.") There were rumors of mass camps for prisoners, and of executions. One young concert pianist who lived in our apartment house, Adolf Baller, disappeared for several weeks, and when he returned he did not say what had happened. (Years later, in California, when he had become the accompanist of Yehudi Menuhin, he told me that he had been abducted to a private home in the suburbs and forced to dig a grave for himself in the back yard, but had been spared at the last moment. His abductors had broken his fingers in a fiendish attempt to prevent him from playing the piano again. They warned him not to tell anyone, and to leave the country. He was smuggled across the border and, fortunately, regained the use of his fingers.)

As I continued my futile pilgrimages to foreign consulates, a series of events occurred that I would never have dared to put in any of our stories nor indeed have believed.

My father wracked his brains to find a way of obtaining a visa for me. He bought a patent, which he thought would have appeal in other countries. It was a little pipe to be installed in the overhead water tank of a toilet, regulating the amount of water for each flushing.

Again I stood in line at various consulates, this time not as a Jewish refugee who wanted to save his life, but as a businessman who would save the interested country millions of gallons of water. Unfortunately, other would-be emigrants had thought of similar schemes, and no consul would grant me a visa.

Then the story of my life took a new twist. Myra, my first girl friend, a chorus girl and nightclub singer (for whom I had written some lyrics), was not successful in Vienna and went on a performing tour abroad. She wrote from exotic places—the Balkans, the Near East, North Africa. She gradually hit the skids and was little better than a call girl, expected to prompt nightclub customers to order more drinks and then to go to bed with them. One night, in Tunisia, a client from Brussels mistook an expression of her disgust with her fate (she wrote that she bit him) for passion. And he became so infatuated with her that after his return to Belgium, he urged her to follow him. He hinted at marriage. At first she was amused, but her situation deteriorated and she went to Belgium. When she heard about my distress, she asked her friend if he could help. He was a businessman, and wrote to the Belgian consulate in Vienna that he was interested in my water-saving device. The consul granted me a one-month business visa!

This was only half the story. While it was almost impossible to gain entry into another country, legal exit from Austria was also difficult. Would-be emigrants were required to have a passport, an exit visa, and confirmations from various Nazi offices that no taxes were owed, no military service required, and no convictions pending. To receive each document it was necessary to stand in line for hours, sometimes days, exposed to every chicanery, even arrest. An increasing number of the endangered decided to cross the border illegally, and there were daily rumors of successful and unsuccessful escapes through forests, across rivers, and over mountains. Names and addresses of smugglers and their prices were passed around; some were swindlers, others were nonexistent. I was not ready for such adventures, and stubbornly tried to go the legal route.

Here our "Aryan" collaborator of plays, Ernst Friese, came to my rescue. He offered to get me the necessary documents. He had "connections," and in Austria connections were all-important. I was able to hide out in the Alpine spa of Bad Gastein where relatives of ours owned a hotel. Few Jews lived in the provinces, and the hunt was not as rigorous as in Vienna.

Bad Gastein is one of the most beautiful spots on earth, surrounded by high mountains, peaceful forests, with a giant waterfall and miracle baths that are said to cure every illness known to old age. It was overrun by tourists from Germany. I kept quiet and wandered through the more isolated parts of the forests. One day I noticed on the path ahead the actress Friedl Czepa, as blonde and "Aryan" as they come. Friese's agent had submitted our play *Lisa, benimm dich! (Lisa, behave!)* to a theater in Vienna, and the director had passed the manuscript on to Miss Czepa as the possible lead. When I left Vienna, Friese had told me that the play would be accepted if Miss Czepa liked it.

I was dying to know whether she liked the play. It was dangerous for a Jewish man to talk to an "Aryan" woman. She could be an ardent Nazi. I walked behind her for a while on that lonely forest trail, then my curiosity won out. I caught up with her, greeted her in my best autograph-hunting manner, and told her that a friend of mine, Ernst Friese, had written a play which, he had told me, she was considering. She was very pleasant, and said she was in the midst of reading it, and that she liked it. I was jubilant, and quietly thanked her.

Another turn in my escape had slowly been developing. Shortly after Hitler's annexation of Austria my father received a letter from one of his former employees. This man, Becker, had emigrated to Trenton, New Jersey, in the twenties. He wrote to inquire if he could help. My father asked him if he could send an affidavit of support for me. Becker answered that American authorities did not consider his income sufficient because he was not a relative. Relatives were given special consideration. My father remembered that a second cousin had emigrated to America as a young man before the turn of the century. My father had never heard from him, and knew only the cousin's name—Karl Beck.

It seems preposterous to me now that my father expected the man in New Jersey to find this long-lost cousin among the 150 million Americans scattered over a continent; my father did not even know the *state* where this Karl Beck was—if, indeed he was still alive. Well, the loyal employee decided to hunt the needle in the haystack. The first thing he did was to consult his own, Trenton, telephone book— and found a Karl Beck listed. It was, of course, not *the* Karl Beck ("Beck" is not a rare name). But now comes the miracle I would never have dared to use in one of our stories. This Karl Beck knew about a namesake in nearby South Orange who had recently died and left a widow by the name of Sophie Beck. And this South Orange Karl (now Charles) was indeed the missing relative!

The rest is almost routine. The "wrong" Karl gave Becker the address of the "right" Karl's widow. My father wrote to her, and she responded favorably to his plea. She promised to take steps to send an affidavit. Father wrote me of this extraordinary chain of events while I was in Gastein.

Shortly afterward my exit papers were ready and I returned to Vienna. Insecurity and fear were widespread. More and more people were picked up at night and disappeared. Swastikas were everywhere, most distressingly in the buttonholes of our gentile friends. From open windows radios kept blaring hate songs, and frequently also Hitler's triumphant voice. Jews were barred from movies, park benches, and from meetings of more than five persons, even in private homes. Illegal flights increased drastically. And here I was the possessor of a precious Belgian visa, and with the prospect of obtaining an affidavit and, eventually, an American visa.

People slipped out of the country unobtrusively. Cousin Arthur had been smuggled into Switzerland, his wife Grete and sister Irma found jobs as maids in England (one of the few available ways to escape, open to women only), and one couple, distant relatives, had disappeared. They later told me in Philadelphia about their flight through Yugoslavia, Italy, France, Spain, and Portugal. All other members of my family stayed behind and eventually perished.

My memory of the last few days in Vienna is blissfully clouded. I only remember, as through a break in a fog, the shattered face of my father when the train pulled out of the station. I dimly recall the rigorous border control in Aachen, first by the Germans and then by the Belgians. Baggage, passport, visa, money. I had a clear conscience, having taken along only one suitcase with my clothes, the allowed amount of money, ten marks, and my portable typewriter. And yet, I had a fireball in my stomach during the checkings. I could not help feeling bitter when forty-four years later my wife and I drove through Aachen and were waved through without even being asked to show passports. All borders in western Europe now open were, in 1938, tightly shut death traps.

Myra met me at the railroad station in Brussels. She did not share my jubilation at having escaped, nor my sorrow at having left my country. Her friend had died suddenly and left her high and dry. She behaved as if he had done it on purpose, just for spite. I was disappointed, too, because I had hoped that he would be able to help me get on my feet, even if he could not use my water-saving gimmick. With other refugees on the train I went to the Jewish

Relief Committee which provided shelter for the night. The next morning the committee gave us some forms to fill out and a small weekly allowance. We learned the rules of the game: no looking for jobs, no loud German in the streets, no large gatherings, no drawing attention in any way. The members of the Relief Committee were concerned that this sudden influx of destitute Jews would create a wave of anti-Semitism, especially if they competed for scarce jobs in an economically depressed country.

Again, Peter Fabrizius brought the solution. From what Max received in London for one short story I could live in Brussels a whole month! I rented a cheap room, sat down at my portable, and produced stories. When I look at them now, I am struck by how indistinguishable they are from those written in Vienna. My world had fallen apart, and I wrote lighthearted tales that had sold in Vienna and that Max could now sell in England. The stories were frivolous but they served a serious purpose. Here I experienced a psychological truth I fully understood only twenty-five years later: an important goal can pull a person out of misery and depression. I typed short stories as if my life depended on it—it did.

My life in Brussels was restricted, yet I was free. I could walk around, sit on a park bench, go to the movies. I remember my delight in the new Disney film, *Snow White and the Seven Dwarfs*. No blaring radios, no flags, I didn't have to furtively check the buttonholes of passersby for swastikas. All the unappreciated joys of day-to-day life were special treats.

But when I thought that earning my own living without taking away jobs from Belgians would give me the right to survive on Belgian soil, I was again too optimistic. A few days after my visa expired, I received a summons to check in at the police station. Some of my fellow refugees who received the same notice went into hiding. I had no reason to hide. I had entered the country legally and could prove I was able to support myself.

We were just a small group at the police station. While waiting, we tried to guess what would happen, but all guessed wrong. Those who guessed right were in hiding. A policeman herded us into a truck which took us to Prison à Forêt. My pockets were emptied, I was photographed, fingerprinted, marched through metal corridors, past steel doors, and locked into a single cell with a cot, table, sink, and toilet. Not until the steel door clanked shut did I fully realize the enormity of this injustice. I lost my head, banged my fists against the steel door, and shouted "I am innocent!" until something in me seemed to split. While banging, I saw myself as if from the outside, shouting and pummeling, and thought of a movie I'd seen, of Captain Dreyfus pounding his prison door and protesting his innocence.

Later the door opened and a uniformed prison official entered. My high-school French was good enough to understand the gist of what he said. The Belgian government had to find a solution to the refugee problem. In the meantime it saw no other place to put us than in an ordinary prison. I was not considered a criminal but had to obey prison regulations. If I had money among my confiscated possessions, I could ask the guard to buy things at the prison canteen. I could have books from the prison library. He even offered to send for a barber.

My native optimism won. Things would work out. Instinctively I grasped another insight that became clear to me twenty-five years later: In unchangeable situations, even in prison, one freedom remains: the freedom to change one's attitude. I could plunge into despair, or plan for the future.

I asked for notebooks, stationery, and a pencil from the canteen. The stationery listed the prison rules in French and Flemish. There was no way to write to my parents without letting them know where I was. I tried to reassure them that this imprisonment was a formality. At least I was safe. I managed to describe the prison like a vacation spot. Then I wrote in my notebook how I really felt, all my fears and exasperation, and felt better.

At 5 A.M. the door opened and the guard set breakfast on the floor: black coffee and a piece of bread. This was a prison rule: nothing to do all day, but breakfast at five. I discovered that I was a morning person. My mind was clear. I sat down and wrote a whimsical Peter Fabrizius short story, with a surprise twist that was our hallmark. I gave it to the guard, who actually mailed it to Max.

The day crept on. I wrote my diary, noted ideas for stories, read books the guard brought me (in French, and tedious), and thought up games I could play by myself. I imagined how various members of my family would behave in a solitary cell. What would

67

grandmother, who behaved like a grand duchess, expecting every-one to give in to her every whim, do in prison? My uncle Camill, the soccer fan, might play a match by himself with a ball of crumpled paper. My father would think up plans for getting out. My mother would worry about everyone except herself. And Max would reflect on whether this relatively humane prison would become a trap if the Nazis were to roll into Belgium.

Several days passed.

Once a day we were led into the courtyard and walked for half an hour single file in a circle. At this time prisoners were allowed to smoke. It was pathetic to see fellow inmates, civilized men, greedily crowding around that one gas flame to light cigarettes before they entered the courtyard. I was glad not to be a smoker.

Although speaking was forbidden, we managed a few words. Rumors. The most alarming was that the Belgian government was shipping refugees back to Austria or Germany. I could not believe it—that would mean concentration camp and probable death. But I could see that day by day our circle changed. Men disappeared, others joined. Every missing person seemed to confirm the unbe-lievable.

After ten days I was led to a prison office. My fellow inmates were there, too. We were told that the Belgian government had found a solution for us to remain in Belgium. We would be interned in a camp near the Dutch border. If we signed a promise to check into headquarters of the Relief Committee in five days, we would be released immediately, to bring our affairs in order. If we tried to hide, we would be shipped back to Austria.

Of course, I signed. I returned to my rented room and called Myra, who did not know where I had been. I learned that I was to be sent to a camp for vagrants picked up from the roads, men who had no jobs or money. They were taken to Camp Merxplas in an isolated region, to do farm work and other labor for low wages until they earned a certain amount of money. Part of this camp was now set aside for refugees.

Objectively, this was better than being caged in prison or returned to the Nazis. But now I was hit by the reality of my situation. I was to be interned in a camp—the very word had horrible connotations—far from everything, deprived of freedom for an unknown time. I went into a deep depression; it seemed the end of the road. I had lost my family, my country, had no future, and was to be locked up in a camp for the homeless, worse off than Belgian tramps. They at least had a country.

I walked through the streets of Brussels with a heavy heart. At the Refugee Committee a man who was also marked for Merxplas had said to me, "What we need is a miracle." I didn't believe in miracles, there was no hope. I came to a park and sat down under a cluster of pine trees. And then the miracle happened, although in a most unspectacular manner. Since then I have come to realize that if miracles happen, they come masked by natural events.

As I was sitting on a carpet of pine needles, suddenly a weight was lifted from me. Nothing in my situation had changed but I knew that everything would come out all right. I was to go to the vagrant camp the next day but I felt at ease.

Only years later, early one morning after a dream and still only half conscious, did I realize what had happened. A ray of sunlight had shone on a twig on the ground. It was evenly shaped, each pine needle in place, the lower part brown and dead, but the tip had fresh green growth. It was a message of hope.

The next morning, twenty "graduates" from Prison à Forêt went by train to Turnhout. There was an attorney from Frankfurt, a judge from Hamburg, a dancer from the Vienna Opera ballet, a high-school student, a Communist agitator from Berlin, an elderly stage director, a physician, a featherweight boxing champ, and bank clerks, salesmen, shopkeepers. The man from the Refugee Committee who accompanied us tried to cheer us up, telling us that the Merxplas camp was a noble social experiment in reeducation. It had no fences or walls; we would not be part of the vagrant rehabilitation program but an independent unit, waiting for emigration. It had required a considerable effort by the Refugee Committee, helped by some Catholic bishops, to persuade the government to accept this interim solution. The committee would make every effort to help us search for possibilities to emigrate.

Despite the pep talk our mood was somber. We changed from the train to a bus that rambled through a vast open heath. No wonder the camp was not walled. It would be difficult to escape undetected.

The camp consisted of many solid brick buildings. We learned later that three thousand vagrants lived here. There were buildings of every size, two farms, a hospital, a church, a slaughterhouse, a school, a quarantine structure, a cemetery, even a little railroad—all off-limits for us. Our bus stopped in front of two huge brick barracks. These had been cleared for the first two hundred refugees. A total of six hundred was projected.

Each building had two dorms with fifty beds each, and no other furniture. I placed my suitcase and my precious typewriter under a cot and joined the others in the dayroom, bare except for benches, tables, and an iron stove. A cluster of men in a giant room.

The uniformed camp director entered and read the regulations. We were to wear camp clothes, just as the vagrants did. Meals would be brought over from the camp kitchen. The timetable: Reveille at 6 A.M., dress, make beds according to specifications, go to washroom; breakfast at 7:15, clean up, then free till noon. Lunch at 12, supper at 6 P.M., 8:30 to bed, 9 lights out, 9:30 silence. He introduced the guards whose orders we were to obey.

He saluted and left.

We sat in silence: prison, after all.

Then something happened I'll never forget. Neidhart, the Communist, began to laugh, loud and hard, exposing two gold front teeth. Then he tore into us. What did we expect? A summer resort? No, here was work to do.

He outlined a plan. We had to show the committee, and indeed the Belgian authorities, that we were not a bunch of parasites but men resolved to build their future. No one would do it for us. We had to prepare for our lives overseas, learn English, Spanish, useful trades, farming. We had to organize ourselves, plan, take charge of our destiny.

In the ensuing silence, the judge said softly, "I could write a constitution."

This struck me as ludicrous. I sensed that others felt likewise. But then the attorney spoke up. "We'll establish a mini-democracy. We, the victims of fascism, will form a democracy."

The idea caught on. The physician made up a list of medicines he would request from the committee. The stage director said he had traveled widely and could teach English. The boxer offered a fitness program. I volunteered to publish a newsletter. We were busy discussing our plans when the guard brought the supper: a kettle of thin soup, black coffee, and bread. We added cooking our own meal to our list. Life had purpose again.

It was a struggle to get permissions for the activities we planned and a minimum of needed supplies. Ours was the first group of refugees. Almost every day brought a busload of new arrivals. We screened them for prospective teachers of courses. A shoe repairman, a carpenter, a barber, an electrician, an auto mechanic. The director of Merxplas was cooperative. He permitted the electricians to open walls for wiring, and the masons to cover up the openings. The committee sent tools, materials, and an old automobile that was taken apart and put together many times for teaching purposes.

I did not see much use in learning a trade. I wanted to remain a writer. It was difficult in the increasing hubbub to discover relatively quiet places, but I found odd nooks and corners, and typed away on my portable. I kept writing Peter Fabrizius stories and sent them to Max. Because there was pressure on everyone to learn something, I joined a course after all: making artificial flowers from wire and wool.

The judge wrote his constitution. It called for each of the four dormitories to elect two representatives to a "council" to govern the camp internally and represent it vis-a-vis the Refugee Committee and the camp director. In addition to taking courses we all had chores. We rotated cleaning rooms, keeping the fire going in the day room, cooking, serving meals, washing dishes. I wrote an article about our "experiment in democracy." Max sold it in England, Australia, and South Africa.

One morning, after three dorms had been filled, and six representatives had been elected to our council, another busload arrived and we lined up to receive the newcomers. A powerful, square-jawed man with a bright red scarf jumped from the bus, followed by a dozen rugged individuals whom he seemed to commandeer. "The Wolff gang," someone whispered, and the word spread. They were a group of rowdies from Vienna. They stuck together, shared the same table during supper, occupied a block of beds in the fourth dorm. When the dorm was filled, they elected Wolff as their representative. It was a lesson in democracy.

After his election Wolff beamed. "Things will get going from now on. If you need something, tell me. The guys on the committee are scared stiff of me!"

News from home was catastrophic. On November 10, during the Night of the Broken Glass, thousands of Jews were shipped to concentration camps. Every mail brought tales of fresh disasters. None of us had received even the promise of a visa. The married men in the camp worried about their wives alone in Brussels. Nerves were frayed. When food supplements didn't arrive from Brussels on time, Wolff staged a revolt. Dishes were smashed, food thrown against the walls. It was not hard to incite a riot.

The reaction of the camp director was swift. He laid down the law. Further violence would have serious consequences. We would lose our privileges and be placed under strict camp rules.

The next day a truck arrived with food supplies. Heavy sacks had to be unloaded. The strongest men, the Wolff gang, were on the soccer field. They kept on playing while we struggled with the supplies. Neidhart stepped up to Wolff. "Now show us what you can do."

Wolff met the challenge with a look of scorn. Neidhart stared back.

"Your men are twice as strong as these professors and book-keepers. Can you control them?"

The red scarf on Wolff's chest swelled like a rooster's comb.

"Hey," he called to his men, "unload the truck."

When the men kept on playing ball, Wolff strode onto the field and grabbed one of the men. They glowered at each other, then the men went to the truck. Others followed.

There were similar incidents. It was clear that Wolff ruled his friends with an iron fist. It was the judge who made a startling proposal. "We have not filled the position of our own chief of camp police. Let's give it to Heino Wolff!"

It seemed absurd. But Neidhart supported the idea, and others came around. Better to have Wolff on our side than against us. To my utter amazement, it worked. Given responsibility, Wolff worked as hard as he had when he opposed the existing order. As soon as he *was* the law, he supported it.

I stayed on the sidelines, finding places to type in relative peace.

My parents wrote that they had been thrown out of our apartment and had to move to a small room. Almost every Nazi-censored letter reported that one of our family or a friend had "gone on vacation," the euphemism for concentration camp.

The more ominous the news, the more we clung to every rumor that promised hope. British Guyana was said to be looking for people to clear the jungle, Paraguay allegedly granted entry permits to those who signed contracts to work in a mine. A man at the Colombian consulate could be bribed to give out visas at a price totally prohibitive for us. We were ready to do anything, go anywhere, just to get away from powder-keg Europe, but none of the schemes panned out, and the committee became less and less hopeful.

In the midst of these frustrations my parents forwarded a letter from a Dave Epstein in Hollywood, one of my namesakes to whom I had sent an appeal! He promised help and requested data so he could write an affidavit. I was stunned. Not only an affidavit, but from Hollywood! In my youthful self-confidence I did not doubt that Peter Fabrizius would be as successful at Metro Goldwyn Mayer as at the *Muskete*. The immediate hitch was that I had to answer Mr. Epstein's letter, and my English was nonexistent. I should have written to Max to have our translator, Akiba, draft one of his masterful letters but I couldn't wait. I approached the teacher of our English course, the stage director. He was the only inmate who refused camp clothes and wore his own threadbare suit. He pinched a monocle in his eye and drafted a letter, which I copied and sent to Hollywood. I never received an answer. Years later I called Mr. Epstein. He told me that he was disillusioned by the terrible English after having been impressed by my (Akiba's) first appeal and did not take my letter seriously. Blissfully, I did not know how empty were the boasts of our English expert. He had been the center of my admiration.

We had conceived the idea of inviting the backers of the committee for a show we were to put on. Our stage director pounced on the idea with contagious enthusiasm. He envisioned a big production that would go on tour all over Belgium, arouse the interest of the press, and result in freedom and visas for us all. He threw himself into the project with the zest of a Max Reinhardt, whose student he claimed to have been. He "commissioned" me to write the script, the carpentry class to build the set, tailoring students to make the costumes, electricians to do the lighting. He held casting auditions. Repeatedly, when something didn't go to his liking, he declared he was "done with the whole dilettante shit" and stormed out, only to return ten minutes later, puffing cigarettes he made from butts he picked up out of ashtrays.

I wrote a parody of camp life, in the manner of our old cabaret skits: professors having to keep the fire going in the iron stove and not having the heart to use a book by Aristotle as kindling; attorneys taking a car apart and discussing injury claims; doctors singing a lively chorus while washing the floor. The camp director was pictured as King of Merxplas, and the members of the committee as angels who in the end flew in and distributed visas among the grateful citizens.

The day of our production came. The road between the two brick barracks was filled with cars from which well-dressed men and women emerged. Women in Merxplas were a rare sight. Reporters and photographers came. Our dancer from the Vienna Opera ballet, the only professional, had quietly directed the production with original ideas, leaving the boastful stage director the illusion that he was the Reinhardt of Merxplas.

Soon afterward I received the long hoped-for news that my unknown American aunt, Sophie Beck, had actually sent her affidavit of support to the American consulate in Antwerp. I was given a pass for a day. On to Antwerp, America, Hollywood, Metro Goldwyn Mayer!

The next day, at the consulate in Antwerp, I didn't get farther than the secretary. My quota number, she told me, was at least one year away. Besides, there were additional conditions. Each American consul made up his own conditions for granting visas, and the consul in Antwerp had the reputation of being one of the toughest. He demanded a blocked account of three thousand dollars in an American bank, ostensibly to make sure that the sponsor really meant to support the immigrant and had not offered the affidavit merely as a formality. Three thousand dollars in 1940 is about twenty-four thousand dollars today. This amount had been deliberately determined by a prejudiced consul, as shortly became known, to scare off sponsors and prevent immigration.

The news I brought back from Antwerp was devastating for those who had hoped to reach the United States. Admission from this consul seemed impossible.

A few days later I collapsed, with severe pain in my stomach. Our physician suspected ulcers, and I was sent to Brussels where a physician from the Refugee Committee examined me. It was a painful examination. I had to swallow a rubber hose so the contents of my stomach could be investigated. Our camp physician's diagnosis was confirmed. I was told that a request would be made to release me from the camp, but prospects were dim.

Once more, Peter Fabrizius found a happy ending, or at least a happy interim solution: Max had learned of a newly approved British transit visa for prospective immigrants to the United States. He wrote that we had earned close to the one hundred pounds required for the granting of the transit visa. I could live with him and his parents until the quota number matured and my visa was granted. His mother was an excellent cook and I would have the diet necessary for my ulcer.

It sounded too good to be true, but this time everything worked. Max proved to the British Home Office that I (Peter Fabrizius) had the money, an affidavit, and a quota number that would come up within a year. Again I was given a camp pass to go to Antwerp, this time to the *British* consulate.

I received my British transit visa and returned to Brussels. I was the first one to leave Merxplas. It is difficult to believe, but I felt sad about leaving that community. We pledged to keep in contact by correspondence. Our camp had served as a model for others, including a much-needed camp for families. No more than half a dozen succeeded in emigrating abroad from Merxplas. The rest disappeared when the Nazis occupied Belgium on May 28, 1940. Merxplas turned into a ready-made trap for people who were deported to German concentration camps.

* 6 *

Learning English for Fun and Survival

1939–1940

PETER

We were united in London, after one year of separation. As planned, Joe moved in with Max and Max's parents. They had a comfortable place on King Henry's Road, with familiar furniture from Vienna.

We had more opportunities to spin stories, especially in the evenings. Instead of discussing ideas while walking the streets as we had in Vienna, we talked late into the night in the room we shared.

For the first time, our situations were different. Max was settled. He considered England his final destination. He had steady employment. His parents were with him, he ate at the same table from the same dishes he had in Vienna.

Joe was in transition. No job, no assurance that he would find one in the United States when and if he got there. His parents were still in Vienna, forced to live in a room they had to share with another elderly couple. They had given up most of their belongings. More and more members of the family disappeared in concentration camps. Joe's father, who until that late hour had still hoped he could survive in Vienna, finally came to the conclusion that he and his wife also had to find a way to leave.

While Max spent every day at his office at the *Jewish Chronicle*, Joe spent much of his time seeking ways to get his parents to

England. The starting place for information and help was Bloomsbury House, the Refugee Aid Committee. Most women refugees to
the United Kingdom were admitted on a "domestic visa," which
meant that British families had to hire them, sight unseen, as
maids. This was one area of employment where demand exceeded
supply; traditionally, London housewives hired servants from the
Continent. This opportunity was occasionally open to married
couples, hired as manservant and maid. Prospective employers at
Bloomsbury House looked over the pathetic piles of applications
from the Continent. Many refugees were there to praise the qualities
of their mothers, sisters, and friends for positions as maidservants—
the atmosphere was a bit like that of a slave market. British
employers got a good deal. Although their new servants had
themselves had maids in Vienna, they were grateful, did back-
breaking jobs, and were much appreciated cooks. Many English
families were introduced to fine Viennese cuisine.

Joe's parents were near their seventies, and he found no willing
employer. Their quota number for the United States was hopelessly
high. They had waited too long. Nor did they have an American
affidavit, and so they did not qualify for an interim visa for England.
The only alternative was to try to become one of those rare cases
when a British visa was granted—as it had been to Max's parents—
on the basis of a guarantee by a British subject. Joe took up the
connection Max had started in Joe's behalf, Josiah Wedgwood. But
it was a lost cause. Joe also tried namesakes and wrote to several
Epsteins in London. He received some replies, among them one
from the famous sculptor Jacob Epstein, who invited Joe to his
home one Sunday afternoon. Joe found himself at a party of artists
and poets who for the first few minutes surrounded him as a
curiosity and overwhelmed him with questions. But Joe's English
was pitifully poor, not even good enough to buy groceries, and
could not stand up under the barrage of sophisticated questions.
Max had told Joe a phrase he had recently picked up and thought
would be appropriate. "Tell them you are hoping for a windfall,"
Max had advised. But the word did not have the magic we expected.
The guests at the Epstein party probably didn't even understand
when Joe said it several times in his Austrian accent. Besides, as we
found out much later, it was not even the right word. What Max

had meant to say was "fluke" or "chance in a hundred" or "shot in the dark" or simply "stroke of luck." Nothing is harder to manage in a newly learned language than idioms. The guests soon lost interest in the peculiar visitor from Vienna. Only Mrs. Epstein had more patience and listened for a while longer, trying to understand Joe. Nothing came of it.

At that time two American Epsteins, to whom Joe had appealed for help a few months earlier, sent letters indicating a willingness to help. One of the letters was from Baltimore and one from New York. Joe, with the assistance of Akiba Schonfeld's King's English, asked them to help his parents instead. But the well-meaning writers did not want to take responsibility for two people too old to work for a living.

We knew few people in London, all emigres from Vienna. Max had Gerda (in a roller-coaster relationship), and his friend Kurt, who was also trying frantically to bring his mother to England. Joe had two relatives in London, both working as maids: cousin Arthur's wife Grete, and Arthur's sister Irma. Harry Freud and his parents were also in London.

One day, Harry called and asked if we could come right away to Maresfield Gardens, where Professor Freud lived. We said we could come as soon as we got properly dressed.

"No," he said. "Come in the oldest clothes you have."

It sounded urgent. We ran over to the house where Sigmund Freud lived with his wife Martha and daughter Anna. It was the home of his son Ernst, an architect who had established himself in London several years earlier. We found Harry, in working clothes, cleaning out the garage.

"Quick," he said. "We have to clean out the garage. The van is on the way with some of my uncle's furniture from Vienna."

We removed trunks and boxes, so that some of Ernst Freud's furniture could be stored in the garage to make room for Professor Freud's pieces from Vienna. Freud had left Austria with the help of the American ambassador to Austria, William Bullitt, and Princess Bonaparte of Greece, one of his devoted followers. Some belongings were shipped at the time of his flight, the rest were arriving now.

After we had done our job, Martha Freud invited us for an afternoon snack. She did not serve Viennese chocolate and cake, but tea English style, with triangular sandwiches. Freud made a short appearance. Because speaking was painful for him (he suffered from cancer of the jaw), he merely nodded toward us and mumbled a smiling thank you.

After tea Freud went to rest in the garden. Harry waved to us, and we sneaked downstairs to get a peek at Freud's (already furnished) study, which looked almost like his study in Vienna. Half his desk was covered with bronze Egyptian statuettes, and tables and window sills were filled with antiquities—masks, busts, papyri, portions of Roman frescoes. In the corner was the head of a mummy in a glass case. In another case were small objects, gold coins, earrings, and pins. Freud was presumably the only person permitted by the Nazis to take so many valuable items from his home.

A large bookcase that filled the entire wall held his works in various translations. At the desk was a chair with a back shaped like the neck of a violin, specially constructed for Freud to relieve his pain by holding his head in place. We also saw a narrow elevator, which Ernst Freud had built for his father.

*

Joe's cousin Arthur Steiner was stranded in Switzerland. His wife Grete in London tried to get permission for him to come to England. During his career as a journalist Arthur had gotten to know many newspapermen from other countries (he even covered the winter Olympics at Lake Placid in 1932), but now none could or would help. He had, however, thought up a scheme similar to Max's in England. He had found a way to beat the strict regulations that prohibited foreigners from accepting employment in Switzerland. Just as Max had used his knowledge of German to find work with an English newspaper, Arthur used his knowledge of English to find work with a German-language Swiss paper. He convinced the Zürich editors of *Weltwoche* that there were enough refugees in Switzerland to justify a weekly eight-page supplement, *Die Sprachstunde*, to teach those who hoped to emigrate to English-speaking countries the secrets of colloquial English. The supplement was published with the title, "It's Fun to Learn English." The trouble was that Arthur's English was as limited as Max's. But Arthur was an excellent journalist with a gift of presenting life and its problems in a light vein. He requested from his wife Grete (the "maid" in London), colloquial phrases, jokes, and words that German-speaking people tended to confuse (such as "gift," which in German means "poison"). Grete asked Joe for help, and Joe asked Max. We sent some of our shortest Fabrizius stories, in German and English. Their publication was an additional small source of income for us. Arthur continued with his "English for Fun" and later published two books on the subject with our assistance. These books were read by Germans and Austrians who immigrated to America after the war.

Years later Arthur told this story about a phone call he received when he lived in New York. A man with a broad Viennese accent said, "Say, Steiner, I have been reading your books for years, and here I am now at the port of New York, and no one understands a word I'm saying!"

While we helped Arthur Steiner teach English to people who knew less than we did, we tried hard to improve our own English. The ladies at the Refugee Aid Committee were a help. They arranged for families to invite us for conversation and dinner, and even an occasional weekend in the country. These visits were delightful but exasperating. We tried to tell our hosts what was happening in Germany, and Max was full of facts and figures from his newspaper monitoring. But when we said that what was happening on the Continent could happen in England, we met widespread ignorance and disbelief. One lady in an exquisite country home thought she had the perfect argument against our warnings. She led us to her rose garden and said, "And you think that your Hitler will come here and destroy *this?*"

The committee also arranged for young people to get together for parties or "rambles," hikes in the beautiful surroundings of London. The green country of Buckinghamshire was a far cry from the charm of the Vienna Woods, but even so evoked memories of Sundays long past. And we were drawn to these outings by the young women who came—mostly working girls. They had never been to the Continent and were attracted by the exotic refugee boys from Vienna. When Max, Joe, and Kurt got to know them better, they said that English fellows were "either shy or show-offs," often more interested in sports than in girls, tending to talk more among themselves than pay attention to their dates. It was a new experience to meet men who listened to what the women said—even though part of our motive was to learn their language. They were also charmed, they confessed, by our traditional "romantic hand-kissing" and "Viennese attitude." For us it was a sweet feeling, after being kicked out of our country, to be appreciated both as men and as human beings.

Max had his Gerda, but Joe was free and became romantically involved with Grace, an attractive telephone operator who had beautiful, clear diction. Joe found two pleasant ways to learn English which he recommended to fellow refugees: have an English girl friend, and go to the movies. He would attend a matinee and sit through three performances of the same film, until evening. He also prepared himself for his future by specializing in American films and learning such useful words as "hot dog" and "shut up"—wisdom he passed on to master teacher Cousin Arthur for his English lessons.

Thus we both improved our English, not in classes but in the school of life—Max in the editorial offices at work, Joe with Grace and the "cinema." Joe also worked on a book, in German, about his experience in the "experiment in democracy" in Merxplas, an experience that left a lasting imprint on him. It confirmed his belief—which had been challenged in our home country—in the basic goodness of human nature.

Our life was a mixture of euphoria and despair. Euphoria because we were together again, thinking up schemes to conquer the world—which now meant the English press. When we mailed off new stories we introduced ourselves with a letterhead individually drawn by a refugee friend, a cartoonist from Vienna. He showed the two of us happily pounding away on a single typewriter, sparks flying. In today's era of mass mailing and photocopying it may seem absurd to produce handcrafted letterheads—but they worked. One after another the bastions of the British newspaper and magazine world fell. They published our stories. The more we published the more we were stimulated to spin our yarns as in the old days. A major publisher, John Murray, published a collection of our stories (in the original German) with a vocabulary in a paperback volume for English students of German. The little book was successful, and three more collections were published in the years that followed.

They persisted through seven editions and were in print for more than forty years.

Yes, our life was euphoria, but also despair. We received letters from our less fortunate friends, caught in Austria, asking us to do something for them. We canvassed everybody we could get hold of for offers of domestic employment for our female family members and friends in Austria. Max placed ads in the *Jewish Chronicle*, appealing to readers to offer household positions to those desperate to escape. On two occasions those ads were successful—a drop in the bucket but a miracle for those two who eventually reached England.

In March, 1939, the most bizarre plant of the Peter Fabrizius collaboration bore fruit. From our "Aryan" collaborator Friese, we received newspaper clippings in which the grand opening of *Lisa, benimm dich!* was announced. The performance took place at the *Wiener Kammerspiele* and was attended by the mayor of Vienna and the governor of Austria (Seyss-Inquart, later hanged in Nürnberg as a major war criminal). Friese sent us rave reviews. The leading lady, Friedl Czepa, with whom Joe had talked in the woods of Bad Gastein, led an Easter parade through the streets of Vienna. We read about these triumphs in our shared room, while fighting for acceptance of each short story.

As we took stock on Max's thirtieth birthday in June 1939, we could look back on many accomplishments in little more than a year: both of us safe and thriving, Joe with his United States visa assured, Max with a job, his parents safe and materially secured. But Joe's parents were in great danger. The Nazi avalanche was gathering momentum. In September 1938, the Allies had betrayed Czechoslovakia and enabled Hitler to occupy its shield, the Sudetenland. In September 1939, we walked on Hampstead Heath; from a hill we looked over London in the glow of the evening sun, with strange blimps holding up steel nets in a naive attempt to obstruct German planes should they attack. It was a peaceful scene. The gleaming buildings of the hub of the empire stretched as far as the eye could see, as if for all time. Soon many would go up in smoke. The invasion of Poland was imminent. The queen of Holland and President Roosevelt tried in vain to deal with madman Hitler. As we left that hill, we realized that something unheard of was brewing that would affect the lives of everyone, in the city and beyond.

Twenty-four hours later we missed a heartbeat when Prime Minister Chamberlain announced that Hitler, defying the world, had invaded Poland, and that England had declared war on Germany. While Chamberlain was talking, an air-raid siren sounded. In a way, this was what we had expected. This would not be a trench war like the last one; within seconds German planes might be over England with poison gas and incendiaries. Gas masks had been distributed weeks ago. The moment we heard the siren Max yelled to his parents to don the masks, and we struggled with ours as we ran to the cellar, which had been staked out as a shelter. On the way we passed the door of the house and, in spite of everything, stepped outside. The street was deserted. One ghoulish Mars man completely covered by a bulging space suit lumbered toward us with a gas mask beneath a flattish helmet. He looked utterly unreal, with goggles and a wrinkled rubber tube hanging from his mouth like an elephant trunk. He motioned with clumsy gestures for us to get back into the house. He was an air-raid warden. England was at war.

It turned out that that had been a false alarm. But the war was grimly real. The thin ice we had been skidding along on had broken overnight. Within hours we were "enemy aliens"—Hitler had chased us out as non-Germans, now we were Germans in the eyes of our hosts. Restrictions were clamped on us, some ridiculous. We were not permitted to own street maps of London (or any maps, for that matter), opera glasses, and cameras. Each of us was assigned a zone, and we could not travel outside of our zone without police permission.

The unpreparedness and general amateurishness in England was appalling. It seemed that no one, from Chamberlain down, had the least notion what kind of enemy they were facing. We watched men on ladders taking off street signs so that the "krauts" would lose their way should they get to London. Men with paint pots obliterated such business names as "Swiss Cottage Laundry" or "Finchley Bakery." The very use of the word "kraut" showed the psychological miles that separated the British from an understanding of the kind of people with whom they had to deal.

A small cannon in Regents Park, a lone toy from the First World War, was readied to fight off Stukas!

Still, we had a respite. The war was on, yet it was not *quite* on.

Hitler turned east, to Poland; on the western front—the *Sitzkrieg*. The French felt safe behind the Maginot Line, and the British were, after all, behind the French. They had time—to evacuate London.

The streets were filled with children, grotesquely equipped with gas masks, being shepherded to railway stations to be taken to the country. Other children were shipped abroad, mostly to Canada. Many businesses moved out of town, among them the *Jewish Chronicle*, which rented office space in High Wycombe, Buckinghamshire. Everyone who knew anybody outside London made arrangements to move and escape the expected bombing of the capital. With much effort we secured permission from the police to move beyond our assigned zone in London, and we found a place in picturesque West Wycombe, a short bus ride from High Wycombe.

West Wycombe was just one street, with a grocery store and one inn, the Apple Orchard. This entire village was a national monument, its houses were historic and could not be replaced by modern buildings or even repaired without permission.

Our house was historic, too. A tiny place, kitchen and living room downstairs, two bedrooms upstairs, no stove, telephone, or proper heating, no rugs. Yet, we were glad to have it. Max's mother bore the brunt, cooking on a single gas-flame burner for a family of four—Joe being her second son.

There was little to do here. In the mornings Max rode the bus to the office in High Wycombe and in the evenings Joe and Max hatched stories. Max was an enemy alien and felt his job was becoming precarious. It was lucky that High and West Wycombe were within the zone assigned to us. Otherwise we were not permitted to move around and had to check in with the High Wycombe police regularly and extend our certificate of registration. To travel to London—an hour by train—we had to have a good reason and permission from the police. From time to time we were visited by English friends who were not bound by travel restrictions. Grace made weekly visits to Joe.

When Max reviewed his situation at the end of 1939, things had greatly deteriorated since his thirtieth birthday in June. Then he had felt settled at home and work. Now he was living in makeshift quarters and was an enemy alien, whose job depended on a revocable police permission. The Rothschild help was about to end and Max decided not to apply for an extension. Instead he would support the family from the payments for his writings and the little he had saved during the past year.

Joe was cut off from any communication with his parents. He waited for his American quota number, yet dreaded the day when he would embark across the Atlantic to an uncertain future. For the time being, at least, we were together.

Not for long. Early in February 1940, Joe's quota number was called and he received a letter from the American consulate in London to pick up his immigration visa. He secured booking on a ship leaving Liverpool. We were to be separated once more.

* 7 *

On My Own in the Universe

1940–1941

MAX

On February 15, 1940, I noted in my diary: "Last night for Joe in our house in West Wycombe. Tomorrow to Liverpool, on ship to America. A piece of myself goes with the friend."

Thus it became still lonelier in our isolated place. However, we made friends with several people in the little town, for whom we were not enemy aliens, and we were invited to their homes. Mother especially won friends wherever she showed herself. Besides, the official attitude was changing. After the first war scare, during the temporary lull, tribunals were set up to separate the sheep from the goats among the "Germans" in the country. We were granted hearings before a judge to establish our identities.

Those regarded as politically unreliable (mostly residents of pre-Hitler Germany) were classified A and immediately interned as enemy aliens. Recent arrivals had to prove that they were not spies who had been smuggled in as refugees. Although it was impossible to prove a negative, many refugees convinced the judge they were harmless and were classified B—not to be interned but confined within five miles of their residence. Finally, those who were employed and had to travel more than five miles to work were classified C and left undisturbed if their employers vouched for their integrity.

Our case was among the earliest to be examined. The tribunals had been set up hurriedly, and the judges were not trained for the situation. Our judge, instead of trying to establish the political reliability of the aliens, merely examined their need to travel more than five miles from their homes. Since I had to travel from West Wycombe to High Wycombe to go to work, while my parents had no such need, I received a C certificate, my parents a B. The difference was to have serious consequences.

Meanwhile, the expected bombardment of London did not materialize. Evacuees to the country became restless. We saw no point in continuing our makeshift living in West Wycombe, with most of our belongings in London. At the beginning of March 1940, we received permission to move back to King Henry's Road in London. My C classification permitted me to commute to work.

The return to London was particularly welcome because Kurt, who had also found refuge in the country, returned to London at the same time, and we were again companions.

Kurt and I resumed what social ties we had in London, visited friends, and again went on rambles. But time was running out. In the spring the German war machine started rolling. Poland had fallen; Norway and Denmark followed. Winston Churchill succeeded umbrellaman Neville Chamberlain as prime minister. On May 14 the Netherlands surrendered, on May 28, Belgium. Nazi tanks crawled inexorably across the western European plain to chew into France. The British sent an expeditionary force to help the French, but the Maginot Line was circumvented. We stared, paralyzed, as we read in the newspapers about the unequal struggle. We read about the fifth columnists, the "quislings" in Norway.

The British became nervous about German-speaking people in their land. Classifications and restrictions were no longer enough. Nonrefugee aliens, classified A, were already interned. Now the screw tightened: The police began to intern those classified B.

Early one morning two policemen appeared at King Henry's Road and asked for my parents. Elderly persons beyond a certain age were exempted. My father was too old, but mother had to go. She was in the middle of preparing breakfast. She took off her apron, said a stunned good-bye to stunned father and me and, completely composed, descended the steep stairs to an automobile. It was to take her, we learned later, to Port Erin on the Isle of Man.

The police left. For the time being, I was protected by my classification C. Father and I shifted for ourselves. But German tanks continued to roll west and the fever rose. The exemptive age limit for Category B was rescinded. During the first days of June, the police came again. This time they took Father. He was dry-eyed when he was escorted out the door but the big question mark in his eyes as he waved his farewell haunted me for days. He was also taken to the Isle of Man, but to Douglas, not Port Erin. My parents remained separated. On June 8, 1940, my thirty-first birthday, I was alone in our flat. My parents were gone, Joe was in America, Gerda and I had amicably separated, she to marry an Austrian with an American visa which enabled her to leave at once. No one else, including Kurt, knew I had a birthday. It was the loneliest I ever had—no good wish, no gift, no telephone call.

I owed my freedom to the accident of my C classification—but how much grace was I going to have? I expected to be rounded up eventually, too. And so I started to work on further emigration—to America.

It had not been my intention to leave England for the United States. I respected the British for their integrity—even for their red tape which, with all its "obedient-servant" mumbo jumbo, seemed merely the symbol for the reliability of everything that bore the engraving of H.M. stationery. England, although declining in power, was a mature and, to us, humane country—a country of gentle men.

But as the tanks kept rolling, we saw the handwriting on the wall. The gentle men, because of their very nature, were not the fighting men of Queen Victoria's days; it seemed terribly late for Churchill to turn the tide, in fact, *too* late for France. On June 14, Paris fell to the Nazi juggernaut; the day after, Himmler's angels of death descended and turned the French internment camps into concentration camps by simply changing the guards. The French, instead of allowing the refugees to escape as best they could—over the Pyrenees or by boat—served them on a platter to the Gestapo, who crunched them out in the extermination camps of Poland.

It was clear that the Nazis would repeat the performance if they were able to cross the English Channel. This was Hitler's chance of a lifetime: to press on at once, invade defenseless Britain, and set himself up as lord of the empire.

I was determined not to become a Hitler victim in England as so many had in France.

In later years I discussed with Joe whether my pessimism was justified or whether I made a mistake in being an unnecessarily nervous Nelly—after all, Hitler did not invade England. Was it a matter of my being right in expecting the invasion of Austria but wrong in England? As I see it now, Hitler, intoxicated with his victory over France, was gorged with triumph, psychologically unable to swallow yet another enemy immediately. He had to savor his triumph, to drool over the victory, as anyone who saw the movie in which he danced a jig in dizzy delight will understand. But that he planned the invasion (dubbed Operation Sealion by the Germans) is today uncontested history—and so is the fact that *he* made a mistake by hesitating and thus missing his opportunity. The military documents for the invasion were found by the Allies in liberated Brussels. The intended invasion was confirmed by Alfred Jodl (Chief of the German General Staff) at the Nürnberg War Crimes Trials, and by Churchill in his memoirs.

The "case of the two invasions" illustrates the difference in attitudes that still permeates Joe's life and mine.

I read the newspapers in 1940 with the same forebodings with which I had read the weekly *Tagebuch* in Vienna in 1937. And I came to the same conclusion: invasion by the Nazis was a clear and present danger, and I did not want to fall into their clutches. I registered at the American consulate for a quota number. Since I registered so late, my number was high, and I could not expect to be called for about a year. That meant I would have to find temporary refuge in a third country. In the meantime I would have to secure an American affidavit of support, such as Joe had received from Sophie Beck.

I wrote to a cousin of my mother in New York for an affidavit. Besides, I knew that supporting letters from prominent Americans carried weight with immigration authorities. As I reviewed in my mind the people to whom I might write to ask for such a letter, an unusual candidate came to my mind.

89

In Vienna I had written a novel, the story of a hitchhiker. That manuscript had been accepted by Zinnen Verlag, a publisher in Hamburg who also published the works of Pearl Buck, an author I greatly admired. When the publisher investigated my "racial" background he canceled his commitment. In London, grabbing at straws, I decided to ask Pearl Buck, my potential "colleague" whom I never met, for a supporting letter. I sent my request in care of Zinnen Verlag but never received an answer.

While working on my affidavit (and on supporting letters), I had to find some way to reach a third country, where I could temporarily stay. The "first swallow" would try to fly again.

On June 17, 1940, Buckinghamshire was declared a protected area. Refugees were not permitted there, regardless of classification. Since the *Jewish Chronicle* offices were in Buckinghamshire, I lost my cherished job.

A few days later, the ax fell. The newspapers reported that category C refugees would now be interned.

I held a war council with Kurt. We had to make it credible to the police when they came to intern us that we were on the way out—show an immigration permit to some country or a paid ship ticket, or some other documents to convince them that internment was unnecessary.

The race to the consulates started again, as once experienced by Joe in Vienna. We cooked up the most abstruse schemes to persuade some consul—*any* consul of *any* country—to give us a visa. One such scheme will serve as an example.

A few wealthy German refugees, who had stowed away funds outside Germany before Hitler's advent, had been able to buy or bribe their way into the Dominican Republic and had started agricultural settlements there. I wrote to the Dominican consul in London, introducing myself as a reporter of the *Jewish Chronicle* who wished to write a series of articles abut these settlements. The consul actually invited me to an interview and I explained my project mentioning, casually, the formality of my needing a visa for my investigating trip to the Dominican Republic. I never heard from him again.

By then Kurt and I were expecting that any day now it would be our turns to answer the doorbell rung by the police. We heard through the rumor-laden refugee grapevine a story so fantastic that we gave it only guarded credence. We understood that there was one country in the world that allowed unlimited immigration—no visa, no landing money, no affidavit. Everybody could come, any time.

Well, it was not actually a country, but a city. And the city was at the opposite side of the globe—in China! The name of the city was Shanghai.

We were in no position to dismiss any rumor outright. Kurt and I investigated, and what we learned was this:

Shanghai, the most important Chinese port city, was not controlled by the Chinese government. The British, French, and a number of other Western powers had wrested Shanghai from the weak Chinese in the nineteenth century and administered the city jointly by a municipal council. They recognized the theoretical sovereignty of China but treated the city as extraterritorial—with its own administration, judiciary, postal system, and immigration policy. The last of these, however, did not exist. The Municipal Council was interested only in the excellent port facilities, and the most rudimentary administration of the city—enough to keep buses running, the water supply functioning, the streets lighted at night, and the like. The city was only the hinterland of the port where ships came and went without port fees to the Chinese. Whatever else went on in Shanghai, especially who came and went, who lived or died there, who flourished or starved to death in the streets (literally) was of no concern to the Municipal Council.

There was another important aspect to the political situation. In 1932 the Japanese occupied vast Chinese territories and conquered the area around Shanghai. But they left Shanghai itself intact. They did not want to tangle with the Western powers controlling the city, which became an enclave in Japanese-held North China.

Thus, a grotesque political vacuum existed in that international city: The Chinese who legally owned it were powerless and had abandoned all functions to the Western-run Municipal Council; the council was uninterested in who was in the city; the Japanese who controlled Shanghai militarily, were holding their horses for the time being. Anyone arriving in the harbor of Shanghai could walk down the gangplank and disappear among the millions of milling Chinese and Westerners. The rumor was true!

Almost true. When it became known in the world of Hitler victims that this remote spot was open, the run on shipping companies was on. Families of prisoners in concentration camps sold their last possessions to secure passage, because in the early years of the Nazi regime thousands of concentration camp inmates were actually released if they could prove they had a place to go. A ticket to Shanghai was that proof.

Italian and Greek shipping lines at once raised their prices. They placed in operation tubs barely seaworthy, transportation under subhuman conditions. Still, the ships were filled to the sinking point and refugees poured into Shanghai—twenty thousand of them before the war in Europe closed the Mediterranean escape route; it was still open from England through the Panama Canal.

Soon the shipping lines were not satisfied even with extortionist blood money. They would sell tickets only to those who could show a bank deposit of two thousand dollars (a horrendous sum at that time, the equivalent of sixteen thousand dollars today) in a Shanghai bank. This was a fiendish scheme to make certain that the refugees had enough money to be transported back, if they could not actually land in Shanghai. After all, for all the shipping tycoons knew, the Municipal Council in Shanghai might from one day to the next close up Shanghai—as the rest of the globe had done.

After days of soul-searching, Kurt and I decided with very mixed feelings to take that route and plunge into the exotic unknown. The bureaucracy was staggering: we needed a travel document (our Austrian passports were obsolete), an exit permit, a shipping ticket—and two thousand dollars in a Shanghai bank.

We started with the two thousand. Neither of us had it. It was here that Peter Fabrizius went into action again. My cousin in New York had written that he was "considering my request for an affidavit favorably." Now I cabled Joe to approach him again and try to convince him to send the deposit to China—I would not use it, but had to show that I had it. I could have written my cousin directly or sent him a lengthy cable, but what was needed was a whip, an efficient and interested friend who understood the urgency and could make others understand.

Joe functioned in the time- and crisis-honored way. I received a return cable—five words only, but all that was needed: "Deposit made Chase Bank Shanghai."

Kurt had a lot more trouble with his deposit. He too had a cousin in New York but it took many anxious days and expensive cables until he had his deposit secured.

*

At this time I received the first news from my parents, in separate communications. Mother adjusted to the hardships of a makeshift camp that lacked the barest necessities. Father broke a leg tripping on the unpaved, unlit camp grounds. He asked for a blanket and other basic articles. What was to become of them? Here I was— history repeating—preparing to leave them behind, and I felt guilty. I could not help them by staying, yet might eventually be able to do so from the United States, just as I could do nothing for them in Austria, but only from England. I could not get rid of guilt feelings despite these deliberations. I summoned my nerve and asked for a Rothschild appointment.

Lionel de Rothschild was out of town, but his brother Anthony received me. He said that at this early stage of the internment program he could not do anything but might later. He was not as cordial as Lionel had been. He was cool when I told him about my Shanghai plan. I could see he felt it was "unpatriotic." There would always be an England. He would keep my parents' internment in mind, he said in a noncommittal way. I was glad that I had not tried to ask him for those two thousand dollars—Peter was a better bet. But Anthony de Rothschild did give me a letter of recommendation to Sir Victor Sassoon, the uncrowned king of Shanghai.

I left St. Swithin's Lane with mixed feelings.

Many additional papers had to be assembled, a skein of red tape untangled—each paper expired after a certain date, yet was required to obtain the next. The various offices were swamped and in no hurry, while our deadlines were approaching. I finally received my travel paper—an identity certificate, not a passport. Stamped on it was the notice: NO RETURN TO THE UNITED KINGDOM. After I left the shores of England, I would be on my own in the Universe.

The Identity Certificate had a short-term expiration date. Before the deadline I had to obtain my exit permit and ship reservation.

No shipping company would issue a ticket without an entry visa to the country of destination. We explained the no-visa situation for Shanghai, and the company cabled their offices in Shanghai to get verification of our deposit from the Chase Bank in Shanghai. Chase confirmed and we thought we had it in the bag. But now the shipping agent asked, where was our transit visa for Panama?

We never knew one was needed. But, surely, it would be a formality. We went to the Panamanian consulate.

A dark-haired man there listened. No. No visa for Panama.

Why not? Sir, we only need a *transit* visa. We do not intend to stay or even disembark in Panama!

Transit visas are granted by Panama only on passports which show a visa for a country of final destination; or a landing permit. Otherwise the passenger may be refused entry, and Panama would be stuck—on the basis of the transit visa the passenger could get to Panama and then disappear there. We tried to explain that Shanghai did not issue visas, that it worked differently, you see—with deposits—the Chase Bank—the shipping line. . .

He threw us out.

We came home, stunned. After all this work and expense, with all the papers in our hands but this one, with a *dated* exit permit— we were up against a wall.

We reviewed our visit at the Panama consulate, and decided we had presented our case miserably. We should have made things simpler; the man did not *understand*. He followed his government's instructions blindly. We had not convinced him that Shanghai was an *exception*, dammit! Shanghai was an exception in everything.

We would try again. We carefully rehearsed our explanation, so that any child would understand. We would bring the telegram from the Chase Bank, and a printed leaflet that explained the deposit-instead-of-visa procedure.

When we appeared at the consulate the next day, the large door was closed.

Mr. X had taken the day off. We looked up his name in the telephone directory. He lived in the suburbs. We decided to visit him at his home.

It was a long ride, but we finally arrived at a rich man's villa. Uneasily we rang the bell, rehearsing every word we would say. He opened the door himself. As soon as he saw us, he shouted at us. What nerve to bother him in his home! He was NOT going to break his government's regulations. We were to produce a visa or never to bother him again. Slam.

We returned home in utter despondency. Here was an impenetrable, irrational block. We were used to talking sense with British officials. No matter how hidebound, they were reasonable human beings. Not so those Panamanians. Our work was for nothing. Our hopes were shattered.

This was a time when I needed Joe's optimism. It would have been justified. Because at the moment when there seemed no way out, a "Joe miracle" occurred.

We told our frustration to the booking agent who had requested our Panamanian visa. He did not seem disturbed. He said he could book us on the *Oronsay* (it would have to be first class—meaning outrageously expensive for us flotsam), due to leave August 10 from Liverpool.

So—? What about Panama?

The *Oronsay* did not go through Panama but to Halifax.

Halifax, Canada??

Yes. Then we could take the train across Canada to Vancouver, and a ship to the Far East.

Just like that, eh? And how about a transit visa for Canada?

Canada did not require one, the man declared.

Holy Joe! From utter despair we were catapulted into highest ecstasy.

On August 10, 1940, on a foggy, drizzly morning, Kurt and I boarded the 20,000-ton wartime-gray Canadian Pacific steamer *Oronsay* in Liverpool, our first step toward an unknown world— China.

*

The *Oronsay* traveled in total blackout in convoy with eight other ships, protected by two destroyers and a cruiser, warplanes overhead for the first two days. We were fifty adult passengers and four-hundred English children being evacuated to Canada. They

95

were a noisy, happy bunch, wearing gasmasks and lifebelts at all times and keeping the stewards busy. The *Oronsay's* bridge had been knocked off by a Nazi bomb in Narvik, Norway, and the ship had been repaired and repainted.

I lay down on my bunk utterly exhausted from the turmoil of the final days in England. It was my first moment of physical rest, but both Kurt and I were still deeply worried about whether we had taken the right step.

We were in a strange situation: in a luxury cabin, preferred passengers, yet with one-way tickets, an emergency travel document, stateless and unwanted—going toward an uncertain destiny to a country under the control of a Nazi ally. War between Japan and the United States could break out any day. What a relief it would be if that disaster should happen—if it had to happen—just while we were crossing Canada, so that our further trip into the jaws of the dragon would become impossible. Today it is forgotten that the "surprise" of Pearl Harbor on December 7, 1941, was no real surprise; war between Japan and the United States was expected: our tickets were stamped with big diagonal letters: NO REFUND IN CASE OF WAR. The question was merely how and how soon. We were traveling first class into war.

Early next morning I was up on deck. I had not slept much and was on the edge of being seasick. There was a shore in the distance. A sailor said: "The Isle of Man." If my parents had looked, they might have seen the outlines of the ship. And here I was deserting them. I was so miserable that I slunk back to my cabin, lay down for the rest of the day, and skipped all meals. I was fighting both seasickness and guilt feelings.

On the third day the ship's bulletin, reporting the radio news from the BBC, announced matter-of-factly that during the night a 17,000-ton ship in our vicinity had been sunk by German U-boats with the loss of forty lives.

The next day I felt well enough to pull out my faithful companion, my portable typewriter, and write some letters and draft a short story. I also kept a diary.

The crossing took nine days. On August 19 we first laid eyes on the New World. The brightly lit city of Halifax—the first city lights after weeks of blacked-out London—was as thrilling to us as the Statue of Liberty has been to immigrants arriving in the United States.

But we were not immigrants, only transmigrants. It took two more nights on board before we were allowed to land. During that time mail was delivered to the waiting passengers. To my great joy, I was among the happy recipients: Letters from Joe, my New York cousin, and, surprisingly, from Gerda (who lived with her husband in Boston). They all said the same: Could we not wait for our quota number in Canada?

Indeed, we thought of nothing else throughout our time in Canada. We boarded a train in Halifax to Montreal, where we were met, unexpectedly, by representatives of refugee organizations who provided inexpensive housing and showed us around town. Para-doxically, we were free—we could do anything we wanted in Canada, so long as we met our deadline, September 8, in Vancouver to board the *Heian Maru* of the Nippon Yusen Kaisha (N.Y.K.) Line for Japan. We decided to make the best of these extra days, pretend to be tourists, and see the sights. While in Montreal, we climbed Mount Royal and, looking south, like Moses viewing the Promised Land, we could see the United States.

Through the organizations we were introduced to a number of people who, we hoped, would have enough influence to convince the Canadian authorities to allow us temporary refuge. We also had letters of introduction from England. Harry Freud had given me a letter—a request for help—addressed to an influential K.C. (King's Counselor) in Ottawa. Our days were filled with a weird mixture of elegant sightseeing and desperate efforts—writing, telephoning, meeting people who might be able to help us change our status from transients to residents, all in vain.

We kept up a positive front as tourists. Our next sightseeing was Toronto. From there we visited Niagara Falls, directly on the American-Canadian border.

A suspension bridge connects the American and Canadian sides of the river that flows from the falls. At the bottom of the falls the water is calm and forms a quiet pool. A small boat, the *Maid of the Mist*, shuttles between the two countries. Passengers on the Canadian side receive Canadian tickets but are not allowed to disembark when the *Maid* picks up American tourists with American tickets. Members of either group may disembark only on their own side, and must prove place of origin by surrendering their tickets. Tickets are passports and visas—nothing else is needed.

On the boat passengers from the two group mingle.

At least this was the situation on that fateful September day in 1940.

In the next hour we passed through the emotionally most explosive episode of our trip.

It was a hazy day but the weather was good enough for sightseeing. It happened to be Labor Day, and thousands of people were milling around on both shores, crowding onto the boat with standing room only, each pressed against the other as in a tightly packed commuter bus at rush hour. Because of the spray from the falls, all passengers were provided with rubber coats that covered them completely—even with a hood that made them look like Ku Kluxers.

Kurt and I sat down by the edge of the water, eyes glued on the *Maid of the Mist*, not Niagara Falls. We did not have to talk, we each knew what the other was thinking.

We were not Canadians or Americans, not even Austrians or Germans. We were stateless. We were not tourists, not visitors, just a piece of existence hanging by the thinnest thread—permission to cross the country by a deadline. We were different from every man, woman, or child of any nationality around us, and the feeling of isolation—and opportunity—was crushing. Across that river lay safety and life. And we were on an invisible conveyor belt carrying us into an unknown, threatening world, driven by the Nazis in Europe into the clutches of their allies in Asia. Would we ever get back alive? Would our quota numbers arrive at the American consulate in Shanghai before war between Japan and the United States trapped us in a Japanese concentration camp?

We squatted on the bank of the river, arms around our knees, our mesmerized eyes glued on that little boat as it puff-puffed every few minutes from our side to freedom, then returned. We decided to take the ride.

We bought Canadian tickets. They entitled us to travel to America—but not to land there. The boat came over with American tourists who remained on board; the Canadians—and Kurt and I—

got on. We slipped into the black raincoats and hoods and squeezed in with the crowd. As the boat returned to the American side, the eyes of the hundreds were on the spectacular falls. Our eyes were on the tickets many of the Americans on holiday held nonchalantly in their hands.

Was there an immigration officer on the American side? Probably not—there was none on the Canadian side. We had carefully watched as the Canadians who had completed the round trip left the ship. They simply surrendered their tickets and stepped back onto Canadian soil.

We looked at the tickets Americans were holding with the fascination of a cobra eyeing a mouse (Canadian and American tickets had different colors). Could we persuade two of them to sell us their tickets? They could claim to have lost them, establish their citizenship, and land. But how could we explain why we needed those tickets? Would they denounce us?

We could just lose ourselves in this crowd, unidentified, a hood among hoods, and float along with the rest on the American side . . . we could jostle someone into dropping his ticket . . . there was a man in front of me, his back actually pressing against my chest, his hands clasped behind his back, the American ticket casually in his fingers, as he stared at the falls. If I pretended to stumble, sliding the ticket from those fingers, then apologized . . . no one would be able to find the ticket among the many feet . . . but what about Kurt? I looked at him and could see from his glassy eyes that the wheels were going round in his head as in mine. Or I could slide the ticket from those loose fingers but not move—no one would ever know who among those sardines did it. The temptation was so overpowering, our excitement at a fever pitch, we saw and heard nothing of what was going on—everybody else's attention was fixed on those magnificent falls and it seemed criminal to pass up this unique opportunity and not act, NOW.

It seemed equally criminal to act. If we were picked up as illegal immigrants, this would be in our American records forever. It would affect naturalization, career, our future. If we *did* get our quota number in China in time, on the other hand, we would be law-abiding immigrants, able to lead normal lives when this nightmare was over.

99

We reached the American side. The *Maid of the Mist* stopped and the Americans, round trip completed, got off. We saw them surrender their tickets to some officer of the company who carelessly tossed them into a bin. I stood on deck, directly beside a post stuck into the water, painted red-white-and-blue. I touched it, shyly, with one hand—I actually touched America! But I was to travel half way around the world before I could touch it with my other hand. And I did not know whether this would ever become possible.

We sailed back as in a dream. From the high pitch of the first half of the trip we dropped into the nothingness of the second. We arrived on the Canadian side, surrendered our worthless tickets, and sat down again by the dock.

We could not take our eyes off that boat as it turned, again to the American side, back and forth, back and forth, all day. We still had the chance. We still could do it. Perhaps we would have more guts a second time. Another idea: We could telephone our friends in New York, ask them to hurry to Niagara Falls AT ONCE, get on the boat with their American tickets, then exchange them for ours. We would get out on the American side, and they could say they lost their tickets; they would prove they were residents of New York. It was a fantastic deal. We looked at our watches—perhaps too late today, maybe tomorrow. But tomorrow would not be Labor Day, the whole tailor-made confusion would be gone, inspection tighter. We would have to try today, now, perhaps simply do some jostling . . .

A voice behind us said: "How do you do."

We turned, and there was a police officer, or rather a man from the Immigration Service. Were we Americans? Canadians? I meant to say, in a belligerent mood, that this was none of his business . . . but, well, it was his business. He asked for our papers, said thank you, and disappeared after what seemed to us a penetrating look.

Well, well, well. Somebody *had* been watching us and perhaps had read our thoughts. Perhaps it was better, after all, that we had done nothing. Only the future would tell. Perhaps it would have been better to sit in an American or Canadian jail than in a Nazi-Japanese compound dying a slow, disease-ridden, sadistic death.

We returned to Toronto, dazed. Everything that followed,

crossing the enormous expanse of Canada, was an anticlimax. We stared from the window of the Canadian Pacific Railroad, resenting the endless uninhabited plains that could give refuge and shelter to millions, yet were declared off-limits by an unrelenting Canadian government that would not permit even the trickle of immigrants the United States allowed.

En route we stopped in a few places and I visited some Canadian newspaper editors, trying to make connections for the future. We stayed in Jasper and toured the Canadian Rockies in their grandeur, mixing with real tourists, indistinguishable so long as we kept our mouths shut.

Eventually we arrived in Vancouver, drained. We made last-ditch attempts with local authorities and organizations to get permission for temporary residence.

Did it not occur to us to go underground? To miss the ship to Vancouver purposely and go into hiding in Canada?

Occur to us, indeed! Throughout the long trip across the continent we were tortured by the thought. The closer we came to the west coast the more we were tempted to do something desperate. But our background militated against this ultimate step. We had been brought up in a world of law and legitimacy; perhaps, had there been a "clear and immediate danger" we might have had no choice. But at that point we still had a choice. To go to China was a gamble against time; to go underground in Canada was illegal. We could not see ourselves as fugitives, hiding in fear, eventually caught and jailed and marked for life. Still, would such a life not be preferable to what we faced? That, of course, was the question we could not answer—but we had to answer it. We were "civilized" people, had legal papers, brushed our teeth in the morning, wore good clothes—we could not see ourselves sleeping in rags under bridges, on the run from the police. As long as there was a chance to survive on this side of the law, as long as no instant destruction was threatening, we would follow our plan.

As I look back now at what happened in later years, I cannot suppress bitterness. Thousands of "boat people" from southeast Asia were given sanctuary in the United States—no affidavits, no quotas, no forced waiting that ended in death camps. Ship jumpers from Russian and Rumanian boats were granted asylum within days. The humanity shown to those unfortunates was not extended to us. No extra quotas were allocated, not even the unused quotas from unthreatened countries were used for us—they were allowed to be forfeited.

In one of the most shameful episodes of American immigration policy, the *St. Louis*, filled with refugees from Germany, was turned back to Nazi Germany, although the ship had reached America. And the British, the gentle and civilized British, sent their warships to the coast of Palestine to keep the wretched survivors who had managed to get out of Germany from landing and joining their kin. And Canada, immense Canada, said no, although we were already there.

No, I do not begrudge the Asians their better fate. They have become model citizens, determinedly learning English, making sure their children do well, far above average, in our schools. They have enriched America. All I am saying is that *our* potential model citizens were martyred in the death camps. Those of us who were allowed to make our homes here have a record to be proud of, and have made contributions far above average. But how many anonymous Albert Einsteins, Sigmund Freuds, Ernst Blochs, Hans Kelsens, Nelly Sachses, Lisa Meitners, were allowed to perish?

On September 8, Kurt and I boarded the N.Y.K. Japanese steamer *Heian Maru* for Yokohama. As the American shore receded we each had a tight feeling in our chests. Would we ever see our friends and families again? In Vancouver we noticed Americans and Canadians returning from the Far East. They did not want to be caught in a possible war zone; that was where *we* were headed.

*

During the uneventful thirteen-day journey we crammed our heads with information from the ship's library about the culture of China, our destination.

In Yokohama we were utterly lost. Nobody met us at the pier, nobody spoke English or German, we could not read the street signs, couldn't ask for street addresses or which bus to take, how to pay for a ticket, where to get off. It was as if we had landed on Mars. We managed to find the YMCA and took a room there.

And yet, and yet . . . the eleven days in Japan, while we were waiting for the connecting ship to Shanghai, were perversely enjoyable. We decided to make the best of a deadly bargain and see this beautiful land like world travelers on a pleasure trip. Psychologically it was easier to enjoy Japan than Canada because in Canada every moment was taken up by tortured efforts to get permission to stay. Now the die was cast. At Niagara we had hardly looked at the falls but in Yokohama, Tokyo, Kyoto, Kamakura, Nara, Osaka, Kobe, Nagasaki we visited temples, shrines, parks, and other attractions with intense interest. We had a Baedeker guide book and an outline of Japanese history, and we plunged into all the new impressions with youthful vigor and curiosity. In an antique store I picked out a pair of chopsticks I liked. When I used them in a restaurant, everyone giggled. I found out I had bought ladies' hairpins.

Our impressions were mixed. We admired exquisite woodprints, and were puzzled by the squat-down toilets. We were enchanted by the beauties of Lake Biwa and Mount Hie, and were frightened by a sudden blackout and air-raid alarm —not the real thing, we learned later.

In general, our attitude was similar to what it had been during our first weeks in London. We made a game out of our precarious situation; we were dancing on a volcano but did not burn our feet.

On October 2, as inexorably scheduled, we left from Kobe on the 14,000-ton *Taiyo Maru* for the last leg of the trip: the three-day crossing of the Yellow Sea. On October 5, after traveling fifty-five days, we saw a mountain chain rising on the horizon: China.

When the *Taiyo Maru* touched the Bund, the embankment of the port of Shanghai, our feelings were in turmoil. Should we be glad to have reached our destination or were we walking into a trap? We were in China, for heaven's sake, a couple of unattached Viennese in China!

At the pier of N.Y.K., an old shabby sign read "N.Y.K. Welcomes You." This commercial slogan, directed at nobody in particular and put up perhaps twenty years earlier—it touched us. We were in such a volatile mood in this outlandish place where we did not know a soul and nobody knew us or cared a fig; we clutched this emotional straw and felt irrationally good about it.

Shanghai was not like Japan. This was an international city. We

could make ourselves understood in English, although the pidgin of
the Chinese was not always intelligible. The city was less strange
than Yokohama or Tokyo. The Bund was not unlike the embankment of a Western city although thousands of Chinese thronged the
port area. Three buildings were prominent: the Sassoon Tower (a
hotel and exclusive business high-rise), the palatial Hong Kong and
Shanghai Bank with its two marble British lions at the front, and
the impressive *North China Daily News* building with its two bell
towers, housing a British-owned newspaper with a circulation far
beyond the city confines. I eyed it with very special thoughts.

We found a small pension, owned by a German refugee, in the
district of Shanghai known as the French Concession. This district
had its own municipal administration, independent of the Municipal Council—a town within a town. Most refugees lived in
Honkew, separated from the rest of the city by Soochow Creek, and
controlled by the Japanese. It had been bombed in the 1932 war,
and the damaged buildings had not been restored. Honkew was the
shady side of glittering westernized Shanghai.

Kurt and I had only some emergency funds. We needed to earn
money. There was a refugee committee, but it had limited resources
and we were determined to stand on our own feet. We advertised as
teachers of German and, miraculously, found a student, Signor Ugo
Tavella, head of the Italian Bank of China.

We were pleased to have some income and to know a member
of a nation allied with the Japanese. We became well acquainted,
and after a while asked his advice about what to do with our
emergency funds: we had dollars, which surely would be blocked (if
not confiscated) in case of war. Changing to Japanese money seemed
risky, and Chinese money was worthless. Perhaps Argentinian
pesos? Signor Tavella shook his head. "Buy a gold bar," he advised.
"It's not liquid, and bears no interest, but it is safe." He offered to
buy it through his bank and do the safekeeping.

It was a ticklish situation. Should we hand over all our earthly
goods to this stranger? We believed him trustworthy. Retaining a
small amount for current expenses, we gave him all we had.

The day after this transaction I took my Rothschild introduction
and visited Sir Victor Sassoon. Although his office on top of the
plush Sassoon Tower was barricaded by Cerberuses, my letter worked

and I was received by the olive-skinned tycoon from Baghdad, where his family originated. He did not say much but gave me his card to give to another Baghdad bigshot in Shanghai, Mr. Horace Kadoorie, a businessman and philanthropist who sponsored a school. I saw Mr. Kadoorie—and he gave me a job as an English teacher in his school!

In London I had to have a translator for our stories, and here I was to teach English! To be sure, the three years in England had left some mark on my linguistic talents, and the innocent kids at the Kadoorie school knew less than I did.

Encouraged by the success of this bit of nerve, I decided to pursue the teaching trail further. I noticed a private high school, run by a Chinese with the unlikely name of Maurice, and asked if they needed an English teacher.

A few days later I had teaching jobs in two schools in Shanghai.

Kurt, meanwhile, had not been idle. With his grand seigneur demeanor he walked into the tradition-bound, British-run, Royal Asiatic Society library and secured a job as librarian. His encyclopedic, scholarly mind made him as much a catch for the library as the library was for him.

And so, we had no need to bite into our gold bar. We had never seen it but Signor Tavella said the gold was safe, and continued taking lessons from us.

The preoccupation with our bread-and-butter survival never took our minds off of what was going on at the other end of the world. In England the blitz had begun. My parents were interned in two different camps on the Isle of Man. Joe was struggling for survival in New York. Shanghai was swarming with refugees, many with stubble on their heads, shorn in concentration camps. A few managed to earn a living; most were precariously maintained by the refugee committee. Kurt and I were aristocrats among them, yet we all were shipwrecks, stranded on this island of Shanghai. In fact, this island was an ice floe melting fast in the heat of impending war.

One German refugee with a little money invested it—not in a gold bar—but in a publishing venture. He founded a refugee weekly, *Der Mitarbeiter* (The Co-Worker), a journalistic cooperative, with one paid editor. I was that editor, and drew a regular salary. Peter Fabrizius short stories, of course, appeared in this exotic outlet. I also participated in a short-story club, mostly of White Russians. They had a link to a local radio station, and on a couple of occasions I read stories by Peter Fabrizius over Chinese air waves.

This dabbling in literary and newspaper work whetted my appetite. One day I heard that the Shanghai telephone directory was going through its annual updating. It was printed in the shop of the *North China Daily News* and I wondered if there was a channel that could be used by an enterprising mole. Yes, they could use a proofreader. Just for a few days. Just part-time.

Few occupations in the world are deadlier than proofreading telephone entries. But I decided to squeeze water from stone, and find aspects in this proofreading that could be developed into a story. According to the format of this telephone book, many times I had to add "and Mrs." to a name from last year's entry—evidence of romance in a telephone directory. I had other thoughts when I had to *delete* "and Mrs." from a previous entry. Sometimes I had to delete a "Miss." Would that same person show up as Mrs. in a different place of the book?

I discovered a number of other colorful angles in that seemingly deadly reference work—and wrote them up in a story. Then I walked into the office of the managing editor of the *North China Daily News*.

Mr. R. W. Davies, an Englishman, was more accessible than I expected. He read the story then and there—and bought it.

That was how it started. The proofreading job ended but the *North China Daily News* was a rich source of feature stories. For instance, the classified ads: "For sale: Wonderful bird. Speaks 50 different words, Shanghai, Mandarin, Foochow, English, imitates dog's barking, cock's crowing, magpie's chattering, man laughing." Another, a want ad for "Two stout Russian body guards" and a sale offer for "two bullet-proof vests in good condition." One ad said: "Tall, dark-haired American gentleman, playing slot-machine at cafe Wednesday, 10 P.M. please communicate with interested lady."

The kaleidoscope of this colorful city was mirrored in those ads, tailor-made for a colorful feature, certainly tailor-made for the newspaper in whose ad section they appeared. Davies laughed and bought the article.

Two weeks later I became "cable editor" of the *North China*

Daily News. I would not have dared to hope for such good fortune when I was greeted by the sign "N.Y.K. Welcomes You." I felt like William Randolph Hearst.

I went to work at the news desk at regular hours and drew a weekly salary. We were a happy and crazy crowd of international staff members—the bosses British, the others from every corner of the earth. The world was going to hell, but I was on top of it.

Nor was this all. Now that I had a good job with the *North China Daily News* I had no time for daytime teaching. I hated to give up that income. I called on the acting dean of the University of Shanghai and asked whether all those Chinese who had fled to Shanghai during the Japanese war might need an English teacher for an evening class?

On February 12, 1941, I was appointed English teacher at the evening school of the university, known as Downtown University. Students were eager to learn, and since they were beginners I had no difficulty holding my own. They did their homework conscientiously and besieged me with questions during recess, after class, and even on the bus on my way home.

I was therefore surprised when, after a while, I noticed some reserve on their part, and sensed that something was wrong. It took considerable prodding until one, acting as spokesman, came forward. They felt that in my choice of study material, giving them such sentences as "The man sat down for dinner," "The cat caught the mouse," I treated them like children. Taken aback, I asked what they expected in their first few weeks of learning the language. "Well," said the spokesman, "could we read Shakespeare?"

For a Shanghai refugee, holding two jobs was an anomaly. In between them I wrote stories that I sold to "my" paper and also sent to former outlets in Europe outside Austria-Germany. Shanghai was an inexhaustible source of fascinating articles; it was difficult *not* to write them.

On one level, Kurt and I led a good life. We had jobs, did not have to touch our gold bar, and felt economically safe with that nest egg. We moved to a better part of the French Concession, attended shows and lectures at the YMCA, made new friends, and had dinners at restaurants. On the other hand, war between the United States and Japan could break out any moment. Since we could not hurry the

ripening quota numbers, we tried again the desperate siege of consulates—Cuba, Nicaragua, Haiti—as interim places, but we were
not considered desirable persons. Because our affidavits had to be in
the hands of the American consul in Shanghai before our quota
numbers became available, both Kurt and I worked on our sponsors
to hurry. Each had a cousin in New York who had promised an
affidavit. But it is a long way between a verbal promise in New York
and a signed document in Shanghai. A sponsor may have a sense of
urgency or not; he may fill the endless forms in a hurry or wait for
the weekend; his enthusiasm may be dampened when he realized how
far-reaching was the requirement for financial disclosure. The affidavit was to persuade the consul that the sponsor was rich, yet the
same sponsor might want the IRS to believe he was poor. These were
dilemmas not likely to speed up the completing of affidavits.

This again was a situation for one half of Peter Fabrizius. Kurt
and I were unwitting guinea pigs in an unintended controlled
experiment. His cousin apparently took things easy, although Kurt
pleaded in urgent cables. I did not need to send cables—I had Joe.
Joe got after my cousin, helped fill requirements, and made me feel
that at least no time was being wasted. He tried to cheer me up, too.
"Shanghai," he wrote, "is an ideal waiting spot because, since it is
practically impossible (because of the war in Europe) to receive
United States visas in Europe, some quotas are scrapped and visas are
given on the basis of affidavits alone." It was a pious rumor. I did
not believe it, and it was not true. But Joe was true. I knew I was
in good hands, and never has friendship meant more than in those
crucial days before the outbreak of war. The outcome of this
controlled experiment proceeded accordingly. To anticipate: My
affidavit came in time, before Pearl Harbor. Kurt's did not.
Although he survived, he had to spend the war years in Shanghai,
cut off from family and friends, under a Japanese regime that
cynically herded the refugees into the bombed-out shambles of the
Honkew ghetto. Kurt lived through four years of agony before he
reached the United States. Joe saved me those four years.

To backtrack:

On April 3, 1941, I received a letter from the American
consulate saying, in words as noncommittal as possible, that my

"informal" application and evidence of "adequate support in the United States" (meaning the affidavit from my cousin) "appear to be" satisfactory and the application was "provisionally" approved. But, the letter cautioned, this communication was not to be construed as a promise for a visa because I first had to pass an examination at the consulate, and I should make no arrangements to leave for the United States.

No one in later years could possibly feel the revolutionary effect of this letter, which, despite all the hedging, appeared to promise a safe future. I did not see the qualifications. I did not fear the examination, which was to test the applicant's ability to support himself and not become a public charge.

On the day of my examination I was interviewed by Vice Consul John S. Service. I was not directly facing him. He sat at a 45-degree angle in front of a typewriter, head lowered as he typed my answers to routine questions. Then he came to the crux of the matter. How had I done financially during the past months in the difficult refugee climate of Shanghai? He had interviewed many refugees, most of them supported by the refugee committee.

The following conversation I know almost by heart—I made notes immediately after the interview. It went approximately like this:

"How much are your living expenses?"

"$400 Chinese dollars a month."

"When you arrived in October of last year, how much did you make?"

"Nothing, sir."

"And in November?"

"$100."

"December?"

"$140."

"January?"

"$200."

"February?"

"$207."

"March?"

"$430."

"Can you make a projection of what you expect to earn this month, April?" "Yes, $1,000. I'll get a substantial raise. I have it in writing from the management of the newspaper."

It was at this point that the consul looked up from his typewriter for the first time, swiveled his chair around, and looked me in the face. "How come you have such a large income?"

I explained that I was holding two jobs—as an editor of the *North China Daily News* (a paper he read daily, I learned later) and as a teacher at the Downtown University of Shanghai.

I was incongruously (in this situation) amused by his surprise. This man was used to dealing with almost faceless people on relief, and here I was, suddenly, a "person." The State Department insisted that the immigrant be a good financial risk, which could only be proved by his immediate past record, and this man, as I saw now, was glad that for once he did not have to be a grim trouble maker but could record information that would satisfy the immigration authorities. He became friendly and asked about my future plans. I had become his star case. He wanted to see some of our short stories. He was not fooled by the grandiose letters of support I had received through Joe's help—letters written by literary agents who professed boundless admiration for my immortal prose and predicted a dazzling literary future for me in the United States. But the consul pulled from my file one sheet of paper with interest. "Ha," he said, "Pearl Buck is putting in a word for you!"

It took me a second to remember that once—a lifetime ago, in London—I had written to Zinnen-Verlag in Hamburg. Apparently my letter reached Pearl Buck, who had written a supporting note. I never saw the note. If immigration files are preserved, it must rest somewhere in the vaults of the State Department in Washington. So here I was, with the endorsement of a Nobel laureate in literature!

I felt good on my way home. I thought, cautiously, that I had won my case.

Two days later Mr. Service himself phoned and congratulated me. The visa was granted! He laughed into the receiver.

Little did I know then that I would see him again under utterly different conditions.

*

During the days that followed I was torn between jubilation for myself and guilt about Kurt. We could hardly speak to each other. I prepared for departure and booked passage on a Japanese liner. My earnings had been enough for my living expenses, but I had not saved anything. I needed money for my ticket.

We had our gold bar, didn't we? I asked Signor Tavella for a personal talk and requested that he sell the bar and divide the proceeds between Kurt and me.

Tavella looked at me. Was there an expression of apprehension or uneasiness on his face? Was everything on the up and up?

It was a Friday, did I realize that? Nothing could be done until Monday; and then it might not be possible to liquidate the bar instantly; it could be a couple of days. . . .

Monday morning Signor Tavella called. The gold bar was sold, the money ready to be picked up. He had realized the urgency and had made a special effort to expedite the transaction. The cash was in American dollars, he said, because my passage would have to be paid in that currency.

I secretly apologized to this honorable man.

Then something unexpected happened. A call from the Jewish Refugee Committee. Would I come to see them?

I had never been there and did not know what they wanted. Mr. Ellis Hayim, a short, graying, friendly man received me. I had received my visa? I was going to leave? Was my ticket in order?

Why, yes, yes—how did he know? What did he care? Apparently the committee was notified when a visa was granted. He asked about my plans and, still somewhat bewildered, I told him.

Then he asked me if I had money. I said yes, I had sufficient American money to spend on arrival, and afterward I thought my sponsor would help until I got settled. "May I ask," he said almost apologetically, "how much money you have?"

"I have eleven dollars."

"You will need some money on board—little expenses. I am authorized . . . He handed me five ten-dollar bills. I almost choked. He saw how moved I was and quickly added: "It's a loan, you know— so we can help other refugees." Then, with a wink: "No particular hurry." It was clear that he never expected to see this "loan" again.

I could hardly say my thanks. But I said something to myself: a firm commitment.

*

On the evening before departure friends arranged a surprise dinner at Sun Ya, the most exclusive Cantonese restaurant in town. It was a sumptuous many-course feast. Yet I could not enjoy it. Kurt was not there, which I could fully understand. He spent the evening with another refugee who had not yet received her American visa and to whom he had become attached during those last days.

She proved a comfort when I, the false friend, left the next day. A few weeks later he married her. The next time I saw him was after the war, when he finally relieved my guilt-ridden conscience by arriving safely in California with Martha and three-year-old Tommy.

I left behind a refugee colony of twenty thousand people. During the war, seventeen hundred died of disease and thirty-one were killed inadvertently by liberating Allied planes.

*

At this point I feel I have to mention the fate of my brother Otto because I introduced him earlier. But since the theme of the book is my relationship with Joe, I will report on my brother in only the briefest outline.

In the mid-1930s Otto was invited by a childless relative who owned a metal factory in Prague to learn the business and eventually take over. Otto traveled extensively throughout Europe for that company and had a promising career ahead of him. But after a few years he joined a group of young people preparing themselves to do pioneer agricultural work in Palestine, resigned his work at the factory, and went to a Zionist training camp in Holland. There he worked at a primitive farm caring for horses, swine, and cattle and tending the fields. It was very hard manual labor. The food was poor, the accommodations were rudimentary, and he got little sleep (he had to get up at 3 A.M. to feed the animals). But Otto was fired by idealism and wanted to earn the approval of the farmhand who was assigned by the farmer to be Otto's boss. He wrote home how proud he was with his accomplishments as a pioneer trainee. But the work was too hard. He ruined his hands with an unusual ailment

112

that immobilized his fingers. Eventually he had to come to Vienna for treatment. On that occasion it was discovered that he had contracted tuberculosis.

TB, at that time, could only be treated by extended rest and nourishing food.

Otto had come to Vienna only a few days before the critical March 11, 1938. On that night, when I left for England, he took the first train leaving for Prague, which he regarded as his second home. The train was crowded with political refugees who hoped to escape over the nearby Czechoslovkian border. But the Nazis were faster. At the border station they captured the most-wanted refugees and turned the train with the rest—my brother included—back toward Vienna. Shortly after the train with the desperate travelers turned back, Otto, abandoning his suitcase, jumped out of the moving train in the dark of night. He then trudged back to the Austrian-Czechoslovakian border, which he reached at dawn. The March River formed the border. He found a small rowboat and reached the far side. There he was caught by Czech guards. He pleaded with them that his home was in Prague and that he was merely visiting in Vienna. (He had learned to speak Czech.) They were unmoved and returned him to the Austrian side. He had no alternative now and returned to Vienna, a city awash with swastikas. He was subjected there to the same humiliations that Joe experienced. After months of paper work he was allowed "legally" to leave again for Prague.

He arrived there on the day the Nazis marched into the city after the Allied betrayal of Czechoslovakia at Munich. He had fallen from the frying pan into the fire.

There was panic in Prague. Otto's former employer, the metal factory owner, rented a private plane to escape from Prague and took Otto and some relatives along, trying to fly into France across German territory. During anxious hours in the air there was no interference by the busy Germans, but when the plane neared the German-French border it developed engine trouble and had to land. The frantic passengers did not know whether it would land on the French or German side. They had landed in France, but the French guards were as stubborn as the Czech guards and insisted on turning the refugees back. Otto managed to get a telephone call through to my mother's uncle, the banker who lived in Paris. Through his influence with the French authorities the refugees were given tenuous, short-term permission to stay in France.

In Paris, and with the help of the uncle, permission was extended long enough for Otto to obtain the coveted permit from Australia to immigrate there.

He left on a French ship and went on a long journey similar to my trip to Shanghai. The *Ville d'Amiens* sailed from Marseille to Algeria to Martinique to Panama to New Caledonia. There, something went wrong, and the ship did not go further. Otto was stuck on that remote Pacific island. It would be weeks before another ship would arrive and he could continue the trip. He decided to explore the interior of the island and travel by himself among the native tribes, using a locally purchased tent for sleeping.

Otto eventually reached Melbourne, his health badly undermined from the weeks of running. Instead of the rest he should have had in Vienna to tend to his TB, the pressures aggravated his condition and he had to be hospitalized. There he lingered for an extended time and then, far away from his family, he died. A pilot dispersed his ashes over the Phoenix Islands in the South Pacific.

Otto had been born on his mother's birthday. He died, thirty years old, on Mother's Day, a delayed victim of the Nazi tragedy.

The
New World

* 8 *

A Temporary Haven

1941

MAX

On May 2, 1941, I boarded the *Kobe Maru* for Japan, on my way to the United States. As the ship receded from the Yangtse-Poo Wharf I saw again that poignant sign that had greeted us on arrival eight months earlier: "N.Y.K. Welcomes You." Two of us had seen it; one saw it now. We passed the stupendous skyline of the Bund—the Cathay Hotel, where Sassoon had received me, the Hong Kong and Shanghai Bank, and the green twin-pinhead towers of the *North China Daily News* building. I had been told that on leaving Shanghai nostalgia sneaks up on every departing traveler. No nostalgia sneaked up on me.

The crossing to Japan (Moji), then the train ride to Yokohama, were uneventful. I was in a different world and paid little attention to the Japanese men in straw raincoats and peaked hats, and to the umbrella-wearing Japanese ladies I saw from the train window— they all looked like Japanese woodcuts to me. I had a layover day in Yokohama. On May 7, 1941, in the late afternoon, I boarded the *Hie Maru* bound for Seattle!

The crossing to Seattle took eleven days. I prepared myself mentally for the immense change that I was facing. And before arrival I had to take care of some business.

A letter from Joe had advised me to anglicize my name. During the First World War discrimination against German-sounding names had been widespread in the United States and was likely to occur again, with war imminent. Kühnel, with its umlaut and unpronounced *h*, had indeed bothered me in London, when I had to spell it repeatedly, especially over the telephone. I was looking for a short name, beginning with *K* to match the markings on my suitcases and handkerchiefs. I consulted the Seattle telephone book on board and came up with Knight.

Thus it came about that Joe is responsible for my name—even as I am responsible for his, having proposed the Fabrizius he later shortened to Fabry.

As we approached Seattle, the immigration officer on board, who checked my papers, asked my name. When I said I was hoping to change it, I expected some bureaucratic procedure, perhaps court action. "What name do you want?" "Knight," I said. He entered the name in his paper, then said: "Knight it is. You can call yourself what you want. We don't care." As simple as that. Perhaps unreasonably, I found it humiliating. I translated his words as: "You are a nameless immigrant; only we make you into a person."

Before I left the ship, I was handed mail. There were three letters—all invitations. This was no longer "N.Y.K. Welcomes You," but Joe welcoming me to stay with him in Connecticut, my sponsor inviting me to come to New York, and Harry Lieser, an Austrian schoolmate and friend of many years who had emigrated to San Francisco, inviting me to share his apartment with him and his wife Trudy. I bathed in the glory of this triple welcome. It seemed obvious that I should join Joe. But, here I was at the West Coast— why not at least see what the opportunities were, and then decide?

I opted for California and have never regretted it.

When I set foot ashore, my name—my "old" name—was called by a well-dressed lady whom I did not know. The wonderful Seattle Jewish community, alerted all the way from Shanghai, had sent a representative to assist the new arrival. How much goodwill in this country from all sides! She was here with her car to take me where I wanted to go. I said I would appreciate transportation to the railroad station.

On the way I asked, somewhat timidly, for a favor. Would she, please, stop briefly at a bank?

She did, in downtown Seattle. I pulled out my envelope with five ten-dollar bills, converted them into a cashier's check and mailed them back to Mr. Hayim. I had left the bills untouched during the trip. I had enough money for my ticket to San Francisco. Before she left, she bought *Life Magazine* for me to read on the train.

I traveled all night. In the morning the train passed a hilly area. Somebody pointed out the window. "We'll soon be in Oakland to catch the ferry to San Francisco; up there are the hills of Berkeley. Beautiful homes of university professors." I looked longingly at those homes on the hilltops.

We pulled into Oakland. There was much commotion and people milled around. I did not know where to find the ferry and was asking for directions when a booming voice behind me called out: "Take it easy, all's fine, I am here!"

Good old Harry had come to meet me. Shortly afterward we arrived at his apartment on Third Avenue and were welcomed by Trudy with open arms.

For the next few weeks I enjoyed the generous hospitality of these two. They had a comfortable place but no guest room. They shared what they had—my nook was a narrow sun porch, which had no bed. But the San Francisco Jewish Committee had been alerted, and one of their board members, Adolph Ermann, partner in a furniture store, showed up, panting up the steps, carrying a heavy wooden bed on his shoulders, a donation for the guest. I couldn't believe it and could hardly thank him. (The firm flourished—under the name of Don Ermann Associates—and I have never forgotten the episode. In my later "affluent" years I purchased most of my furnishings from that firm to fill my home, located in those same Berkeley hills viewed from the train window.)

I did not allow myself many days of rest. I was driven by an intense wish to start life in America at once, make the necessary connections, earn my keep, relieve Harry and Trudy, and stand on my own feet.

As a newspaperman, I thought I'd start out with the *San Francisco Chronicle*. I made an appointment with its literary editor, Joseph Henry Jackson, whose book reviews I greatly admired.

Jackson received me soberly but with friendliness, and heard my story. Could he do something for me at his paper or introduce me to somebody with literary connections?

When I said that I had lived in London, he had an idea. "There is a British writer in Berkeley—do you know C. S. Forester?"

I didn't but I should have. He was the creator of the Captain Horatio Hornblower novels of the sea.

The following day, armed with an introduction from Jackson, I rang the bell at a luxurious, Spanish-style home at 1020 Keeler Avenue in Berkeley. A tall, lean, somewhat absent-minded man in a bathrobe opened the door to an immense living room with two-story windows looking out over the Pacific Ocean: C. S. Forester.

The following dramatic few minutes are etched in my memory, and I am sure my quotes are close to what was said. I presented my story to Forester in grotesquely abbreviated form. Then:

"So, so. You just arrived from the Orient; a new immigrant. Where are you staying?"

"I have no real place: friends in San Francisco let me sleep in a borrowed bed in their apartment."

"Would you like to stay with us?"

Was I hearing right? Was this famous man who had known me for less than ten minutes offering me a home? He gave me no time to answer.

"Tell you what," he said. "Talk to my wife. She's taking a nap on a cot outside under the trellises." He called through an open door leading to the garden: "Hey, Kitty, come in a minute." Some inarticulate noises outside, then a petite figure, which did not seem to fit the tall man, came through the glass door, hair tousled, half asleep.

"This man is a refugee just arrived in America," Forester explained. He has no place to stay. How about him staying here?"

It was as direct as all that.

"Sure," she said. "A good idea, come along, I'll show you your room." Without hesitation she took my hand and walked up that grandiose stairway to a gorgeous little room, with a balcony over a garden, overlooking the Golden Gate. It was tastefully furnished, with fine draperies, a pink-tiled private bathroom, the works. The sun shone brilliantly through the windows. I cannot even say that a dream had come true. I never dreamed anything like that. It all seemed like watching a movie.

But it was pinch-your-arm true. "When do you want to move in—tomorrow? the next day? Whenever you have your things arranged."

C. S. Forester was no longer interested, she had taken over. I was still stunned.

"Mrs. Forester," I said, "this is a fairy tale. But you surely understand that I want to do something to earn your generosity. Could I have some function in this house, make myself useful in some way?"

She immediately understood. She had quick, jerky movements, like a lizard, which seemed to reflect her flexible thinking. "Yes, yes. You want to do something." She thought and I felt the wheels go round. Then, like a dart: "Can you make coffee?"

I was embarrassed. "I can learn, I suppose."

"Sure you can. I'll show you." And, as before, she took my hand. She led me down some steps into the kitchen. (After Shanghai, what a kitchen!) She showed me where the coffee was and the pot and how to fix coffee. I stared at a note pad over the sink, used for a shopping list, and marveled at the abundance of the planned purchases. Right between apples and rice and butter were such items as "a bicycle for John" and "a new refrigerator."

John, about thirteen, the older of the Foresters' two boys, and George, about eight, were not home at the moment.

"Mrs. Forester, making coffee is not enough."

The wheels went round again. "Yes, yes, not enough. Let me see." Pause. Then, rather apologetically: "You know, there's one thing I hate to do every morning. Maybe, maybe . . . you could . . ." She hesitated, then blurted out: "I have to polish four pairs of shoes every morning, and I detest it. . . ."

Thomas Alva Edison started his career selling newspapers. I started my career in America shining shoes.

*

Life with the Foresters is among my fondest memories. With one stroke all material worries were wiped out. I not only got room and board there, I was a son in the house, the older brother of the two children. All my daily needs, even laundry and toothpaste, were taken care of. I was chauffeured around in Mrs. Forester's fancy red sports car and was taken on weekend trips to Yosemite with the family and to the Orinda Country Club for swimming. The Foresters were the center of a literary circle to which, among others, belonged George Stewart (author of *Storm*, *Fire*, and *Ordeal by Hunger*), the Hollywood movie writer Niven Bush, and Joseph Henry Jackson.

*

Meanwhile, Joe was in Connecticut, working in a cotton mill, trying to write on the side. In November 1940 he had taken a big step—he had married. In describing his wife, he noted especially her interest in words and language, crowning his letter by saying she was a "a female Max," the highest praise. (I read this letter to their children many years later, on Joe and Judy's fortieth wedding anniversary.)

I tried to make myself useful. Polishing shoes did not seem much compensation for the Foresters' largesse. I started to give the boys German lessons. It was a disaster. They had no tradition of sitting still, doing homework, expending any sort of effort. After a short time, in which discipline was a major factor, I gave up. Then Mrs. Forester became interested, and I gave her lessons. She asked me about my background and my life story, and thus learned about Joe. I had an ulterior motive in steering the conversation toward him. There was this charming little garden house in the backyard of the Foresters. The Foresters had no gardener, see? It was a triumph of diplomacy: I could write Joe that a gardening job was waiting for him in Berkeley. To my delight, he immediately accepted.

* 9 *

An Ancestor Arrives

1940–1941

JOE

I arrived in Boston March 3, 1940, long before Max reached California. Today there is no place on earth that cannot be reached from any other place within a day: it took me a year and a half to go from Vienna to the United States.

Our ship, the *Newfoundland*, traveling in convoy, crossed the Atlantic in sixteen days. I had never been on an ocean liner, and the *Newfoundland*, even in her gray war paint and blacked-out at night, seemed magnificent. I shared my cabin with three other exiles. Two were older men who had left behind great fortunes and considered their lives over, the third was my age and almost always seasick. I had my share of seasickness but in the calm periods I pondered how lucky I was not to have had great fortunes to lose. My possessions were not in the past, but in the future.

In spite of several storms, a rumored attack by a German U-boat, and discouraging news from Europe in the ship's newsletter, the mood on the *Newfoundland* was upbeat. Relief at having escaped danger was stronger than fear of uncertainty ahead. The young women on the ship had the time of their lives with Canadian soldiers going home on furlough. There was a lot of frolicking, laughing, and kissing, and many a matron reported at breakfast that her cabin mate had not come to bed all night.

My mood was mainly curiosity. A whole continent lay ahead, a land of unlimited opportunities. With my fifty stories, my book in manuscript, and future productions, I would conquer that land, bring over my parents (America was not yet at war, so direct communication with Vienna would be possible), and all of us, Max included, would go back to Vienna when Hitler was defeated. I was cherishing the typical delusion of refugees: that their side would win, that they would return and pick up their lives where they had left off.

We stopped briefly in Halifax, where the Canadian soldiers left, and arrived at Boston before dawn. The city was brightly lit, a promise of normalcy after months of blackouts in England. Yet, when the disembarking began, I felt anxiety. I was concerned less about the more distant future than the next few days. We hadn't been told that the ship would land in Boston. I didn't know a soul there. In New York I knew a few other refugees, including Harry Freud, and Sophie Beck was nearby in South Orange. How would I get from Boston to New York? How far was it? What would the trip cost? Why did my ship have to land in Boston instead of New York, as the others had?

It turned out that landing in Boston had advantages. Ours was only the second ship with European refugees to land there. The officials checking our papers and baggage were sympathetic. Reporters waited for us, flashbulbs flashed. We were news. I tried to interest one of the reporters in our short stories but he said his paper did not publish fiction. A loudspeaker announced that arrivals from Europe with no place to stay should meet in a nearby warehouse. There were more than a hundred of us. The warehouse was big enough for a circus, cheerfully decorated with red-white-and-blue streamers. Long tables were loaded with large trays of sandwiches. Well-dressed women of all ages brought us coffee and pancakes. They sat down and had breakfast with us. The woman next to me was about my age, attractive, cheerful, and chatty. She said what I would hear from many Americans over the next few years: that my English was very good, and my accent cute. I was new in this country and believed her, and it made me feel good.

She asked me if I would like to stay with her family for a couple of days to catch my breath. When I enthusiastically agreed, she took me to a parking lot, and I realized that each woman had come to offer temporary shelter to one of us.

The name of my angel was Gladys, and her shiny car took me to a house in the suburbs, with a snow-covered front lawn, a play yard in back, and a double garage. Every room had furniture that looked as if it had just been bought yesterday. Two children's rooms were full of toys, kitchen and utility room sparkled with appliances that I recognized only from American movies. Gladys showed me "my" guest room, which had its own bathroom. The children came home from school, and I was introduced as "our visitor from Vienna" and we all had ice cream. When I went to my room to rest, I was convinced that this rich family would help me get on my feet. Gladys's husband presumably was a business tycoon with connections, perhaps even in the newspaper world. I was looking forward to get to know him.

I met the husband at dinner time. He was friendly but quiet, which confirmed my impression that he was an important man in an important job. After the children went to bed, I told Gladys and her husband of my hope to establish myself as a writer in America. Gladys said she was sure I'd be successful.

When I came down for breakfast the next morning, the children were already eating, and Gladys fixed bacon and eggs for me. Then her husband joined us. I swallowed my surprise. He was in overalls and carried a hard hat and a lunch pail. He ate hurriedly, kissed Gladys good-bye, and left.

I burst out: "Is your husband a laborer?"

She nodded cheerfully, not noticing my class prejudice. "He's an auto mechanic," she said proudly.

This was my first lesson in Americanism.

I stayed in Boston two days and visited newspapers where I was told the identical story: American papers rarely printed fiction, and those that did bought it from syndicates. Short stories were published mostly in magazines.

I looked at the magazines on display in drug stores. Most of them had editorial offices in New York. I took the bus to New York, reassured by Gladys's confidence in my success.

*

Harry Freud met me at the bus station. In Vienna he was the only one of my classmates whose parents had owned an automobile, and now he had one in New York. He took me to a rooming house where many new arrivals from Germany and Austria lived. I rented an inexpensive room on 96th Street off Broadway with shared kitchen privileges. The room was not much bigger than my Brussels prison cell, but this was home.

The next morning I went to the public library and made a list of magazines with editorial offices in New York. I was quite confident. Peter Fabrizius had conquered many European countries, including England. I had fifty translated stories, I could not fail.

But the reaction was consistently negative. I met with other European writers and their experience was the same. They had given up trying and were making a living any way they could. In contrast to England, we were allowed to seek and accept employment, but the Depression was still felt and jobs scarce. Ernst Weiss, a Viennese playwright with whom Max and I had briefly collaborated on a movie scenario, and whose plays had been performed in many European theaters, now carried blocks of ice from a basement to a hotel on the third floor. Another writer had a job holding chickens while they were being injected with serum. I was determined to be as successful in the United States as Max had been in England, and not to waste my time looking for stupid jobs.

Harry Freud's cousin was Ernst Waldinger, an Austrian poet. When we met in New York, Waldinger was depressed. He even envied me. "You write short stories," he sighed. "They are difficult to get published but they do get published. No one here is interested in German poetry." I asked him how he knew that stories did sell. He gave me the address of an agent, Franz Horch, who placed stories of refugee authors.

Franz Horch was a breath of fresh air. He had been assistant to Max Reinhardt in Berlin, and knew the prominent German-speaking writers in exile. He had struggled to establish himself as their agent in New York and had been able to sell their stories. Of course it helped that they carried such by-lines as Thomas and Heinrich Mann, Franz Werfel, Carl Zuckmayer, and Stefan Zweig. Even so, there were many rejections before each acceptance. The outlook for short shorts was poor, he told me. Although our kind of story had been invented by an American, O. Henry, magazines preferred long stories with character development, mood pieces, and human interest angles. "Facts," Horch said. "Give me facts. They sell more easily than fiction."

I didn't have factual stories translated into English. Nevertheless, I left a number of our short stories and my book manuscript about Merxplas with Horch. There were some book publishers who read German. There was hope.

Shortly after my arrival in New York I called Sophie Beck's daughter, Blanche, who was the secretary of an investment broker on Wall Street. She invited me for lunch. I walked in awe through the canyons of downtown New York, an ant among towers of Babel. This was a world with purpose—even the buildings reached for the sky. In Europe, church steeples dominated the cities. On Wall Street the church was dwarfed by skyscrapers. I was early for my date but found myself rushing with the rushing crowd. The little church chimed twelve, and hundreds of revolving doors spewed out thousands of people. I realized I was in a different world, taller buildings, faster people—with different tastes in short stories.

Blanche was a refined, middle-aged woman who listened with quiet amusement to the story of my odyssey and to my plans for conquering America. No, her boss had no connection with magazine editors. If I really wanted to try to make a living from writing, that was my choice, but she made me feel she didn't think that was the best way. She listened to me with a cocked head and a strained expression on her face, as if hard of hearing—the way Americans listened who had difficulty understanding my accent.

Her mother wanted to meet me—could I come to South Orange for Seder?

Seder, the Jewish celebration of the miracle of the Exodus from Egyptian bondage, a celebration of freedom, was appropriate to my situation. Blanche took me by train to South Orange. Sophie Beck was a sweet old lady who reminded me of my father's sister, not so much in looks as in European hospitality. She was genuinely interested in my father's side of the family, to which her late husband had been related. Other guests arrived, and I realized that I had at least as big a family in America as I had left in Europe—I just had never heard of them. Sophie had five children, a dozen grandchildren, one great-grandchild, and an assortment of aunts, uncles, cousins, their spouses and children. I was introduced as "cousin Joe" and I bathed in the missed feeling of belonging to family again. The Seder had been one of the few Jewish celebrations my immediate family had observed.

Sophie's oldest son presided over the recital of Exodus, interrupting several times to explain to the children the parallels between pharaoh and Hitler, Exodus then and now—cousin Joseph the living example—and the hopes for another miracle. The ceremony ended with the traditional sumptuous dinner and songs I recognized from my Seders in Vienna. I was a great success with the children: I let them ride on my shoulders, swung them up to the ceiling, and told them some of our short stories. They had no trouble understanding me; at least they did not ask me to repeat and didn't cock their heads. It was a wonderful evening, crowned by Sophie's slipping me a twenty-dollar bill which paid for two weeks' living in New York.

Horch, meanwhile, had collected a number of rejection slips, but was optimistic. I, too, kept going after the editors. They consistently said no, our stories were not what they wanted. "Facts!" Horch urged me, "Facts!" I looked over our stories that could be rewritten as factual reports. I selected one in which a woman, suspected by the police of carrying a plan for a bank robbery, is thoroughly searched, but nothing is found. Yet she delivered the plan. It was not, as the police thought, sewn into her dress, it was the dress. When she met her accomplice, she took off her dress, ripped the seams, and—presto!—the pattern of the dress was the plan. This was after the Nazi invasion of Norway. I made her into a Norwegian patriot smuggling a plan of German fortifications to Norwegian guerrillas.

In my research on drugstore racks I discovered a new magazine, *Friday*, and I went to their offices, hoping they were not yet overrun with manuscripts. The editor glanced over the "Norwegian" story, then sat down, read it right through, and said he would buy it—could he rewrite it a bit? An American in my rooming house had corrected my English but it probably needed more work, so I gladly agreed. The editor made out a check for fifty dollars, which doubled my rapidly dwindling resources. I wrote Max a triumphant letter: I had sold the first Fabrizius story in the United States!

There was more to come. I had mentioned to the *Friday* editor that I had a collection of documents that illustrated my flight—papers the Nazis required, releases from the Belgian prison and the Merxplas camp, and official mementos from England about my stay there. He asked me to bring them. He said he would write a story using my documents, and paid me another fifty dollars.

These payments topped even what we had received in England. I could hardly wait to see myself in print. The spy story appeared two weeks later, "A Stitch in Time" by Peter Fabrizius. The style was smooth and American. When I came to the surprise ending, the surprise was on me. Tacked on were two paragraphs that showed my heroine double-crossed by British agents who were described as foppish and arrogant. The story ended with a slur on the British as imperialists.

I was puzzled and disappointed; the British had been good to me. But worse was to come. Two weeks after that a story appeared in *Friday* with my documents. None of the Nazi difficulties were described. The story was that of a poor homeless man hounded by Belgians and British, arrested, treated as a vagabond, refused work permits, and persecuted as an enemy alien. Fortunately my name was blotted out in the documents, and Peter Fabrizius was spared the shame of authorship of this scandalous distortion. I went to Horch who had not known about this new publication but had been pleased that I had discovered "a new market." He made some inquiries and we learned that *Friday* was a front magazine for the American Communist party, and the party line was to blacken the "imperialists" while protecting Hitler—Russia's ally following the Molotov-Ribbentrop pact. (Ten years later, during the McCarthy period, I still felt apprehensive at the thought that I had once contributed to a Communist publication.)

The capitalist press, however, continued to be unreceptive, and Horch's rejection-slip collection grew. But the hundred dollars buoyed my spirit, and I was more than ever resolved to break through the editorial barrier. My book manuscript, Horch reported, received friendlier rejections than did my short stories. Viking Press almost accepted it. Novels were easier to get accepted than short shorts, he told me.

So I would try a novel. I was used to spinning my stories with someone, and I began to collaborate with Ernst Weiss, who had a room not far from mine. He lugged ice blocks all night, then had a few hours' sleep. I worked with him in the afternoon, and we concocted not one, but two novels. Weiss had a knack for light, sophisticated plots and snappy dialogues. But our collaboration differed from mine with Max. We would discuss the plot, flesh out details, then I would go home and spend the rest of the day typing (in German). Weiss was exhausted from his job, but I was fresh and eager to produce while my money lasted. Both novels were escape tales, at a time when we, and the world at large, needed to escape grim reality. The theme of one novel was a letter written by Casanova, said to have magic power: women fell in love with whoever possessed the letter. In a series of episodes the letter slipped into the lining of a tailcoat, and the unsuspecting owner became the center of romantic attention. Our trick was to have the coat change wearers, and many hearts were won and broken.

The other story was about a charming playboy, son of an oil magnate (we had Cary Grant in mind), who thought more of sports and girls than the empire he was to inherit. He wanted to prove to his father that his unorthodox ways of doing business could be successful. And unorthodox they were! He was sent to buy a newly discovered oil field in Turkey, which fanatical followers of the dethroned last sultan would not sell because it belonged to the revered house of the monarch. The playboy won the heart of an American girl traveling with her boarding-school class. And who does she turn out to be but the only surviving daughter of the sultan, who had entrusted her as a baby to the captain of an American ship. We laughed at ourselves as we were writing.

We worked all summer, but the result was not sensational. The German-reading publishers suggested Hollywood, and Horch sent English synopses to his movie agent. Years later we thought we discovered similarities between our Casanova story and the film "Tales of Manhattan." A suit by our attorney resulted in an out-of-court settlement. The Turkish story was published in installments in a Swiss German-language newspaper in San Francisco.

Collaboration with Ernst Weiss had unexpected consequences. Ever since I had arrived in the United States I had wanted to start life afresh. I had been deeply wounded, my roots were cut; my family was being annihilated. Every letter from my parents told of another member of the family "gone on vacation." They also told of increasing difficulties with their own emigration efforts. Sophie Beck sent them an affidavit but it needed to be supplemented. My parents' quota number was high. Difficulties in obtaining exit permits increased. My parents tried not to sound alarmed but when I read innocent-sounding phrases like "it's getting a bit hard," I wept. I looked for supplementary affidavits, but every hurdle I overcame was replaced by another. My usual optimism was put to the test, and a question emerged that would stay with me for years to come: What was the meaning of it all? Did life have any meaning?

As so often happened, one insignificant incident provided a hint of an answer. I chatted with a woman who helped Horch translate his German authors. She was a seventh-generation American, her ancestor having come two hundred years ago. I said, I wished I had an ancestor like that, and she replied: "Why, *you* are an ancestor." This chance remark shifted my attention from shortcomings in the past to potentials in the future. I lost my family in Europe but could start my own in America!

The uprooted family tree needed new roots. Because I was starting over, I began to think about a new name. I was escaping from my past—but escaping to what? Something in me was trying to express itself, a search had begun for a new relatedness, a belonging. I wanted to sever links, yet at the same time I wanted to retain them.

Once more a hint from heaven was masked by natural events. In the building where Ernst Weiss lived, he shared a hall telephone with the other tenants on his floor. They often doodled while they made their calls. One day, when I used that phone, I found the note pad covered with doodles around names of callers they noted down. One of the names was Fabry.

This was the solution—a new name, and yet a link; not with Epstein but with Fabrizius. I remembered that on occasion by way of a lame joke people had asked which of the two halves of Fabrizius was Fabri and which was Zius. Franz Horch had mentioned several times that Fabrizius was not a good pen name for America, people could not pronounce it. Max was in Shanghai, our literary cooperation was in peril. At least, these were my rationalizations. Actually, I liked that name, the first half of Fabrizius. I began using it, and made it official when I became a United States citizen.

I never considered that appropriating my half had left Max with the impossible remainder "Zius." It was a "betrayal" (I think my only one), but when we had occasion to talk about it, much later, he laughed it off.

A second by-product of my collaboration with Weiss was more far-reaching. He was engaged to a refugee from Frankfurt, who lived in the Clara de Hirsch Home for Working Girls. I met her several times, and she decided that a bachelor like me should not go to waste when so many Hirsch girls needed husbands. She openly informed me of her match-making scheme and I was receptive. I was thirty years old and lonely, and if I was to become an ancestor a wife was a good idea. There were at least fifty eligible girls in the Clara de Hirsch Home, and within a week she had whittled down the candidates to three. Another week, and my private marriage broker had made her choice. The lucky winner was Judith Lieban, American-born of Austrian parentage, secretary to a German psychoanalyst, and popular with the refugee residents because she helped write job applications, fill out forms, and do other tasks requiring a knowledge of English. It seemed a reasonable choice to me, and I let Judith's friend arrange a date.

A slight delay increased the suspense. Sophie Beck invited me to spend two weeks in her summer home in Bradley Beach on the New Jersey coast—an opportunity to relax too good to pass up. It so happened that my matchmaker's choice also went on vacation, to friends in Connecticut. I decided to write her a postcard, introducing myself. I wrote it tongue-in-cheek, in Peter Fabrizius manner. She answered in the same spirit. By Labor Day when we were both back in New York, we had managed a delightfully sophisticated exchange of letters. We met two days after Labor Day, September 4, 1940.

Judy was different from the "movie-star" girl friends of my past. She had a simple, fresh beauty, and the quick mind which I knew from her letters. I felt comfortable with her and we had much in common. Her parents had both died within a year, five years before. She too was lonely, although not rootless. She had two brothers, many relatives in Europe, and a few cousins, uncles, and aunts in New York. She had spoken German in her home and perfected it during two years in Austria attending school in Vienna. She could type, and knew both English and German shorthand.

What did she see in me? I was penniless, jobless, with no marketable skills. A stranger in a strange land, a dreamer in a world of reality. Yet, she introduced me to her friends and relatives as if I were a rare catch. What she saw in me was not what I was but what I might become, "the butterfly in the caterpillar," as she put it. We were married November 2, less than two months after we met.

I wrote the news to Max, and received an enthusiastic reply from Shanghai. I still treasure his letter. "I cannot sit still," he wrote, "even while I am writing this letter. Every few moments I jump up, embrace you. You did it! You did exactly what we dreamed about." We had dreamed of marrying women who would become part of Peter Fabrizius, compatriots in the land of the short story, a foursome instead of a twosome. We would have houses next to each other, a yard without a fence, our children would play with each other. One plus one equals three would be expanded to two plus two equals infinity.

My marriage announcement was one of the few cheerful events in Max's life in this period. He had given up a budding career in Vienna and fled to London and succeeded in an amazingly short time in laying the foundation of a new life. With an invasion of England apparently imminent he broke up that life and fled to the only rathole still open. And Shanghai truly was a rathole, a ghetto overrun by the desperate. Max left the fire-bombs-to-come for the hot, humid, explosive, frying pan of Shanghai. He had registered late for his United States immigration, and did not yet have an affidavit of support. To help him come to the United States became my high priority, while I tried to save my parents, place Fabrizius stories, and write novels with Weiss.

By the time I married Judith, Max had given me two names of persons who might have been in a position to provide an affidavit for him: A brother of his father, who had lived in the United States since the turn of the century, and a cousin of his mother who, although himself a recent arrival from Austria, seemed able to send an affidavit.

I first visited Max's uncle. As a close relative he was the most plausible sponsor. I pleaded Max's case, but it turned out that this man had already given an affidavit to his sister and her husband, and felt he could do no more. I tried to convince him that even a supporting affidavit (added to somebody else's weak affidavit) would be a great help. Perhaps he would have relented but his wife was stubbornly opposed, and I could see that this was a hopeless situation.

I turned to the cousin. He was friendly, and said that he had already written to Max in a favorable sense. He was prepared to sign an affidavit, but was not rich and his guarantee was too weak by itself. His son, who had immigrated a few years earlier and was well established as a successful advertising artist and magazine illustrator, could be asked to co-sign. But the son was out of town, and there was one delay after another. The son was in no hurry. It was my task to make the urgency of the situation clear to this man, and so I went after him relentlessly as Max's alter ego. I finally scored and telegraphed Max the happy news.

But that was not the end of my Peter Fabrizius mission. I persuaded Horch to write a letter testifying to the publication potential of Max's stories in America. Through Harry Freud we also received a letter of support from his father who, as Sigmund Freud's brother and an internationally known trade economist, would carry weight.

Although I was trying to convince the American consul in Shanghai that Peter Fabrizius had a great future in America, I began to have my doubts. We didn't seem to write the stories American editors wanted. My money, including the precious hundred dollars from *Friday* magazine, was melting away, and I came to the conclusion that I had to look for a job, however temporary, until the American publishing world would see the merits of the new O. Henry. Or until we learned to write what was wanted.

During my breathing spell in Bradley Beach I had had time to think over my situation and seek counsel from my American relatives who shared Aunt Sophie's cottage. They advised me to take any job and work my way up, shoveling snow, raking leaves, whatever. Hard labor, they said, strengthens character. They almost sounded like the Viennese Nazi laborer who had shown me his callused hands while I cleaned graffiti off sidewalks. My American cousins meant well; they revealed aspects I had never seen as a middle-class Viennese. I also thought of my host in Boston, the auto mechanic in overalls with the princely home. This country had a different value system, and as a future American I needed to experience it.

As so often in my life, a job fell into my lap. While my fellow refugees spent weeks chasing after any kind of work, I was spared this humiliation. My uncle's stepson Willy Beer, also a recent immigrant, had opened a small factory, making ski bindings. He had owned a ski-binding factory in Vienna, made business trips to the United States before, and had some money here that helped him start anew after losing his Vienna factory to the Nazis.

Willy and I had little in common. He lived in a business world and had poked fun at my ambition to be a writer. When I visited him in Brooklyn and asked if he had a job for me, he felt vindicated in his judgment that writing was not a way to earn a living, and offered me work at twelve dollars a week. This was enough for me to get by on, and I gratefully accepted.

Willy did not think much of my mechanical skills and assigned me the simplest task: assembling parts of ski bindings into a box, at a brisk pace. After a few weeks Willy expressed his grudging amazement that a dreamer like me could actually assemble a dozen items in a box. When I married, I asked him for a raise. He granted me one extra dollar—thirteen dollars a week—and since Judith earned twelve dollars, my male pride as main provider was saved.

We rented a room from a refugee family at Washington Heights. So many German exiles lived there that it was called "the Fourth Reich." Our combined income of twenty-five dollars was barely enough to pay for room and board. Our honeymoon consisted of spending one night in a small hotel across the Hudson where Harry Freud, my best man, drove us. The next day, a Sunday, we walked on foot across the George Washington Bridge. We went to work the following morning.

It was a happy and busy time. Judith translated and typed a

synopsis of the Casanova novel, we walked around Yonkers where Judith had spent some of the years of her childhood, and we visited the New York World's Fair. In the spring the ski season ended, and Willy Beer's factory closed for the summer. Worries about the future made my ulcers flare up, and we decided to move to the country in North Grosvenordale, Connecticut, where some of Judith's family friends had a farm. She and her family had spent many summers there, and she had an open invitation.

The Einsles were a hard-working couple, pre-Hitler immigrants from Austria, and through them I got to know a different kind of America. Their farmhouse was without electricity or running water. They rose and went to bed with the sun. To get water they had to go outdoors to a well. One morning, when I hoisted a bucket of water with a frog in it, Mrs. Einsle told me that frogs keep the water clean because they catch flies and spiders that fall into the well. We took our baths in a galvanized laundry tub on the kitchen floor. The Einsles' little girl was bathed in the kitchen sink. They had no car, but there was a tractor in which we all took occasional rides. The mail was delivered to a post office box two miles away. Next to the farmhouse was a ramshackle barn with cows and a hayloft that Judith and I used as a trysting place.

The closest neighbor was half a mile down the road. Others were within hiking distance. The neighbors were of German and northern European stock. We were far away from scare headlines, rushing people, automobiles, flashing neon signs. It was a time and place for recuperation.

Yet we had to make a living. I had lost my job, and Judith had to give up hers. A neighbor who worked in a cotton mill in the village of North Grosvenordale said they needed a "beam boy." He took me to town one Monday morning, and an hour later I was the beam boy. The job consisted of taking, on a dolly, an empty beam (a twelve-foot long spool) to the spinning machine that filled the spool with cotton thread, then returning the full beam to the storeroom. It was as back-breaking as Ernst Weiss' lugging ice blocks but after a while I learned to handle the dolly.

The same neighbor took me to and from work in his Ford, and I paid him a dollar a week for the transportation out of my paycheck of eighteen dollars, a considerable improvement over my income from Willy Beer. We contributed to the Einsle food expenses, and splurged from time to time by taking hitchhiking trips on weekends, enjoying the luxury of an occasional hotel room. I got a glimpse of rural America's morals when my boss called me to his office one Monday morning and asked: "Who was that woman who hitchhiked with you on Saturday?" Only when I assured him she was my legally wedded wife, did he let me go back to my dolly. I believe he would have fired me had I hitchhiked out of wedlock.

I did develop the calluses on my hands that the Nazi laborer in Vienna had been looking for, and also some physical and psychological muscle. But it was wonderful to come home to Judith in the afternoon. We went to bed by kerosene light.

In May we received a jubilant letter from Max. He had arrived in San Francisco from Shanghai and was staying temporarily with a schoolmate who had preceded him to California. There was never any question that we should join—either we would go West, or he would come East. I'll never cease being grateful for our decision to go West.

Neither Max nor I had anything to lose by moving from one end of the continent to the other. Judith had friends and relatives in New York but she was adventurous. Besides, her brother Ralph had volunteered for the Army and was doing basic training at Fort Ord, south of San Francisco. All summer, letters flew back and forth. Max again carefully built his ladder, for the fourth time, from the bottom. In early August he wrote that he had a minimum of security—not *as* a writer but at least *with* a writer, C. S. Forester of *Captain Horatio Hornblower* fame, in Berkeley. Max had persuaded Mrs. Forester to let Judith and me live in the garden cottage in exchange for our helping in the backyard. At least we would have a roof over our heads. Somehow we would be able to earn our groceries.

In August we said good-bye to the Einsles, the farming neighbors, the cotton beams, and went to New York to find the cheapest way to cover the distance to Max. We heard of an agency on Times Square that arranged shared-car rides. Within days they found two young men who were driving to Lincoln, Nebraska; another couple would pick us up there and drop us in Berkeley, California. All for twenty-three dollars each.

On August 20, Harry Freud took us to Times Square with all our belongings: two suitcases, my portable typewriter, a radio, a folding table and four folding chairs (wedding gifts from Judith's psychoanalyst boss and Blanche Beck). Our drivers managed to pack it all in, there was no foot space left, but we cuddled together comfortably. Off we went.

We stayed overnight in Chicago but saw hardly anything of the city. In Lincoln we were dumped, and were a bit nervous about connecting with the next ride. But the other couple came early next morning and were even more in a hurry. They drove, alternating, day and night. Endless cornfields, open space, crops, the magnificent Rockies, Salt Lake, the desert, the famous Sierra range, orange groves, palm trees, California.

We arrived in Berkeley September 6, 1941, and were left standing on a street corner in midtown, with our suitcases, folding table, and radio. I sought a public telephone and called Max.

* 10 *

Two Emigrants Become Immigrants

1941–1946

PETER

After two journeys halfway around the world, Peter Fabrizius was united again. Kitty Forester graciously chauffeured Max to downtown Berkeley to pick up Joe and Judith at the street corner.

When we arrived at the Foresters, the sun was setting and the intensely orange sky covered San Francisco Bay with its islands and boats in a brilliant glow. The city floated on the far edge of the Bay like a *fata morgana*. A flashing red light blinked from the graceful arch of the Golden Gate Bridge. As we looked through the floor-to-ceiling bay windows the sky changed from orange to purple to gray, and one by one the lights of San Francisco came on.

The three of us stood silently, marveling about the dying day displaying such beauty. In the months and years to come we often talked about the comfort nature affords, just by being harmonious and beautiful.

Joe's garden cottage was on a lawn surrounded by eucalyptus trees on a steep, terraced backyard. The cottage was a one-room rebuilt tool shed with kitchen and bathroom added. No door connected the room and kitchen, so it was necessary to step outside to go from one to the other. But the cottage was comfortably furnished and proved a perfect honeymoon nest.

In our first quiet moment Max told Joe that he had to settle a score with him. Each time Max sold a story in Shanghai, to the *North China Daily News* or other publications, he put half the fees in an envelope, in cash. Although Joe had no part in writing and placing these stories, and did not even know about them, Max felt that he had to share the payments. Now, in the garden house, Max handed Joe a nice fat envelope, Chinese currency changed into U.S. dollars. Joe showed no surprise. Instead, he pulled out an envelope with cash *he* had collected for stories he sold while we were separated! When we counted the contents, they were so close that we did not bother to even out the pennies—each returned his envelope to his pocket. None of our joint episodes, before or after, illustrated our relationship so eloquently.

We now lived in our own little paradise while the world was in turmoil. Although we were busy with our own livelihood, worry about our parents hung over our heads.

Max's parents, interned in May 1940, were released in February 1941—to London, a city under daily German bombardment. They had no apartment of their own and lived with a family for whom Max's mother kept house and cooked in return for rent.

Joe's parents were the only family members not yet transported to concentration camps, and there was a ray of hope that they could still be saved. They had the affidavit from Sophie Beck, exit papers, Joe had money for ship tickets, and their quota number was coming up. One last problem: ship passage could not be booked until they had their visa, and the visa was granted only when proof was given that ship space was available, which was extremely difficult under war conditions. Joe was trying to break that vicious circle.

*

Kitty Forester was an avid gardener. She spent hours planting, trimming, pruning, spraying, and showed as much pride in her flowers as the lady in England who told us Hitler would not dare invade her rose patch. Joe mowed, watered, and raked leaves from the ever-green and ever-shedding eucalyptus trees.

We took walks on the university campus, a park with ivy-covered buildings around the Campanile with its musical chimes— a far cry from the dark, fortress-like University of Vienna. The campus spread out into the hills, and high on top was a strange building, round and domed. This, we were told, was the "cyclotron," where they "try to split the atom." We knew from high school that atoms were the smallest particles of matter, and trying to split one seemed like splitting a hair. We shook our heads over the useless things professors do.

Max fell in love with the university. Just as he had aimed at the *Neues Wiener Tagblatt* in Vienna, the *Jewish Chronicle* in London, and the *North China Daily News* in Shanghai, he decided that the University of California was where he would eventually have his office. An academic career appealed to him but he did not want to give up literary ambitions. It didn't take him long to discover the University Press as a place where academia and writing/editing could be combined.

Max got himself an introduction to the chief of the Press, Harold Small, to inquire about chances for employment. Small asked about Max's background. Max felt uneasy about not having a specific publishing background. All he had was a well-rounded general education. As it turned out, that's what Small wanted: the Press published books in all disciplines except agriculture, and the interview became more encouraging by the minute. Whenever Max mentioned one aspect of his past activities, Small would say, "excellent," or "that's just what we want." Eventually Max, no longer able to contain himself, blurted out: "Well, if everything fits so well, Mr. Small, can you offer me a position?"

"I'd love to," said the chief, "but I have no place for a desk for you."

Max did not take this for a final answer, but it took him nine years to break this peculiar deadlock.

Meanwhile, Max had to have an income. He freelanced several articles for the *Oakland Tribune* and, in the last week in November of 1941, asked for a desk job there. He told about his experiences doing newspaper work in Vienna, London, and Shanghai. The interview took five minutes. Then the city editor pointed to an empty chair in the horseshoe arrangement of copy editors. "Sit down, start work."

This was incredible. America, truly, was the land of unlimited opportunities. The city editor handed Max a news story that had come on the ticker, and told him to write a headline for it.

Writing headlines requires a special skill of which Max was unaware—counting spaces, considering the width of letters, length of words. He peeked at what his neighbor was doing.

The city editor took Max's headlines silently, scribbling something on the sheets. Did he rewrite them? Correct them? During lunch break Max pumped a colleague for information, picking up as much as he could, then dashed off a short letter to his parents that he had landed a job at a big newspaper.

He struggled along in the afternoon, rapidly learning by trial and error. The errors were Max's, the trial the city editor's. At 5 P.M. Max was fired. This was Max's first job experience in America, not counting the shoe shining.

Joe, too, needed to earn food money and he, too, tried the university—but at a lower level. He became janitor at the Hillel Foundation, the meeting house for Jewish students, cleaning rooms after lectures and parties.

Kitty Forester was sensitive about our embarrassing position and found occasions to ask for our help, not as servants but as house guests. She also sensed that, since Joe married, Max felt isolated. In her direct way, she attacked the problem openly and asked if Max, too, was thinking of getting married.

"Thinking, yes," he replied, "but I cannot even support myself."

"You don't have to get married right away," she said. "But you could look."

She did not smile. Max could just visualize her writing on her shopping list over the sink, among three pounds of rice, one bicycle for John, two loaves of bread, "one wife for Max."

A few days later she handed him an envelope. "Here is your future wife," she said. "Christmas is a month off but this is my Christmas gift. Open the envelope and you'll see why I give it to you so early."

It was a membership card to the Sierra Club and an announcement of the annual Christmas dance for members. "Go to this dance," said Kitty. "You'll find your wife there."

At the dance Max felt uncomfortable, an enormous hall and zillions of people. He didn't know anybody. He did not dance but stayed on, watching. At 1 A.M. the last dance was announced. It was ladies' choice. A blonde came and took him to the floor. She was direct, a bit coarse, talked a lot. She invited him to a party the following Sunday at her house, which she shared with another woman.

When Max arrived at the party he found several people, mostly paired up. The blonde, Sue, introduced Max in a way that made it clear she considered him her catch. Another woman entered, bringing in a tray with coffee, tea, and chocolate. This was Charlotte, Sue's housemate. Later, when Max told Joe about her, Max said she reminded him of a painting by Jean Etienne Liotard, *La Chocolatière*—the way she held the tray with both hands in a friendly offering, a gesture of feminine caring. Charlotte paid no attention to Max, and Max paid no attention to Sue, except when she mentioned she would go to a concert Tuesday night.

On Tuesday Max phoned. Charlotte answered. "Sorry," she said. "Sue isn't home."

"I know," Max said. "That's why I am calling. I want to talk to you."

Charlotte was surprised but said okay. He described Charlotte in a letter to his parents. "She is Canadian, naturalized, in Berkeley to take her M.A. in anthropology and psychology, and works for the California Department of Employment. She has a fine, beautiful face, delicate nose, and lovely brunette hair with a coquettish premature white strand in front. When I first saw her she had a red flower in her hair, which struck a sensitive chord. I looked at it in wonder. The spark flew."

(The wedding was seven months later, in the Berkeley Rose Garden, the first time this lovely background was chosen for a wedding ceremony. It was performed by a judge because neither Max nor Charlotte were religious, although Charlotte came from a strongly Baptist background. Not only was there no minister, there was no family—Charlotte's was in Canada, and Max's in England, Australia, and the death camps in Europe. Joe was best man. The Foresters opened their house for a reception.

Sue moved out and Max moved in. She forgave him only when, years later, she also married. Kitty's shopping list had worked, with the surprise Sue/Charlotte twist worthy of a Peter Fabrizius story.)

*

Shoe shining, leaf raking, and house cleaning left us time to spin the new stories we sent to our agent, Horch. During this interval we learned something about C. S. Forester's working habits: he wrote all morning, and in the afternoon read the *Encyclopedia Britannica*. This, his wife told us, was where he collected information for his historical stories. Facts, as Horch kept telling us, facts! Perhaps we had to shift from fiction to well-researched factual articles. Horch backed this idea. Fiction, he told us, was difficult for foreign writers because they don't have the ear for nuances of speech. Words that sound all right coming from a businessman sound false coming from a taxi driver.

Luckily, Judith's brother Ralph was a gifted writer who did "have the ear" we needed. He visited Joe and Judith from his army post at Fort Ord on weekends and slept on the floor in their cottage. He reviewed our stories and made them more idiomatic.

During one of Ralph's visits Max came running down from the Forester house, and it was clear from his expression that something terrible had happened. "Quick," he called out. "Turn on the radio!"

Pearl Harbor had been bombed.

Ralph immediately returned to Fort Ord, and we spent the day listening to increasingly grim news. Then President Roosevelt's voice came over the air. Here was the inspiring confidence we, America, the world, needed. Only two years earlier we had heard Churchill's deeply confident and convincing voice talking of victory at a moment of greatest unpreparedness. In some tragic way, the involvement of America vindicated us, the refugees. No longer were we alone trying to convince people who would hardly listen of the burning need to fight the evil empire in Europe. The mighty United States of America, despite the blow it had just received, would win out.

World news and personal news were intertwined. Our parents, regardless of their immigration status, were trapped in Europe, like Kurt in Shanghai. And we? Would we become enemy aliens again?

Not this time. Within weeks, we heard that shipyards in nearby Richmond were hiring workers. No experience necessary, not even American citizenship. We qualified on both negative counts.

We went to the hiring office and joined a long line of job

seekers. Unlike other lines in which we had waited, this one moved
fast. Everyone received a slip with a job assignment. Ours said
"shipfitter." We asked someone in line what a shipfitter did. "Beats
me," was the answer. "Report to work and find out."

Ride pools were arranged, and we entered a new world as
crowded and rushed as Wall Street, but here the people wore overalls
and hard hats and carried lunch pails like Joe's host in Boston. The
yard was arranged like an American city: A, B, C streets running
one way, 1st, 2nd, 3rd streets the other way. They were streets
without houses but traffic was thick with trucks, movable cranes,
little trains, and people carrying steel plates and wooden templates.
At water's edge were the ships, or rather halves of ships, thirds,
quarters, and tenths of ships. Huge cranes carried big chunks of
prefabricated units and dropped them in place. The whole ship city
sparkled with the flashes of welders.

So we started in this world where you don't say left and right,
but port and starboard, where your nose is on your forward and you
sit on your afterpeak. The crew on our assemblyway consisted of
ranchers, garage hands, miners, salesmen, teachers, retired people,
and later housewives, from California, Texas, Oklahoma, the
Midwest, New England, and the Deep South. From them we
learned American English "as she is spoke" and "developed an ear."

Shipfitters, we found out, marked up the steel plates according
to blueprints so that girders, beams, and brackets could be welded
in place and holes cut as needed for pipes. Cranes picked up
completed units and placed them on the growing ship. It was a new
method of shipbuilding. Someone told us that ships the size of
Liberty ships, as we built them here, used to take a year to
complete. We built them in six weeks, and hoped to do better.
Flotillas of ships were needed for the war.

In those early days, the quickly hired workers had no experience
with this kind of shipbuilding. On that first day Joe and Max stood
around waiting for orders. Ours was a new crew hired only yesterday
to build a ten-thousand-ton ship. Our foreman and the supervisors
were on their hands and knees studying blueprints. We joined the
other crew members watching them. It was a good opportunity to
"develop an ear," especially for cuss words. Apparently the men had
run into trouble and couldn't figure out details on the blueprint.

After a while, during a brief break in the cursing and shouting, Joe timidly said: "I think the staggered line means the bracket goes on the other side." Everybody turned and looked at him. "Can *you* read a blueprint?" Joe answered, almost apologetically, "I learned it in high school." He was immediately drawn into the inner circle, and they restudied all the blueprints.

On the way home Joe glowed. After having been flotsam for two years, he again felt useful where it counted. And he got amused satisfaction from the fact that the high-school teacher who had given him the knowledge to help, however little, in the American war effort, had been a Nazi.

Joe's days of glory were quickly over. The units were mass produced, and as soon as the supervisors knew what the mysterious blueprint symbols meant, Joe was no longer consulted. We were just laborers, snapping chalk lines, punching holes, carrying brackets. It was heavy routine work, eight hours a day, six days a week. Yet, we never missed a day, had no time to be sick. This was work with a purpose that didn't allow boredom or exhaustion. A war had to be won, arms transported, troops shipped. We were both rejected by the draft board because of deficient vision, but in the shipyard we were participants. Setting beams in place may seem to be a meaningless routine, but we felt we were sharing in an important national effort. We could see how every little steel bracket we welded became part of a unit that became part of a ship. The ship grew before our eyes from the pieces we assembled and was launched to help win the war against the brown-shirted killers and their allies. We saw how our part fitted the whole—a psychology of work motivation that only now is being recognized by American management and, ironically, borrowed from the Japanese against whom we built the ships.

During 1942 we worked side by side as shipfitters' helpers. The weekly check of sixty-two dollars made long-cherished dreams possible. In July Max had married Charlotte; at the same time Joe could notify his parents through the Red Cross that they were to become grandparents. A small chance to save them had reopened. Although escape to the United States was no longer possible after Pearl Harbor, persons with an American affidavit were admitted to Cuba. Joe wrote this to his parents, but communication through the

Red Cross took weeks. His parents probably never received that last message.

Max had moved in with Charlotte, and Joe and Judith found an apartment with a nursery room. In the fall of 1942, our shipyard work took an exciting turn. Our foreman informed us that our crew had been selected to assemble a Liberty ship in record time! These ten-thousand-ton ships were being built in shipyards on both coasts, and there was a race between them. In the half year we had already worked in the shipyard, the time from keel laying to launching was cut from six to four weeks. They wanted to cut this even further.

The launching date of the record ship was set for early November, and the entire yard, especially our crew, bubbled with excitement all through October. The foreman talked about a five-day ship. Here was a purpose with a capital P. A challenge for all, and for us an opportunity to write about it, with "facts"— an article we planned to send to Horch for *Readers Digest*.

As it was explained to us, the bottleneck in shipbuilding was the shipway: a new keel is laid only after the previous ship is launched. The solution was prefabrication. A ten-thousand-ton ship contains two hundred fifty thousand pieces. Before the war, each piece was taken to the hull separately. When Henry Kaiser introduced prefabrication to shipbuilding, the cranes lifted about one thousand preassembled units to the hull instead of a quarter of a million single pieces. During our seven months in the shipyard, the units had become bigger and fewer. The aim was to assemble the ship with the fewest possible units in the fewest days between keel laying and launching.

Our assemblyway was the focus of this giant effort, but units were prefabricated all over the yard, and beyond. Four Whirley cranes hoisted units weighing up to one hundred tons. They lifted boilers assembled in Los Angeles, ventilators from Chicago, a compass from Boston, an anchor from New York, propellers from Eddystone, Pennsylvania, and lifeboats from Kokomo, Indiana. The captain's room was lifted into place, complete to the inkpot on his desk, and the galley fully equipped for immediate use. The entire ship, the *Robert E. Peary*, was built from November 8th to the 12th in four days, fifteen hours, and twenty-nine minutes.

It was a personal triumph for all who worked on the "Wonder

boat." Although this record was not repeated, prefabrication cut the average building time to eighteen days.

We wrote the story and sent it to Horch. It was the closest we ever got to *Readers Digest*. However, the magazine had one of its own writers cover the event—a disappointment for us.

We were not aware of it then, but Peter Fabrizius was going through an identity crisis. The era of the light, humorous short story, the cabaret skit, the flippant comedy had come to an end. The shipyard helped our Americanization but Peter Fabrizius could not be naturalized. Joe became a volunteer field reporter for the shipyard magazine *Fore 'n' Aft*. He also began to write a book about the workers in the shipyard. His foreman, a frustrated writer himself, showed some of Joe's chapters to the Labor-Management Committee, and Joe was encouraged to finish the manuscript. (By the time it was finished, the war had ended and no one was interested in war stories. The manuscript lay in a basement for forty years until it was published, as *Swing Shift*, in 1982, when a younger generation wanted to know what Pop and Mom did during the war.)

Max was restless. He felt that his abilities could be used more productively. Since American Japanese were interned at Tule Lake, the military had hardly anyone who could speak Japanese for prisoner interrogation and intelligence work. So Max enrolled at the university and attended classes in Japanese in the morning and early afternoon, leaving just enough time for the swing shift at the shipyard. It was a grueling regimen. The Japanese-language courses were keyed to war purposes and ruthless in intensity. Some homework had to be done at night, after swing shift, but Max, interested in linguistics, still could enjoy this furious bulldozing pace. He appreciated his White Russian instructor, Professor Peter Boodberg, who taught the Chinese characters that are part of written Japanese. His interpretations gave Max insight into the history of these characters and thus a glimpse of Chinese culture. What he learned tied in with his experience in Shanghai.

*

In May, 1943, Max received an invitation to a hearing by a commission of the Immigration Service in Washington, D.C. He had sent an affidavit for his parents in London. Although financially weak, a son's guarantee was given special consideration. Max's affidavit was supplemented by his New York cousin. The commission was to consider whether to approve the parents' application for immigration.

Max couldn't afford the train, and went by bus. Yet he knew he had to impress the commission that he was a solid prospective American citizen, and that neither he nor his parents had, heaven and the commission forbid, Communist leanings.

He put on his best suit and a necktie. He wanted to convey the image of "upper middle class." To promote that image he had with him a miniature portrait of his mother, in oil on ivory, painted in her younger years. It was artistically framed in bronze, and her looks and bearing were those of a princess, with her distinguished dress and fine shawl draped on her shoulders. No Communist, surely, would dress like that or indulge in the bourgeois luxury of a miniature oil portrait on ivory, Max figured.

On his way to the hearing he had one misgiving about his own appearance. He wanted to look "American" but did not know whether wearing a tie pin was American or foreign. He stopped at a street corner and checked out fifty men walking by. Only six wore pins. That settled it.

The hearing was short and painless. The ivory miniature scored. It was passed from hand to hand by the commissioners' panel and earned smiles of approval.

The decision would not come for six months, but Max left with confidence.

Even the cheapest transportation, the bus, had drained his wallet and he decided to try his luck and earn his fare back. He walked into the offices of the *Washington Times Herald* and asked for a job. Did he have any experience? Yes, Europe, the Far East. And the United States? Yes—the *Oakland Tribune*. He didn't say how long.

This time he managed to hold the job for twelve days before he was fired. It paid for travel expenses and a brief visit to his sponsoring cousin in New York. He also dropped in at the German department of the Office of War Information in New York and gave a shortwave radio talk to Germany about the experiences of an emigre Austrian doctor of law as a laborer in a California shipyard. He had ulterior motives.

The Office of War Information in San Francisco had no German department, only departments that broadcast to Far Eastern countries. And this, Max tried to convince Joe and himself, was an advantage. As the experiences at the *Oakland Tribune* and the *Washington Times Herald* had shown, our English was not good enough for the American press. But at the Office of War Information the English did not have to be perfect because it was translated by various area specialists into Chinese, Burmese, Vietnamese, Thai, Tagalog, and some languages we had never heard of.

After his return from Washington, Max laid siege to the Office of War Information in San Francisco in his very limited spare time. Finally he heard that they were setting up a Manchuria desk.

Manchuria? Where was Manchuria? He trotted to the university library and armed himself with the information that its capital was Hsingking, plus a handful of other vital statistics. Then he applied for the job.

It was a curious interview. Max's strategy was to play the shy man, seemingly understating his knowledge about Manchuria. The interviewer didn't know much either and desperately needed someone for the job. So the roles were reversed, Max "modestly" (but ah, how truthfully!) stating that he knew very little about that area, and the boss trying to convince Max that his knowledge was what was needed. Whenever Max mentioned a few words he had picked up the day before in the library—Manchukuo . . . the Manchu dynasty . . . the last puppet emperor . . . the Yalu River . . . Hsingking— the interviewer nodded enthusiastically.

Max was hired but skated on thin ice. When he heard that a job was available in the Chinese section, he went to see its chief. This man knew China, and it was not as easy as it had been with his colleague to convince him that an Austrian ex-attorney was the ideal person to interpret the war in Europe to Chinese guerrillas behind the Japanese lines. With some skimpy bits of evidence—having lived in Shanghai, taken university courses in Chinese script, worked in the Manchuria unit—Max succeeded. For the fourth time, and in a fourth country, he found employment in his own element, as a writer.

*

Because we both were married to American citizens, the waiting time required for citizenship was shortened and we attended evening classes to prepare for the naturalization test. During our adult lives, we had never known democracy. Just as we reached voting age, Austria abolished democratic elections. Joe had had his limited experiment with democracy in the vagabond camp of Merxplas, and we had participated in the little melting pot of the shipyard within the big melting pot of America. We had plenty of experience with dictatorships. As law-school graduates we relished, perhaps more than others, such democratic safeguards as the Bill of Rights, the balance of power, the Declaration of Independence with its guarantee of liberty.

We became citizens October 11, 1943, sworn in side by side in the Superior Court of San Francisco, and voted for the first time in the presidential election of 1944.

When Max felt sufficiently at home in the Chinese section, he embarked on a special mission. He asked for an interview with its chief and told him about Joe Fabry and his "exceptional qualifications" for a job in the Office of War Information. There was sufficient substance in the recommendation. The directives of the Office of War Information called for emphasis on the cultural and scientific life in the United States, to counter the impression in the ancient Far Eastern cultures that America was a land of cowboys and eccentrics. Joe, with his long-standing interest in the theater and literature, had kept up with the American stage and literary scene. He also understood the need for basic research and would be able to allay the widespread belief abroad that America was only good at practical applications of basic research done in Europe.

In December, 1943, Joe left the shipyard and started as a script writer for the Chinese section of the Office of War Information. We were united once more, not as Peter Fabrizius but as writers of informational broadcasts. Every morning we received teletyped guidelines from Washington on what to emphasize. We were not to fabricate, but could accentuate. For instance Max, writing editorial roundups, selected editorials that made the points the guidelines recommended, with a sprinkling of contrary comments for credibility. Joe, in addition, was assigned broadcasts dealing with sabotage. This, too, was done according to guidelines. He never encouraged the Chinese to blow up a railroad, but told in detail how Yugoslavs derailed trains.

Our group of writers, translators, and the American supervisor who checked the translations, formed a little family. We perfected our intimacy with things Chinese and our skill with chopsticks by having lunch together in nearby Chinatown.

From time to time we were shown cables from the American listening post in Chungking, behind the Japanese lines, or received a visit from a State Department official who told about responses to our broadcasts from the other end of the world. On one occasion, Max bumped into one of these visitors in the hallway. To Max's utter amazement, the man said: "Hello Max, how nice to see you here! How are you doing in America?"

It was John S. Service, the former consular official in Shanghai who had issued Max's immigration visa! This man had processed hundreds of visas, but still recognized Max and remembered his name. This was also the man who later became the focus of a McCarthy witch hunt because he correctly predicted the victory of Mao Tse-tung, a "crime" for which he was stripped of duties and livelihood, and publicly maligned. It took him years, fighting all the way to the Supreme Court, to rehabilitate himself and be reinstated—with back pay.

Meanwhile the ivory miniature of Max's mother had done its job, but the mills of the Immigration Service ground exceedingly slow. It took a year and a half until visas were issued, another three months until Max's parents could get passage on a ship. A day before they left London they received a farewell message from the Nazis—a bomb hit a building next door and severely damaged their house. They were not hurt, and managed to pick up their belongings from the rubble. After another delay in New York, they arrived in Berkeley on April 12, 1945, to move into a little house Max had rented for them.

On the same day, another end point was reached. The center-piece of our Office of War Information was the teletype machine, continuously ticking away with news and guidelines from Washington. When an important news item was about to come over the ticker, the machine rang a bell, once, twice, or three times, depending on urgency. On April 12, 1945, the teletype started ringing, and continued perhaps twenty times. When we reached the machine, others were crowded around and we could not read the print-out. The chief, first to reach the machine, was ashen-faced. "All it says," he stammered, "is that President Roosevelt is dead."

We stayed overtime to handle the news, Max to write about the life of Roosevelt, Joe about Truman, others about America's tradition of continuing on a steady course while changing presidents. We looked at each other while typing our stories. No one spoke—we were choked up.

Three weeks later the war in Europe ended.

This was the moment we had waited, worked, and hoped for. The nightmare was over. The world had changed—and so had we.

It was time for stock taking. We didn't want to go back to Europe. Our families and friends were gone. Joe heard that in August, 1942, his parents had been shipped in a cattle wagon to the concentration camp Theresienstadt following a prostate operation on his father. Joe's father died on arrival at the camp, his mother three months later. Vienna was a graveyard of memories, the past too darkened with grief. Self-preservation demanded focus on the future.

We both felt well established in our new country. We were married, Joe had a child, and Max and Charlotte intended to have one. Max's parents had arrived. We had work, friends, were citizens, had voted. We thought of anchoring by buying our own homes.

Many people we knew owned houses in Berkeley. It didn't seem out of reach. Once we scraped together the down payment, monthly payments were no more than rent; eventually we would own our homes. Judith's brothers were ready to help with the down payment, and Max's father had unearthed a distant relative who was willing to give him an interest-free loan; so was ever-helpful Kitty Forester. We began to look at houses. We knew the risks. We still had "war jobs." In peacetimes there would be no Office of War Information, no need for ships. By now, however, we had learned the language, and could chance peacetime work as writers.

Max went on the job-hunting warpath again. Using his chain-introduction method, he investigated possibilities. Joe decided to stay with the Office of War Information, hoping his job would develop into a peacetime position. For the time being, broadcasting to China was more important than ever—the war was still being bitterly fought in the Far East.

Not for long. On August 6, 1945, the war in the Pacific also ended. San Francisco exploded with cheering, shouting people. Almost everyone seemed to be swinging a bottle, and the effects were soon evident. Men, especially those in uniform, hugged and kissed passing women, chanted, yelled, turned over streetcars, smashed parked automobiles. It became uncomfortably similar to street scenes in Vienna on the day of the Nazi takeover, except that the mood of celebration was not directed against us.

We were troubled about atom bombs, which destroyed two cities in two short attacks. We didn't know much about this awesome force but had forebodings that one era of violence had come to an end and another was about to begin.

But our desire for peace and a normal life was stronger than all forebodings. We both continued looking for houses, and Max for peacetime work. He discovered a small financial newspaper, the *Daily Commercial News*, which regarded itself, without justification, as a western *Wall Street Journal*. He knew as much about stocks and bonds as he had known about Manchuria, but was able to talk the editor into hiring him for reporting on speeches given at business lunches, editing commercial releases, interviewing company heads, and maintaining a channel to the Chamber of Commerce. He enjoyed reporting on one aspect in the busy port of San Francisco: international trade. Here the parochial concerns of San Francisco businessmen broadened into interest in the world at large.

The war was over but, surprisingly, the Office of War Information continued. One important story was the birth of the United Nations in San Francisco. Delegates from all over the world wanted to make real a dream we all shared. Joe, the "expert in sabotage," was sent to interview former underground leaders from Yugoslavia, France, Norway, the Netherlands, now official delegates to the United Nations. One was Georges Bidault, later president of France. He presented Joe with his autographed photo. Joe dug out his old autograph books and collected signatures of such world leaders as Field Marshall Jan Christian Smuts of South Africa,

General Carlos Romulo of the Philippines, Paul-Henri Spaak of Belgium, and V. K. Wellington Koo of China.

In December, 1945, we both found suitable homes, not side by side as we had dreamed, but both in Berkeley, no farther apart than we had been in Vienna.

We were each making a living but still did not feel secure. Max as a financial editor was in a field he knew little about and did not see his job as a career. Joe held on to his work at the Office of War Information, where there was talk about its becoming a peacetime agency, but we had our doubts. We started to spin again, not about stories but about our future work together. We knew now that our kind of short story was not suitable in the United States. Horch placed few, and only in minor publications—not a basis for supporting two families. We had to find another strategy.

We asked ourselves as so often before: how can we put to use what we specifically have to offer? As always, the answer seemed obvious once we had thought of it. We lived in one of the most attractive areas of the world. People everywhere wanted to know about the American West—our first jointly published story years ago in Vienna had been about Indians in New Mexico. The European press, including German and Austrian publications, soon would be open to us. True, the German-language press was in shambles, and most of our former battlefields of glory, including the *Neues Wiener Tagblatt* and the Rob publications, no longer existed. But the German press still existed—largely produced under American auspices. Besides, we could submit articles in English to countries whose newspapers employed translators.

We decided to establish our own feature agency, writing reports about people, places, and events on the West Coast—"facts," written in the readable style we felt was our strength. We had little trouble agreeing on a suitable name: Pacific Features. This described what we had to offer. It retained the initials of Peter Fabrizius, which felt good.

First contacts with former outlets in Switzerland, the Netherlands, the Scandinavian countries were soon established, but payments were low. As before, when we were still in Vienna, these fees provided little more than pocket money. But we no longer lived with our parents, we had our own families to support. In Max's case, the situation was reversed: his parents now lived with him.

We kept our jobs while building up our feature agency. We could now in good conscience sell the same story several times—nobody in Switzerland minded if the same feature was published in Sweden.

Material was plentiful. The local press provided leads, Joe's Office of War Information broadcasts on cultural events could be rewritten for our private purposes, and Max's work with the *Daily Commercial News* offered opportunities for feature articles on economics and industry. We felt the thrill of creativity, establishing our own enterprise. We celebrated every new conquest, and cultivated regular subscribers. Among them was the *Delphian Quarterly*, a Chicago-based publication of the Delphian Society, a national organization that sponsored women's discussion groups and published articles on education, science, and literature that would stimulate discussion; the Swedish magazine *Industria*, which published articles based on material that Max came across in his newspaper work; and *Aufbau*, a German-language weekly published in New York with a West Coast supplement for which we became correspondents.

The activity was great, but the income small. It was clear that much work and patience were needed to build our mini enterprise. We had to hold on to our jobs, insecure as they were. Max did not know how long he could last in the unfamiliar (and to him basically distasteful) world of commerce. And Joe did not know how long an office of "war" information would last in peacetime.

The decision was made by the U.S. State Department. It changed the name to Office of International Communication (later renamed "Voice of America"), but curtailed its activities. The San Francisco Division was dissolved and a token force of its Far Eastern language sections was transferred to headquarters in New York. Most of the agency's writers lived in San Francisco and didn't want to move. But it provided an opening for Joe if he wanted to apply for the transfer.

We had long discussions, the four of us. Joe had no leads for a job in San Francisco, and he and Judith were expecting their second child. Judith was homesick for her relatives and friends in New

York. Eventually we decided that a temporary separation had advantages. Joe would use his presence in New York to widen the scope of Pacific Features by introducing himself to the many small special-interest magazines with editorial offices in New York. This would build up our feature agency and, when it was strong enough, Joe would return to Berkeley.

Joe applied for and was granted the transfer. One last obstacle was finding a place to live in overcrowded New York. An ad in the *New York Times* helped—a swap was arranged with a family who owned a house in Brooklyn.

In July 1946 Joe boarded a plane with a handful of other Office of War Information writers. Judith and Wendy would follow in September. This was Peter Fabrizius' only voluntary separation.

* 11 *

From Surviving
to Living
1946–1948

JOE

Personal history repeated itself: Harry Freud and his ever-useful car picked me up at the New York airport and took me to the family in Brooklyn with whom we had arranged our housing swap. Harry had been in the U.S. Army in Europe and brought an Austrian wife back to America. He told me about the strange coincidence that Sigmund Freud's grandson Anton served in the same British parachute division as George Bryant (Breuer), grandson of Josef Breuer, Freud's oldest collaborator. During the last phases of the war the grandsons of these two Austrian pioneers of psychoanalysis had jumped side by side, as British paratroopers, into Austria.

The house in Brooklyn was drab, utilitarian, on a gloomy street. I realized how spoiled I had become during those four years in California. Other New Yorkers told me how lucky I was to find a house in the city, but I did not look forward to bringing up our three-year-old Wendy in these surroundings. She and Judith were to join me in two months. I had been told the house was near a playground. It turned out to be a little square of asphalt, with a swing and a sandbox. Not a blade of grass anywhere. No tree grew in this part of Brooklyn. It was July and sweltering.

The commute in a tightly packed subway to my office in Manhattan was a far cry from the comfortable train ride across the

Bay Bridge, when I used to read the morning paper and occasionally play chess with a co-rider. My work, however, was even more challenging than it had been in San Francisco. The Office of War Information had become the "Voice of America," part of the State Department. It was a strange feeling to be a member of the same government agency that had placed so many obstacles in the way of my coming to this country, and I marveled that it now allowed me to be one of its spokespersons. Our responsibility was to present America at its best, and I had no compunctions in doing that.

Only much later did I learn about the State Department's role in interpreting immigration laws as narrowly as possible (permitting consuls, like the one in Antwerp, to make granting visas practically impossible) and its tendency toward anti-Semitism. But in July 1946 I felt grateful to the United States for having helped free the world from Nazism, for having accepted me, however hesitantly, and for having provided me the opportunity to gain a foothold, however arduously, and start a new life.

It was my job to scan newspapers, magazines, and wire reports for material showing the positive side of the United States. I was assigned to the English section, the core of the division that fed features to all language sections. There they were translated into the various languages, including Chinese (we had brought two Chinese translators from San Francisco) and even my native German. I was now an American writer!

One bonus of my job was that I had access to material that I used for stories I wrote in my free time for Pacific Features and sent to Max at our agency "headquarters."

Judith and Wendy joined me in September, and our Brooklyn house became a home, not a mere shelter. Wendy was three years old and the world was opening to her. It was a world different from mine when I was three. She became my teacher. She would come home from her nursery school and say, "Daddy, sing 'Baa, Baa, Blacksheep'" or she would ask "Tell me about 'Jack and the Beanstalk.'" I consulted her books. I played games with her I never knew. ("Daddy, do pat-a-cake with me.") I realized that you don't enter a new culture through cotton mills, shipyards, and offices but through the country's songs, stories, and games. I went to market with the little pig, and with Alice into Wonderland. For my child, through my child, I became an American, three years after my official naturalization. I wrote up this experience in a story I published in *Common Ground* magazine, under the title "Today's Foreigner—Tomorrow's Ancestor," my favorite theme.

On November 30 our second daughter, Claire, was born, another leaf on our family tree. After the hot summer came a freezing winter. Our house was heated with oil, and there was an oil shortage. Twice we could not get oil and the pipes froze. We had to move to a hotel with the children. Judith was not happy in her native New York, and we considered packing up and moving back to California.

Here were two dilemmas: Our house in Berkeley was occupied by the people from Brooklyn, and, more decisive, I had an ideal job in New York, and no prospect of work as a writer in California. I had no other skills, and we now were a family of four. Even Max, so fabulously successful in finding work with newspapers in three countries, went through a desperate struggle. Our feature agency still was in its infancy and helped with additional income, but it certainly was not sufficient. I had to stick it out in New York.

My position at the International Broadcasting Division was not secure. In the spring of 1947 a heated debate developed in Congress over whether shortwave broadcasting should be sponsored by the U.S. government. There was a widespread feeling that government broadcasting interfered with private enterprise, and that our office should be abolished. Eventually Congress decided to fund international broadcasting by the State Department, but only for one year, and to review the question again in 1948.

Because I had been living hand-to-mouth for the past eight years a year seemed sufficient security. I threw myself into feature writing—for my office and for Pacific Features. The world was beating swords into plowshares and this brought crises as well as opportunities. In my work with the State Department we stressed the opportunities, which agreed with my personal views. America pioneered a new age—more sophisticated industrialization, expanding uses for chemicals, plastics, atomic energy. New production methods created jobs for the returning veterans, new building methods created prefabricated housing as we had created prefabricated ships. Scientists showed new ways to solve old problems.

Articles, ideas, drafts, corrections, final versions flew back and forth between Berkeley and New York, at five cents an airmail letter. This was a novel, transcontinental cooperation of Peter Fabrizius. Our targets were scattered throughout Europe, South America, Australia, Canada, and the United States. I discovered that even the stinginess of Congress in providing funds for international broadcasting had its silver lining. Since the language sections did not have enough money to hire their own script writers they contracted with freelancers. I made arrangements with our German section to order from us features about the American West. I also found that the U.S. Army had an office in Washington that supplied articles to the American-controlled newspapers and magazines in Germany and Austria. We contributed specially written features to that office. The editor of a new Austrian monthly published in New York, *The Austro-American Tribune*, commissioned me to write a column of satirical comments, a welcome relief from the serious features. Horch also got into our act. We finally wrote "facts" and he placed some articles in American magazines.

All this, and family life. When I came home from work, Judith often reported sayings by Wendy, which I shared with Max ("I was afraid. I know because my belly tasted funny," or to a playmate: "I don't like you any more, not even next week!") As July approached, we decided to rent a summer home. Judith's friends found a little house at Greenwood Lake (New York) where she and the children stayed and I visited weekends. We dreaded the return to Brooklyn and were lucky to find an apartment in Queens. The rent was higher than we could afford but by subrenting one room we managed.

Another icy winter of discontent—the coldest in memory, we were told. The news from Max was not encouraging. He lost his job at the *Daily Commercial News*, was trying to live on Pacific Features, couldn't make it, and was on one of his intensive job-hunting rampages. Although we longed to be together, he warned me: stay where you are, the job situation in California is very poor.

But my job situation in New York was also precarious. The ax fell and chopped off the entire English section of the International Boadcasting Division. Congress decided to turn over all English shortwave broadcasting to private companies—CBS and NBC. The foreign-language sections were left in government control, but reduced funding prevented any chance for employment in the German section.

Neither CBS nor NBC was prepared for shortwave broadcasting. Each corporation announced it would hire two writers from our office. Fourteen applied. This was the perfect excuse to go West again, but since there was so little hope for work in Berkeley, I did the "reasonable" thing and applied too.

It was a peculiar situation. All fourteen applicants had to take a test. Each was handed a sheaf of wire reports as they had come over the teletype, and told to write a five-minute news report. I had never done this before. I was a feature writer. As I faced the batch of copy and my typewriter, I felt relieved. I knew I couldn't do it, and I wanted to go back to California. I didn't want to pass, but there was this old treacherous voice that had pushed me so often into doing what I felt was duty.

I looked over the material and, relaxed, began typing. We were allowed one hour, I handed in my news broadcast after forty minutes. The next day my boss congratulated me. I was one of four to remain in New York. I would be on the news staff of CBS.

Surely, if I had wanted the job badly, I would have tensed up and never made it. I happened to see my personnel file a few months later. It contained my news broadcast, with a scribbled remark, saying: "A pretty good news spread from a dull day. Writes good features, too." It was a boost to read the note. But in all the time I worked for CBS I never had to write a news broadcast.

I had a wonderful time writing features for CBS. My immediate boss had no experience with shortwave writing for abroad, and was not really interested. We still received guidelines from the State Department, but on the whole I was on my own. I had a CBS press card, was granted interviews, attended press conferences, and wrote features, for CBS—and separate versions for Pacific Features for Swiss and Argentinian papers, the *Delphian Quarterly*, and other publications. Everything was divided fifty-fifty just as the articles Max wrote in San Francisco, mostly about economic topics. The San Francisco correspondent of the *Christian Science Monitor* also accepted our contributions.

But the pull to Berkeley became stronger. Having seen the Promised Land of California, I felt New York was no place to bring up children. They played on the street. People huddled on tiny patches of grass in the midst of asphalt, to catch a ray of sunshine. Coney Island and other places of "fun" were nightmares. In Berkeley we had our own little house, with a backyard, our own swing, and a playhouse I had built for Wendy.

There was another consideration. For the past year we had been working on bringing a cousin of mine, Irma, to the United States. She had been able to reach England from Vienna on a domestic visa and had been a "maid" until England entered the war. She was bombed out twice in London, and fled to a small town in Scotland where she earned a living as a dressmaker. Her brother, Arthur Steiner, was with the American occupation forces in Munich where he worked for the U.S.-controlled German press. She felt alone, and we were in need of a substitute grandmother for our children, who would never know their grandparents. We wanted to reunite the remnants of a once-large, extended family. Now, since emigration from Europe was no longer a matter of life and death, many restrictions were removed. Although my income was skimpy for a family of four, my affidavit of support for a fifth was accepted. Because there was no longer a desperate run on the consulates by the endangered, quota numbers came up faster. Shipping was again available. Irma wrote happily that she would arrive in New York in early April.

Judith by now had all homesickness for New York out of her system and longed for California. She realized my job difficulties, and did not press me to make the decision. To live in our own home in Berkeley, with our expanding family, and be reunited with Max was a great temptation.

I considered the pros and cons of moving back to Berkeley. A number of publications abroad printed our contributions regularly. Max had cultivated publications for articles on economic subjects. *Aufbau* would take an article every two weeks for its West Coast page, the *Delphian Quarterly* a story four times a year, the *Austro-American Tribune* once a month. I discovered that a radio station in Toronto broadcast twenty-minute radio scripts of humorous sketches, and we rewrote a few of our old short stories into radio pieces. We could count on them to take one every month or so. Then there were a number of trade magazines that took stories whenever we had something in their field. They ranged from *Iron and Steel* to our pet, *The Popcorn Times*. We rediscovered that incidental information could be worked into a full-blown story—a familiar practice since we had turned finding a button into our first short story and Max had converted a Shanghai telephone directory into an article for the *North China Daily News*. A routine item on milk delivery to a prison made me follow up this lead and sell a story "Milk Goes to Prison" to the *American Milk Review*, which thus was added to our list of prospective clients. We later focused the story on the West Coast, and wrote another feature, "Milk Goes to Alcatraz."

Besides, with increasing frequency we contributed West Coast features to the German section of the "Voice of America" and to the Army, which controlled newspapers, magazines, and radio in the American zones of Germany and Austria. With these prospects for Pacific Features I was tempted to risk our return to Berkeley. But I was not sure if such a move would be an act of courage or foolishness. I sensed that New York was still part of my running away, of being the refugee. New York linked me with the past, California with the future. New York was survival, California was living. The time had come to start living.

I remember an evening with old friends from Vienna. They were struggling to build careers and openly said that I was crazy to give up my job at CBS and return to California without any prospects.

"What are you going to do there?" one asked. "You cannot live on sunshine."

"We'll have our Pacific Features," I responded.

"Oh yeah," he said, and added sarcastically, translating "Pacific Features" in a facetious way: *"Ihr seid halt zwei schöne friedliche Gesichter"* ("You are two beautiful peaceful faces").

But the pull was too strong. Judith backed me when I finally came to a decision. She would work as a secretary again. The children could be put in a nursery. And so on April 5, 1948, I walked into my boss's office and announced my resignation.

He was matter-of-fact, wished me well, not aware what a momentous decision it was for me. I'll never forget my feeling of triumph when I walked out of his office. Only much later did I realize that at this moment a new person was born. All my life I had done what other people wanted me to do. I had studied law because of my parents, left my country because of Hitler, become a published writer because of Max, even married Judith on the recommendation of a friend. I had yielded to outside influences, well-meaning or otherwise. This was the first time that I took a stand, truly my own against all "reasonable" advice. For the first time, I made my own choice. I had no idea where it would lead but it felt glorious.

A few days later I picked up Irma at the port of New York. Although she was my first cousin I knew her less than my other family members. She was twenty-two years older than I, had lived most of the time abroad, been widowed twice, and had fled to London from the Nazi threat. Now, at sixty-one, she looked for a quiet life with our reemerging family.

It was a tearful reunion. She told me about the bombings and her struggle to make a living as a dressmaker. "I'm so glad to be here," she said.

I told her, "We're going to California."

Irma immediately assumed her part as grandmother, spending much time with the two girls, who were delighted with her undivided attention. Irma was a gourmet cook and offered to do our meals, an offer Judith gladly accepted. I still commuted to New York where I wound up my career as a script writer for CBS.

On Friday, April 16, I received a telegram from Max: "Drop everything. Come at once."

I made reservations for a flight on Sunday. The family would follow when I knew what it was all about.

* 12 *

The Tale of Two Jobs

1946–1948

MAX

After Vienna and London, Peter Fabrizius was separated for the third time. Joe broadcast the virtues of America from New York, and I reported on speeches made at creamed-chicken-and-peas luncheons with businessmen in San Francisco. It was sobering to see their parochialism, their preoccupation with profits, their indifference to (and mostly ignorance of) the world abroad. I carved a narrow ledge of common interest by concentrating on world trade. On one occasion the State Department wired the editor of the *Daily Commercial News* for permission to shortwave broadcast a series of commentaries on world trade I had written. Sure enough, Joe was behind that request. I had sent him the clippings, which he maneuvered through the proper channels. Thus articles from an obscure local paper were beamed to the world. It was the word "commercial" that determined the policy of the paper—and my disgust with it.

I was glad to have the job but I knew it was only a bridge until I either found something more to my taste or Pacific Features could sustain two families—a long shot.

The paper was a good listening post for stories and made me aware of publications interested in world-trade subjects. At the San Francisco consulates I saw foreign-trade magazines that looked like good targets, and I sent stories ("Pacific features") directly to them. I developed a firm correspondent's relationship with the prestigious magazine *Industria* in Sweden, *Arbetsgiveren* in Denmark, *La Semaine Economique* in Paris, the *Evening Post* in Wellington, New Zealand, *The Eastern Economist* in New Delhi, India, and trade journals in western Europe and South America.

At the same time local dailies (*San Francisco News, Call Bulletin*), trade journals (*Shipping Register*), and magazines (*San Francisco Life*) were hospitable to Pacific Features contributions. I joined the Press Club and attended meetings watched over by the club's mascot, sculptor Benny Bufano's famous marble Cat. Although on the fringes, outwardly I belonged to the gang.

Inwardly, I knew I did not belong at all. My turf was the academic, not the commercial world. Far in the distance beckoned the University of California Press.

The end of my excursion into the world of the dollar came suddenly and unexpectedly. The editor of the paper retired. A new editor took over who disliked my international outlook, and, within days of his takeover, fired me.

I had lasted one day at the *Oakland Tribune*, two weeks at the *Washington Times Herald*, two years with the *Daily Commercial News*. The abrupt firing did not seem rational and, as it turned out, only three weeks later, the new editor made other arbitrary and irrational moves. He had a mental problem, and was placed in an institution. In Vienna, Joe had gained a job when an editor had a mental breakdown; in San Francisco, twelve years later, I lost mine for a similar reason.

I was sorry to have lost my income, but happy to be rid of work I detested. I was free—as free as a shipwrecked sailor on the ocean. Now came an interregnum for me, *die kaiserlose, die schreckliche Zeit*, as I had learned in high school ("the leaderless, the terrible time"—when thirteenth century Germany had no ruler and lawlessness stalked the country), the period between jobs, from November 1947 to April 1948.

I was on a double track: seeking approaches to the university and vigorously pursuing the leads we had opened for Pacific Features. Family was pushing. In January 1947 it had grown to three when Anthony arrived; we had carefully planned his arrival to coincide with my "permanent" job. Now I had no job, permanent or temporary. (We did not own a car. When Charlotte's time had come, I took her to the hospital in a taxi.) In addition, Charlotte, who at that time worked for the California Department of Employment, lost her job when this department, which operated under the War Manpower Commission, was newly organized after the war ended. With a new baby at home she would have had to quit anyway. Still, with determined efficiency, she soon took on various part-time jobs at the University, while my mother cared for the child when Charlotte worked, and prepared our meals. But this was not my idea of running a family. I wanted to support it myself. I typed away in my den twelve hours a day. Joe in New York was creating cultural articles, and I was writing economics commentaries for Pacific Features—I actually did better in these anxious months than I had done on a salary. But this free-lancing hand-to-mouth existence did not reassure me—I needed the peace of mind of a monthly paycheck.

Pursuing my double-track approach I wound up with a double result—and thereby hangs a happy tale.

In my free-lancing efforts to open new avenues for placing contributions I made an interesting discovery. The Division of Agricultural Sciences of the University of California published brochures for farmers in specialized areas. I asked the manager of the publications office to let me edit one of those brochures, prepared by scientists who were experts in their specialties but not in writing. He agreed, and gave me a manuscript—on walnuts.

After my expertise on Manchuria and on finances, I had no trouble editing a brochure on nuts. Soon one on swine followed; I developed a tenuous working relationship with Agricultural Publications.

But I needed more. To make additional contacts I signed up as "rapporteur" (glorified unpaid secretary) for a conference on the Far East conducted by the World Affairs Council in San Francisco. Chairman of the conference was Laurence Sears of Mills College, Professor of American Philosophy and Political Theory. But Sears was a man with a broad world view, widely traveled in the Orient and Europe. He had an open mind toward East European countries, and had authored a number of books on philosophy. It was the man and his attitude, his frank face, his natural presentation, which interested me more than his impressive record. I felt as though I had known him a long time, he seemed accessible. Although I had not met him before, I walked up to him after a lecture and asked if I could speak to him. In private, I had to tell him something important to me—but not here.

He showed no surprise at the awkward request. I lived in Berkeley? So did he—would I care to see him, say, next Saturday? He gave me his address.

I felt in my bones that here was a man to trust. This stranger was a friend. He invited me to sit down, but he himself stood by the window and looked out while I talked. And I talked.

I poured it all out: about the lost years after reaching the first career rung at the *Tagblatt* in Vienna; about the little empire I was building with a friend; about hoping to combine writing with an academic career based on my education.

Professor Sears listened. What a rare blessing to experience somebody who truly listens! From time to time he nodded his handsome gray head or briefly murmured ("sure," "true," "what a shame"). I felt secure and on the right track. I sensed that this was a key moment, and that I was being convincing. In all my job-hunting projects, in Austria, England, Shanghai, California, I had developed an ear for those almost imperceptible sounds a person makes who wants to help. Sears, I sensed, wanted to help. And was in a position to do so. I asked him outright: Could he find me a research assistantship at a university?

Despite my confidence, I expected to hear a dozen reasons why this was not possible.

But he gave no such reasons. Nor did he promise anything. He thanked me for the visit (*he* thanked *me*!), and said he would call.

I was all hot on my way home and I "rehearsed backward" what I had said. Did I omit something? Did I say something wrong?

I didn't. I had said it right and I knew it. I also knew that this interview was a milestone and a turning point.

*

Early in April 1948 I received a letter from Professor Easton Rothwell at Stanford University, vice chairman of a Carnegieendowed project at the Hoover Institute, saying that he had been approached by his colleague at Mills College, and would I visit him at my convenience.

My "convenience" was the next day. We had a lengthy interview in which I confirmed the information he had received from Professor Sears. A week later, Professor Rothwell mailed me a copy of a letter he had sent to·the vice-president of Stanford University: "I should like to recommend Dr. Max Knight for appointment as deputy executive secretary in the Carnegie project at Hoover Institute. The appointment is for one year beginning June 15, 1948, at a salary of $350 per month."

The project was called RADIR, which stood for Revolution and Development of International Relations. It was a so-called elite study, research into the backgrounds of the primary political decision makers (members of governments) in five countries—Britain, France, Germany, Russia, and China—between 1890 and 1933. The study was based on reference works, and on close analysis of newspaper editorials in those countries according to a system worked out by Professor Harold Lasswell of Harvard University. I was assigned to study German newspapers (from the comprehensive holdings of the Stanford Library) from the time after Bismarck to the advent of Hitler. At the end of the appointment (it could not be extended according to the terms of the Carnegie endowment), my results and those of four other researchers (for the four other countries) were scheduled to be published in separate volumes by Stanford University Press.

To gild this stupendous lily, somebody was on vacation at the Institute until June 15, and I could freelance until then—beginning Monday, April 19, 1948.

I was about to send a telegram to Joe telling him about this development (we still used telegrams, not the telephone), but something happened to change my wording.

When I returned from Stanford, I received a phone call from my nuts-and-swine manager at Agricultural Publications. A colleague of his, at the Agricultural Information Office of the University, had an emergency and needed a news and feature writer immediately. If I was interested, I could start work at once, next Monday, April 19.

I was born a Gemini. I had lived through many doubles before—my work as Peter Fabrizius while getting a position at the *Neues Wiener Tagblatt*; a foothold in London while keeping a place in Vienna; freelancing with Joe in England while finding work at the *Jewish Chronicle*; trying to build up Pacific Features while starting an academic career. This was another major "double" and more would come. I sent a telegram to Joe. Instead of saying that I had found a job for myself, I merely wired him to come at once. I didn't explain—it was to be a surprise.

It was characteristic of our relationship that I knew he would come. He was about to return to Berkeley anyway, and I knew he was prepared. He arrived Sunday night, and my mother prepared a welcome dinner. I told him that I was expected to start two jobs tomorrow, and that he was going to have one of them. Though he believed in miracles, he was doubtful that my scheme would work. I was flushed with success and was sure we could pull it off.

Next morning, at 8 A.M. sharp, we both appeared at Agricultural Information on the Berkeley Campus of the University of California. It was a two-room office, and an elderly man, smoking furiously, hacked away on a typewriter. He was Harold Ellis, the chief.

He looked up, probably puzzled to see two of us.

"I'm Max Knight," I said. "I know you expect me to start work this morning. Apparently at Publications they did not know that I was not available. However, you need a competent editor at once, so allow me to introduce my friend Joe Fabry who has the same background and qualifications described to you for me." I was so obliging. I would not let poor Mr. Ellis down without help in his emergency.

He actually seemed relieved. He got up and pointed with his pipe at some papers next to the typewriter. "We have to get out a news story about aphid control on roses by 10 A.M.," he said. "Two hundred and fifty words."

He went to the next room, Joe sat down at the typewriter, and I was on my way to Stanford.

We did not know it then, but this was the moment when our true careers began in the United States. My appointment at the

Hoover Institute was limited to one year, but led to a permanent position elsewhere. Joe was to be a replacement for an editor suddenly called away by a family crisis in the Midwest and hence Ellis did not care whom he hired "for a few days."

Joe remained with Agricultural Publications for the next twenty-five years.

* 13 *

Life Begins at 39

1948–1963

JOE

During the summer of 1948 I should have been intensely insecure. I had a wife, two children, and an elderly cousin to support, and a job that could last anywhere from a few days to a few weeks.

And what a job it was! I was to gather material for news releases from the agricultural departments of the university on the Berkeley campus, where basic research was done, and on the Davis campus, sixty miles north. At the Davis campus, called "The Farm," applied research was carried out in fields, orchards, and on livestock. The Office of Agricultural Information consisted of three men. Harold Ellis was an experienced editor, near retirement, newly married to a younger woman, and getting away with as little work as possible. The second man had a daily radio show on agricultural subjects. And I was to supply news and features to California papers to convince the taxpayers, especially farmers, that the Division of Agricultural Sciences was worth supporting. The radio man did not spend much time at the office; he had other radio assignments and used the information I dug up.

The Berkeley and Davis campuses were rich digging grounds. At the Office of War Information and CBS I had relied on ticker tapes and newspaper articles for stories, but now I had to go to original sources, the professors who did the research. I found them delightful people pursuing fascinating work. There was Max Kleiber who showed me the first radioactive cow. He fed her radioactive hay and followed the feed through her body with a Geiger counter to see how much went into flesh, milk, and waste. This helped him determine what feed was most effective for milk cows and for beef cattle. Roy Bainer and his staff of agricultural engineers revolutionized harvesting by inventing automatic tree shakers for harvesting nuts, and mechanical tomato pickers that distinguished a green tomato from a ripe one, which it picked without squashing. Bainer worked with agronomists who developed tomato varieties whose fruit ripened at the same time, so that the machine could pick the entire field at once. There were geneticists who traveled all over the world to find a wild spinach that carried a gene resistant to a disease threatening California's spinach crops. Through selective breeding, that gene was introduced into the highly marketable California spinach. There were the biological control people who prevented a potentially disastrous invasion of giant snails by finding a natural enemy that killed them, making pesticides unnecessary. There were entomologists who studied the language of bees. I had the pleasure of meeting Professor Karl von Frisch from the University of Graz, Austria, who pioneered that study. Though Professor Frisch understood the language of bees, he had difficulty understanding his California colleagues, and I served as interpreter.

I was like a bee myself, gathering agricultural information. Unlike shortwave broadcasting beyond the oceans, where we never knew who listened, writing news releases for the California press was rewarding. A clipping service provided us with my stories as they were printed all over the state. I filled three scrapbooks the first six weeks. I collected the printed releases because I wanted to show potential employers what I could do. I was not too worried. The university was fertile ground for Pacific Features. Ellis permitted me to use the material for national magazines and for publications abroad. Pacific Features produced many agricultural stories that summer. Our articles appeared in specialized journals such as *The American Fruit Grower*, and *Hoards Dairyman*, and in such notable general publications as *Farm Journal* and *Country Gentleman*. Foreign magazines, too, were interested in farming methods that were pioneered in California.

Pacific Features peaked, and I hoped to be able to make a living even after the regular editor returned. But then, just as my temporary job at Rob Verlag in Vienna had become permanent, so did my job at Agricultural Information. The man who left for an emergency never came back. Ellis asked me if I wanted to continue as a permanent staff member.

Did I! I was delighted. Although my experience in agriculture was limited to raking leaves for Mrs. Forester, I felt competent as a feature writer. My high-school biology and chemistry helped. The scientists I interviewed felt my genuine interest in their work and, after initial resistance against what some considered an intrusion, opened up and showed me what they were doing. They sensed my respect for their research and compared it favorably with the cynical approach with which newspaper reporters sometimes hid their ignorance. I, too, was ignorant in many of the subjects on which I reported, but turned ignorance to advantage. I freely admitted when I did not understand the scientific terms, and the professors explained in ordinary language. My rule of thumb was: if I don't understand a term, many readers won't either. Ellis received compliments saying that the news releases were now clearer.

There was one hurdle still to overcome. I received a call from the office of the president of the university and was interviewed by George Pettitt, assistant to President Sproul. Pettitt had heard good things about me, he said. And then he came to the point: I now represented the university—and here I was with my Austrian accent. I knew my job depended on my answer. I told him: "For the past five years I worked for the State Department representing the United States. I think I can represent the university."

He scribbled something on a sheet and a few days later I received my permanent appointment.

On November 6, 1948, I turned thirty-nine. According to folk wisdom, life begins at forty. Mine began at thirty-nine. Again.

After ten years of running, I was safe. I had arrived. Not at a goal but, as it turned out, at a start: to begin *my* life, according to *my* visions, toward *my* goals. But who was I? What were my visions and goals? The value structure on which my early life was based had been shattered. None of the homilies embroidered on wall hangings, supposed to contain eternal truths, stood the test of my experience.

"Do justice and justice will be done to you"—this was not what happened these past ten years. "The foundation of life is the family"—mine had been murdered. "Love thy neighbor"—but look the other way when they are carried off to an unknown fate in the middle of the night. "Father knows best"—mine believed he could survive in Vienna until it was too late. "A penny saved is a penny earned"—for the Nazis who had taken our savings.

I had a home, a new family, job security, yet was restless. While running for my life, the fight for survival had filled my existence and was "fulfilling." But what now? To save our skin is instinctual. Animals fill their days with the search for food, shelter, security. For humans this is not enough. After our animal needs are met, human longings surface. We want to find out who we are and what we can become.

These are philosophical and religious questions. But philosophers like Nietzsche had provided the foundation for the superman concept that ended in genocide. And religion had not saved but destroyed my family. Where was solid ground to build a new life?

Help came from an unexpected source. Wendy came home from kindergarten with disturbing questions. What was this Christmas the other children were talking about? Who was baby Jesus? Why didn't we go to church like the others? And finally: "Daddy, do I believe in God?"

This was a question I would have liked to answer for myself. How could I believe in a God that permitted concentration camps?

At this time we met a couple whose son was in kindergarten with Wendy. The mother was Catholic, the father Baptist. They told us of the Unitarian Church of Berkeley, which accepted everyone, no questions asked. Jews too. In fact, the Jews in Berkeley had no synagogue then and met at the Unitarian church. The minister talked sense, the couple reported, and their boy liked the church school.

Judith and I decided to investigate. We took our two girls to Sunday school, where we were received without formalities. We went to the church building and I entered with misgivings. The word "church" had painful associations. It was the place where "they" went, and in Vienna "they" had evolved from "Christians" to "Nazis." Although the church building was of warm redwood and had none of the symbols and paintings found in other churches, I felt uncomfortable, like a traitor. The organ, the hymn singing, the choir made things worse. When the minister, J. Raymond Cope, stepped to the pulpit in his church robes, I was ready to leave. I looked at Judith. She looked uncomfortable too.

I cannot remember what the minister said that morning but I know he answered questions I had not even known to ask. I remember one simile he often mentioned that provided comfort and confidence for years to come. He said we have a gyroscope inside that keeps its balance no matter how much it is thrown off center. During the past years I had been thrown off center so many times that it was good to know that something within me kept its balance. At the church door, shaking hands on the way out, I told him I was Jewish. His eyes lit up and he asked questions, holding up the line behind us. He made me feel that Jewishness was an asset, quite the opposite from my past experiences.

I was suspicious at first. Was he trying to snare me? I was no great catch, could contribute neither much money nor theological wisdom. The church was full every Sunday, the Sunday school overflowing, they had to rent rooms nearby. What did they need me for? One day the minister told me: "You have gone through a lot. You've had experiences. We can learn from you."

Once more, what I thought was a drawback turned into an asset.

His appreciation of my Jewishness was no ploy. He found something praiseworthy in every religion, stressed common human features rather than differences, and had a special admiration for the Jewish faith, which he credited as being the roots of Christianity. He always spoke of "our Judeo-Christian heritage." I became aware that the essence of Judaism lay in an ethic that had survived four thousand years of suffering, including the destruction of the homeland, the Inquisition, pogroms, and concentration camps, and that was proclaimed by the prophets of whom Jesus was one. Cope made me see religion in a new way: as a universal human longing for a reality transcending the world in which we live and suffer, and which we approach from many directions: Jewish, Christian, Buddhist, Islam, humanist, agnostic, even atheistic.

Wendy, too, came home from Sunday school with answers that satisfied her. Christmas was the celebration of the birthday of baby

Jesus, born to Jewish parents. He was a teacher, a light that still shone brightly, and Christmas was the festival of lights celebrated by other Near Eastern religions. As to God, she seemed to have received answers that made sense to her. One Sunday morning, when we left for church, a neighbor, probably in doubt about whether Unitarianism was a real religion, asked her if God was in her church. Wendy's answer: "Yes, He's there if I bring him along."

Judith and I were both drawn into the activities of the church. Cope learned of my love for the theater and literature, and invited me to review books in a group and lead discussions. His wife found out about Judith's love for music and soon had her playing the Estey mini-organ in the children's worship service that met in the small chapel then newly fashioned by church school parents. We met people with different backgrounds, who shared our search. The gyroscope kept its balance, regardless.

For me, a turning point came when the minister's wife called and said: "The head of the Religious Education Committee has to leave. Would you like to be the new chairman?"

I had never been on any committee, let alone as chairman, I told her. But she said: "I believe you would make a good chairman. Think it over."

This was the first time someone had trusted me with something with which I had never trusted myself. I accepted, and did something which later I found to be a logotherapeutic technique: "acting as if." I acted as if I were competent to lead ten people in establishing a church-school curriculum, a teacher-training program, parent education, and in running a Sunday school. By acting "as if," I became competent.

At the same time, Judith was made co-leader of the worship service for small children. Just as my search for self-esteem came through discussions, hers took the path of worship and music. She joined the San Francisco Municipal Chorus and taught children French and German through fairy tales, songs, and circle games. Cousin Irma took over many of the housekeeping chores.

The year 1950 brought many changes to anchor us in our new life. Our third child—a son, Richard—was born, moving us further on our path to ancestoring. We learned to drive, bought a car, and

I felt as if I had grown wings. We moved to a bigger house since we now were six.

During the previous two years Pacific Features had run on automatic control. Max and I had full-time positions, and the need for extra income was not pressing. We had less time and opportunity to actually work together. Max's contributions were articles for economic and academic journals, mine for farm publications, and there were our old customers in the United States, several papers in Europe, and the German section of the "Voice of America." We still had the refugee mentality that prevented giving up sources of income, and were work-driven nights and weekends. We met often to exchange drafts and manuscripts for final checking.

*

One of my jobs in the Unitarian Church was program chairman who invited guest speakers for evening programs. The university was a reservoir of experts in all conceivable fields. At that time, nine Nobel laureates worked on the Berkeley campus. Among our speakers who later received Nobel prizes were: Wendell Stanley, who told about the secrets of viruses; Glenn Seaborg discussing the atom; Melvin Calvin telling about the origins of life. And on two occasions I invited a young graduate student in astronomy to give illustrated lectures on his vision of the universe—Carl Sagan.

By inviting such speakers I satisfied my curiosity about "reality." I wanted to know how things "really" were. But I understood that even Nobel laureates in physics and chemistry did not have the entire truth. Scientists could explain what things were but had no explanation for the ultimate why. I wanted to explore that evasive why— why Hitler? How could the nation of Kant and Goethe establish death factories for millions? What turns people from good to evil?

Our program committee arranged discussions of the works of philosophers, psychologists, and theologians—Lewis Mumford, Erich Fromm, Paul Tillich. My "search for ultimate truth" induced me to lead a Great Books group for seven years, and our readings ranged from Aristotle to Freud.

Max was wrapped up in his own new world of academic publishing. The output of Pacific Features reflected our widening interests. We wrote articles on the changing city, the ethics of car insurance, how grass makes solar energy available, the Great Books movement, and "How to be Happy in Times of Crisis." The latter, published in *McCalls* magazine, reported about a college girl who had written to famous philosophers and writers for advice. "I want my life to be happy," she wrote, "but also to spend it in a way that will provide some good for others." She received fifteen answers including letters from John Dewey, George Santayana, Albert Schweitzer, Carl Jung, William Faulkner, and Carl Sandburg. If their answers were condensed to two words, they would be: "Be yourself." Good advice for us, too.

All this is not to say that we became brooding philosophers. We still wrote light-hearted articles about the American scene, mostly for the European press. We went on family camping trips, and wherever we went we described the American West—Disneyland, ghost towns, the giant redwoods, gambling casinos—for Pacific Features.

My cousin Arthur in New York was the American correspondent for the German magazine *Quick*, and occasionally called with a quickie request for one of the sensational stories for which his magazine was notorious. A West Coast murder, the first heart transplant in a rabbit, or our favorite—the engagement of a woman who, after a transsexual operation, became male, to a man who by a similar operation had become female.

Max became dissatisfied with such pot-boiler activities. One day, out of the blue he said: "We have written enough for the wastepaper basket. These features for newspapers are printed today, forgotten tomorrow. We have to write books."

"What kind of books?" I asked.

"I don't know. Books that will outlive us—and are worthwhile."

It was a seed that would take years to sprout.

*

My responsibilities at the church increased. I became a member, and eventually president, of the board of trustees. I was "trusted" to help direct the activities of an entire church congregation! One incident remains etched in my memory.

As a consequence of the McCarthy hysteria, the California legislature passed laws requiring individuals, and later organizations, to take loyalty oaths. I had taken one as an employee of the University of California; I saw it merely as a silly duplication of my avowal, on being admitted to this country, not to overthrow its government. A new law was now on the books that required tax-exempt institutions to require employees to sign a loyalty oath or lose tax-exempt status. The question came before the board whether to recommend that the congregation sign the oath. The church struggled to meet its modest annual budget and was in no position to pay the extra two thousand dollars in yearly taxes. It seemed a foregone conclusion that we would sign.

One board member, however, spoke up. He had signed the loyalty oath as a state employee because he had a wife and three children and could not afford to lose his job. But the church, with its six hundred members, he argued, could take a stand. He would be proud to belong to a church that blocked the first step toward thought control, and he believed others felt likewise.

His arguments were convincing. I should have thought of the implications of this oath before.

What followed was an inspiring discussion among the nine church board members, ranging from freedom of religion to the practical consideration of how to raise the extra two thousand dollars every year. The result was a unanimous recommendation that the congregation not sign.

The congregation was not prepared for our recommendation. Most members thought this would be a routine vote. I had written a one-page statement summarizing the board discussion about alternatives. It stated that our decision was based on our belief that "not signing the 'loyalty' oath would be the expression of deepest loyalty to the principles on which our fellowship and this nation are founded." The board decision was attacked and defended.

Finally Fred Wood, a respected member of the congregation, a judge of the San Francisco Superior Court, spoke up. He had come prepared to vote for signing, he said, but after hearing the debate he decided to support the refusal, and he spelled out his reasoning for his decision.

The vote not to sign and to pay the taxes was overwhelming. As we learned later, only a dozen of the twelve thousand churches in California did not sign. Three, the Unitarian churches of Berkeley and Los Angeles, and a Methodist church of San Leandro, went to court. The case eventually went to the Supreme Court where, by unanimous decision, the state loyalty oath for churches was declared unconstitutional. The court case took three years, and the church got the tax money refunded, with interest.

For me that was a perfect example of democracy at its best. I have mentioned it often to people who maintain that one individual makes no difference in a modern state. One man on our board did make a difference: his stand led to a major decision of the United States Supreme Court with consequences for the state of California, and for McCarthyism.

*

Not everything in my life was going well, however. My euphoria with the job at the university waned. Our office was reorganized, news releases were transferred to Agricultural Extension, and I was made editor of agricultural bulletins (what Max had called the nut-and-swine bulletins when he had edited them as a freelancer). I found this work much less challenging than interviewing scientists about their current research. Some of the badly written bulletins gave me a chance to do rewriting, but a well-organized manuscript left me with little to do besides copy editing. My marriage, too, had tended to become stale, and although I enjoyed seeing the children grow up, I often felt irritated by their demands. Writing bread-and-butter stories for Pacific Features turned into a chore; I resented the deadlines. I was in a midlife crisis, and asked myself whether this was all that life had to offer. Would I go on like this for the rest of my life?

Frustration was probably the reason I became more involved with church activities. But after I had done my stint as president, there was a letdown even there. Ten years earlier I would have been happy to be as settled as I was; now I was restless.

At this point something unexpected, and at first even irritating, happened. Judith became "religious" in a way that went far beyond my own "search for truth." Cope had spoken about the difference between "religion" that can become rigid and fanatical and lead to pogroms and killings, and "the religious search" that was beyond denomination, a search for truth, reality. I had heard him but it had not registered. With Judith it had.

She spoke of a "religious experience" and had it confirmed in a private ceremony with the minister, some close friends, and myself. She said something like a credo, about love and forgiveness, then bowed her head and the minister gave her a gift of a simple silver cross symbolizing the transformation. Later she added a Star of David to indicate her continuing commitment to her Jewish heritage.

To my surprise the ceremony affected me too. What I witnessed made no rational sense but for the first time since I had left the shelter of my family I felt I belonged. The term "web of life" came to mind, and I was part of it. I had had a glimpse under the pine trees in the park in Brussels, and it had comforted me. I was grateful to Judith for an awareness I had not had before.

Our relationship after that ceremony was on a different level. When I married her she was rooted, I was floating. She was my guide to life in America. During the ensuing years I had become a leader, and she acknowledged it. Now she led in a new, spiritual dimension. We were both "guides"—we were equal partners.

It was as if I were married to a new wife, with strengthened commitments.

Max was not at the ceremony. His absence was not in protest. It was quietly understood by both of us that the church was not Peter Fabrizius territory.

*

About this time my job situation also improved. My new boss, Bill Calkins, probably as bored as I with agricultural bulletins, got himself extra assignments writing speeches for Claude Hutchison, dean of the College of Agriculture, and for vice-president Harry Wellman and other university spokesmen in agriculture. Calkins would outline a speech, and ask me to get the data he needed to make his points. This allowed me to interview professors again and do research in the library. I was able to dig up some significant or amusing information which I then saw quoted in newspapers; for example, figures indicating that the agricultural income of the state in one year was now greater than the value of all the gold found in California during the gold rush.

Occasionally, when Calkins was busy, he asked me to write one of these speeches myself. My day of glory came in the spring of 1960 when Chief Justice Earl Warren gave the Charter Day address on the Santa Barbara campus of the university. For some reason the regular university speech writers were not available, and the assignment came to Calkins, although this fell outside his area. Calkins had to go on a trip and gave me the task. The only instruction I received was that Justice Warren wanted to pay tribute to State Senator Tom Storke of Santa Barbara, an old friend who had just celebrated his eighty-sixth birthday. This was meager information for a twenty-minute speech. Was it really up to me, a refugee from Vienna, to decide what the chief justice of the United States Supreme Court would say? I thought it appropriate to trace the advancement of science during Senator Storke's life ("When Tom went to school the automobile was an 'impractical idea.' Today, three man-made satellites circle the sun.") I threw in a few ideas of my own. I was amused when the *San Francisco Chronicle*, in reporting the speech, said: "Chief Justice Earl Warren said today that the ultimate role of education in a free society is not to teach but to test democracy. [Democracy] must be maintained by experimentation and probing. The chief justice said that universities must serve as the brain of a free society."

I was proud but also disappointed that Chief Justice Warren had read my speech word for word. Disappointed, because I realized so very clearly that what great men and women say is often what ghost writers concoct. But I was proud that Earl Warren apparently agreed with what I had written.

*

In 1959, when I turned fifty, Max gave me a true gift of friendship. It was a hardbound book with the title imprinted in golden letters on the title page:

ALL ABOUT PETER FABRIZIUS

by Peter Fabrizius

Presented on the occasion
of his fiftieth birthday to Peter Fabrizius
from Peter Fabrizius

Published by Peter Fabrizius, Berkeley, November 6, 1959.

It was a scrapbook of our common work, with a special introduction tracing our "ancestry" from Fabricius Luscinus, mentioned by Plutarch, through an assortment of Fabriziusses (mostly Fabriciusses or Fabritiusses) who were physicians, astrologers, painters, entomologists, and authors, to the contemporary Dutch writer Johann Fabricius, and Fritz Fabritius, the "Führer" of the Rumanian Nazis.

The book contained tear sheets of our stories from the thirty-nine countries in which they had appeared, mementos from the production of our play, a list of universities where our collections of stories were used in German classes; leaflets, announcements, photographs, and anecdotes. The second half of the book was blank, with a note: "Room to grow for the next fifty years."

*

Shortly after I passed my half-century mark I became assistant editor of *California Agriculture*, a monthly journal reporting current research. This assignment was more interesting than editing bulletins, but the editor let me do only routine tasks, and often changed what little I was allowed to write. I realized how thin was the line between self-confidence and self-doubt. My work at the university, the church, and Pacific Features had boosted my ego. Yet when the editor rewrote my contributions, without explanation, I was devastated. I always felt how much I missed editing a magazine. The happiest period of my professional life was when I was in charge of the Rob Verlag publications in Vienna. Whenever I could I edited a magazine of my own. I published a little mimeographed newsletter for the church school, and later a monthly sheet for the West Coast region, called *WREN* (Western Religious Education Newsletter). When Calkins took on the editorship of *ACE*, the magazine of the American Association of Agricultural College Editors, he asked me to help. I became so active editing and writing that Calkins let me be in charge of the publication. But my heart was set on becoming editor of *California Agriculture*. Calkins promised me the job when the present and ailing editor would retire. Shortly afterward Calkins changed jobs and a new director took over. In 1963, when the editor of *California Agriculture* retired, I reminded the new boss of Calkins' promise, but another man was hired. I did not even remain assistant editor of the magazine.

This was a blow. With Calkins out of the picture, all hope of taking over *California Agriculture* was gone. Putting commas in bulletins was no challenge.

Then, as so often before, something happened that pointed me to new directions and turned everything around. Looking back I see that not getting the job as editor of *California Agriculture*, far from being a disaster, was the best thing that could have happened.

* 14 *

Breakthrough

1948–1963

M A X

On the day Joe started his "temporary" job as newswriter in Agricultural Information I started work at the Hoover Institute (now Institution) at Stanford. The interregnum was at an end. I had finally landed at the edge of academia. No one talked about profits and dollars—except how to spend them. Hoover was well-funded, my work delightful. Again, as in London, I could use my German. By now I was fluent in English and found it rewarding to use my bilingualism. My associates (researchers for the other four countries) were exceptionally pleasant to work with; all became distinguished scholars. The head of the project, Professor Rothwell, hovered over me like a guardian angel, encouraging and protective, and I was fond of him from the moment we met—I felt about him as I did about Professor Sears.

Many interesting persons walked in and out of the great tower on the Stanford campus where the institute was housed. I specifically remember two visitors.

One was a fine-looking, well-dressed man (the institute secretary in announcing him placed her finger on her lips and whispered "he is first class") with the bearing of a diplomat. He conversed easily with us on a person-to-person basis, although his status was far above ours. He was the Washington head of the RADIR project. His name: Alger Hiss.

The other was a ruddy-faced, hang-jowled old gentleman, who slouched into the atrium of the Hoover Tower to be feted on his birthday. A flower-decorated, thronelike chair had been placed there, and the entire staff assembled in a half-circle to listen to a warm birthday eulogy. The head and eyelids of the honored guest became increasingly heavy until both drooped while the speaker rattled on. But, as a sleeper on a train wakes up when the train stops, our celebrity awoke when the speaker stopped, rose, and answered in well-turned phrases which contained no allusions to the unheard speech but had the polish of a thank-you he must have made on similar occasions. The name of the birthday guest: Herbert Hoover.

I liked my work, my associates, the Stanford campus atmosphere. There were two clouds on the horizon: the job would end after a year; and it was in Palo Alto, two-and-a-half hours by train from Berkeley. Despite my Americanization I still had not yet graduated to a car.

I did not mind the trip but I had to think about what to do when the year was over. Working at a university, my old hankering for an academic career became strong. In San Francisco I attended a UNESCO conference, that swarmed with academic people; I wrote to Harold Small, editor of the University of California Press, expressing the hope that during the past seven years somebody was able to solve the complex problem of finding room for a desk; and I talked with Professor Rothwell.

I told him that, when my Hoover appointment expired, I would continue building my feature "empire" with my friend, but I also wanted to qualify for an academic career if our enterprise should not be fully successful. I wanted to enroll in a Ph.D. program at the University of California in Berkeley, in international relations— with the aid of a research assistantship.

Professor Rothwell did what Professor Sears had done: he approached a colleague, the head of the Political Science Department at U. C., Professor Peter Odegard—the third in my three-star constellation of sponsors.

My reception by Professor Odegard was as encouraging as my

meeting with Rothwell and Sears had been. Was I available for studies at the university? I wasn't—my appointment at Hoover ran for many more months. Well, it would do no harm to apply for a research assistantship anyway—none might become available for a long time. And I should look for some backing.

I applied at once. I obtained the backing of Professors Sears, Rothwell, Boodberg (my teacher in Japanese in 1942/43), and Hans Kelsen, my much-revered teacher at Law School in Vienna, now professor of political science at Berkeley, truly a galaxy of supporters.

In the spring of 1949 an assistantship became available and my Ph.D. program in Political Science/International Relations could start. Odegard asked me which I would choose, Stanford or the University of California?

I was not going to give up the Hoover appointment nor to pass up the chance at Berkeley. I was a Gemini, I would ride two horses. First I talked with Rothwell and received permission to come to Stanford only two to three times a week, and work the rest of the time at home. Then I talked to my prospective U.C. advisor who told me I could pursue my studies without attending many lectures: I could take a "reading course"—study assigned books on my own—and be examined at the end of each semester.

So far so good. Actually, I rode three horses, because I had to earn my keep as research assistant at the library of the Bureau of International Relations. But things were not difficult there; hours were flexible.

There was a fourth horse, Pacific Features. I had no intention of relaxing in that saddle. In fact, Joe and I made our enterprise official by registering it in a notarized and published certified statement as a partnership.

I did not sleep much in 1948 and 1949. In Vienna we used to say, indelicately, you cannot dance with one ass at two weddings. Here I was dancing at four. It was a strenuous but happy carnival. I did my reading, worked for seminars, and particularly enjoyed those given by Professor Kelsen on international law and by Professor Condliffe on international economics. These seminars provided sources for a number of essays for our feature enterprise. One was seen in abbreviated form by A. P. Giannini of the Bank of America and he requested the full version.

My happy association with the Hoover Institute ended early in 1949. The resulting monograph, *The German Executive, 1890-1933*, was published by Stanford University Press in 1952.

All class requirements for the Ph.D. program were completed by July 1950, including the language test.

At this convenient moment the bubble burst.

One day, the librarian of the Bureau of International Relations told me she heard of a vacancy in the editorial department of the University of California Press!

I had waited nine years for that moment. Finally, somebody must have found space for a desk there! I knew all along that this was the right place for me—just as the editorial offices in Vienna, London, and Shanghai had been before. It was the right place because it combined my interest in writing/publishing and scholarly work.

I abandoned the additional part of the Ph.D. program, the dissertation. Since I had completed the main part of the program I did not even have the feeling of a dropout. The dissertation would have been no problem—ironically, in the following years I helped a number of doctoral candidates write theirs, and even gave a summer course at the university for Ph.D candidates in how to write dissertations. In choosing an academic editorial position in preference to a purely academic (probably teaching) position I secured for myself the best of two possible worlds. I never regretted my choice.

On November 1, 1950, I started work as Editor Second Class at the University of California Press in Berkeley.

It was to be my professional home until retirement, twenty-five years later.

*

Almost ten years had passed since my arrival in America, yet it was only now that I felt my odyssey had ended. Integration into a new country ("Americanization") has two phases: acceptance of the new country by the immigrant, and acceptance of the immigrant by the "natives." The first phase was reached when I became a shipyard worker; the second when I was accepted where I wanted to be. The shipyard, Office of War Information, *Daily Commercial News*, even the Hoover Institute had all been jobs. The Press was the beginning of a career. Finally, in 1950, I was back where I left off with the *Tagblatt*, in 1938. I did not mourn the twelve years; when I reflected on what had befallen so many others in my situation I could only be humbly thankful.

My starting salary of $310 a month was small but regular and budgetable. It was never my ambition to make big money, but it always was my ambition to have a secure income. I earned more as a freelancer during the "interregnum" but was more at ease now. Still, although Charlotte was employed and contributed, and Pacific Features also yielded extra income, we felt the pinch especially when, three months after I started at the Press, Charlotte presented our four-year-old Anthony with a little brother, Martin. The next two summers, when my new colleagues went on vacation, we spent ours "in residence," and enjoyed every minute. We were a large family now: the "ancestor," his wife, two children, his parents, and Vicky, our black dachshund.

For once, I did not have to pretend. I did not have to pose as an expert on Manchuria, a shipfitter, or a financial genius. Of course, I had to learn the ropes. It was my task to edit scholarly manuscripts for publication by the University of California Press. Countless details had to be checked; I was keenly aware that after I had gone over the manuscripts there was no further human eye between them and the printing press. I, newcomer to the language, ironically, was supposed to supervise the grammar, punctuation, style, and even the structure of native authors—university professors. Years later, when I taught classes in writing for publication at University Extension, one American student, after a three-month course, warmly thanked me for what she said she had learned, and added with a twinkle: "Do you know what chutzpah is?" Then, without waiting for my answer she explained: "*You* teaching *us* English—that's chutzpah!"

The first months were rough. I felt insecure and consulted batteries of dictionaries, style books, and grammars before I dared to add or delete a comma. More important than the reference books were my colleagues. I walked a fine line between pumping them for information on usage and not pestering them. I judiciously spaced my inquiries. I kept a noteboook with their answers, to make sure

I would not ask the same question twice. (This notebook eventually became the teaching text of my editorial workshop at Extension.)

*

The content of our Pacific Features articles changed over the years. Just as Darwin's finches at the Galapagos evolved the shape of their beaks according to the food available on the various islands, so our features developed according to the "food" available in our different jobs.

The conditions for our working together were now ideal. We both worked on the campus, and our offices were so close that I could see Joe's window when I looked out of mine. We met every lunch hour, went to the university library for research or to the swimming pool at the men's gym. We walked a stretch of wooded campus on a path we called Peter Fabrizius Way.

We still had what Joe called the "refugee complex," which prevented our passing up the chance to write for a magazine even if it meant writing on subjects that did not interest us. We still contributed to such egregious publications as *Popcorn Times* and *Knitted Outerwear Journal*. The end of that never-letting-go came, strangely, with *The Delphian Quarterly*, for which we wrote stories that interested us—on education, culture, and science—and were used in adult discussion groups. One day, a woman wrote us that she was denied membership in the Delphian Society because she was black. We checked past issues of the *Quarterly*, which regularly printed photos of local member groups. Indeed there was not one black or Asian face among them. We asked the editor about their membership policies. She wrote back, evasively, that they did not discriminate, but our suspicions were aroused. For the next issue we wrote a piece on discrimination, and for the first time one of our contributions was rejected, with a labored excuse. We spent a few soul-searching hours at the university swimming pool, then decided to drop the *Quarterly*. From then on, it was easier to drop other magazines. If we could live without the Delphians we could manage without the popcorn sellers.

Pacific Features kept producing, on a more selective basis. Besides, our old collected Peter Fabrizius stories made their debut in

America, in the original German, simplified, to serve as textbooks for German classes in American universities. Appleton-Century-Crofts published them in two volumes—the same stories that Murray in London kept reprinting. The books were called *Wer zuletzt lacht* . . . (He who laughs last . . .) and . . . *lacht am besten* (. . . laughs best). We imagined the quandary of the cataloguing librarian at the Library of Congress faced with the problem of recording a title beginning with an ellipsis and a lower-case letter. The stories were used in the German departments of Harvard, Princeton, Yale, California, and other universities. One volume was illustrated by Fritz Siebel, the artist who had furnished the supplementary affidavit for my immigration.

In 1953 I edited a book by Professor Lawrence Price, *English Literature in Germany*. It was published by the Press and the professor asked me if I was interested in doing a translation. I was and it was published by the noted house of Francke in Berne, Switzerland. It received devastating and embarrassing notices in the press. "One senses at every turn the compulsion under which Knight labors," wrote the *Journal of English and German Literature*, "when he uses a German idiom foreign to him. His German sounds like a dead language. As a translation exercise for an advanced student the text might receive a good grade; as a book to be read by a German audience it is unacceptable." (I was reminded of a theater critic who once wrote wryly about Siegfried Trebitsch, the German translator of George Bernard Shaw's plays: "Shaw and Trebitsch have one thing in common—neither knows German.")

Had it come to that? Did I no longer know German? The reviewer, deceived by my "English" name, thought I was an American. It was a warning. I had been careless. In my later translations I took those reviews to heart.

Actually, the reviewers were right. I felt more comfortable translating *from* my native tongue than *into* it (the latter being the direction usually taken by translators). I had recently ventured into another unusual translation project, translating German poetry into English. My favorite German poet since high-school had been Christian Morgenstern, who wrote whimsical, grotesque, humorous "nonsense" verses, sparkling with word plays. My first self-concocted poems, published in the youth section of the *Neue Freie Presse* in Vienna, were pale imitations of Morgenstern. I wondered about this extremely popular German poet's standing in America, looked him up in *Cassell's Encyclopedia of World Literature*, and read: "Morgenstern's parodies, punning, and satiric truculence succeeded in creating an Alice-in-Wonderland climate which endeared him to millions of readers throughout the German-speaking world, but which, of course, defies translation."

The "of course" of this entry was a challenge. How much fun it would be to make the encyclopedia eat its words! I wanted to share the poems with my American friends, and I decided to try. I played around with this poem or that, off and on, trying to find equivalent wordplays, to tame rebellious rhymes, and then brought the drafts to the swimming pool. Joe made his Peter Fabrizius comments, a better word here, an improved line there, and I gradually built up a collection of translated poems. I took my time.

*

At this time our relationship was put to a serious, unexpected, awkward test. One day I saw Judith wearing a cross, combined with the Star of David.

Joe lives near the El Cerrito Sunset cemetery, and we often walked in that parklike area for quiet and personal talks. On one of these walks I asked him for an explanation.

What he said was a shock. I was never a religious person. I was raised to be considerate, ethical, moral, honest—all the good adjectives in the vocabulary of a humanistic upbringing. In our assimilated environment, described earlier, my heritage meant little to me. Religion was not discussed. It was not avoided, it simply was not an issue.

Hitler and the anti-Semitic years made me conscious of my roots. I was placed in a category I hardly knew existed. I was arbitrarily made a target, first of ridicule, then of discrimination, deprivation, expulsion, and finally destruction, although I escaped the worst. It was during the years of my flight on three continents that I became defiantly Jewish, in solidarity with the persecuted, in loyalty, in compassion, in acknowledgment of a shared destiny. Jewish diet laws and other restrictions still seem anachronistic to me, and the belief in a caring deity seems almost obscene after Auschwitz. My consciousness of my heritage is political, not religious. I accepted it because I identified with those who had survived the brown scourge and, in supreme sacrifice, established an island of self-respect in Palestine, in a world of hatred and murder.

With this background, I was shocked that Judith wore a cross. It seemed a betrayal of the martyrs who had been targets of such wearers. I did distinguish between Nazis and innocent cross-wearing Christians. Nevertheless, with or without a conjoined Star of David, the cross, since and before the days of the Inquisition, was a symbol that, I felt, was out of place on her.

Joe and I walked up and down the well-tended paths among the dead in El Cerrito. He was in anguish (or so I perceived) about my rejection. I never doubted his sincerity. He shared my feeling of solidarity with a culture persecuted for millennia, and with the haven in Israel, which would have saved millions had it existed during the time when the world closed its doors to them. He, too, had felt the "betrayal" when Judith veered in a direction for which the cross was the symbol. But his long "search for reality" and Judith's religious experience had led him into territory into which I could not comfortably follow, although I could understand that the Unitarian Church allowed him to strengthen his Jewish roots and yet to reach out into a broader, more inclusive area. He compared this position aptly with being an American and yet being part of the United Nations.

We argued, as we often had, about the meaning of such words as "God" and "religion." I was the stubborn heathen, and he was frustrated by my narrow interpretations and rejections. We realized that arguments ran deeper than words, and that we could not resolve them. I knew how important the search was for Joe, and I made up my mind that this argument was not going to raise a wall between us. We had shared a long and battle-tested path, and this difference in attitude was not going to interfere with our relationship.

It didn't. Both he and Judith stuck to their guns and I to mine. I knew that her interpretation of wearing the symbol had nothing to do with "betrayal of the martyrs," and my discomfort was not caused by a sense of such betrayal. She said that the cross meant something different from what it might mean to the world at large. My point was that others could not divine her private interpretation, and that appearance was important in a world where no one lived in isolation. Wearing a cross and saying it is "a symbol of concern for human suffering" was like wearing a swastika and saying it was an ancient Indian fortune symbol.

After our cemetery walk, Joe and I did not talk about it any more—it was not necessary. We agreed to disagree, we accepted each other's position—it was not an issue. Joe himself never wore the symbol. And I, on my part, reflected on what he called renewal of marriage vows, a ceremony many marriages could benefit from. Including my own.

Peter Fabrizius passed the test.

*

With the family complete and a steady living assured I indulged in a luxury I could not afford while struggling for economic survival: seeing the "old country" again. I was not homesick for a land whose people had forced me out; I was not nostalgic for the "gemütlich" Viennese whose "Sieg Heil" at the railroad station on March 11, 1938, still resounded in my ears. What I missed were the glaciers of the Tyrolean Alps and the meadows beneath them (the "Almen"), irrigated by the melting ice, fresh and green all summer. Ever since my father had taken me to the Alps at age four my heart was anchored there.

There are mountains in California too. I hiked them with Charlotte in the summer and skied them in the winter, sometimes with Joe and other friends. I am a life member of the Sierra Club (which had "sponsored" my wife). Yosemite and Sequoia and the redwood country are beautiful and I love them. But they do not move me. Anyone who grows up by the shore is moved by the sea, and those raised in the desert are moved by the desert. I missed the Alps and the meadows. The Sierra Nevada also has "meadows" but they are swampy and mosquito-infested, the wild flowers have names I do not know. Except for a few weeks in spring, there is no natural greenery in Berkeley. The Berkeley hills are dry and barren.

A native once pointed to the brown slopes and said with emotion: "Aren't they lovely, those golden, tawny hills?" To me they were dead—hay, not grass. It all depends on where you walked as a child.

I had hiked in the Vienna Woods every weekend. In the summer the family vacationed in the lake country near Salzburg or the spectacular high country in Tyrol. I always felt a transcendental attachment to the mountains and meadows and on a mountain peak I was full of what Joe called religious emotion. Apparently, what the Unitarian experience is for him, nature is to me. I have always cared for wildlife and wild flowers, and to this day I collect the beautiful crystals I find when hiking.

I wanted to see the Alps again. After two summer vacations "in residence," enough money was in the kitty for the big splurge—for one person. Charlotte understood what the trip meant to me and let me go. With two small children, it was out of the question, as yet, for all to go. We caught up later.

So I went. In Vienna I avoided shaking hands with strangers— how did I know what those hands had done from 1938 to 1945? I had not come to visit the people of Austria; I had come to the mountains—and they were innocent. A few people whom I trusted were still around. When they asked me why I had returned, I said because of the green grass.

I streaked through the Alps from the Vienna Woods to the Grossglockner, the Matterhorn, Mont Blanc. I kept a diary and wrote a long letter to the Sierra Club about my feelings of being back in "my" mountains. When I returned to Berkeley, the editor of the *Sierra Club Bulletin* asked me to write a fuller account for their annual issue. It brought a warm response.

While in Switzerland I made a pilgrimage to the mecca of all Christian Morgenstern devotees. Morgenstern was an adherent of anthroposophy, an offshoot of theosophy (a mystical philosophy with affinities to the Gnostics and Neoplatonists). Its headquarters are in an impressive building, the Goetheanum, in Dornach near Basel. I looked at the symbols and exhibits of anthroposophy with the eyes of a curious tourist, and was fascinated by the library and bookstore that featured books by and about Morgenstern. I wondered whether, one day, my draft translations of Morgenstern would graduate into a published book to be included on those shelves.

On my return to California I continued work on the translation of Morgenstern's poems with drafts on slips of paper to discuss with Joe. I learned much in the process about the translator's art, and formed my own attitude toward the perennial controversy about whether translations should be "literal" or "liberal." It became clear to me that there is no single method, and that some works—here poems—are best rendered literally and others in an interpretive, more liberal version. To illustrate the difference, two poems follow (each in the original German and in English translation), the first more or less literal, the second "free":

Der Lattenzaun	*The Picket Fence*
Es war einmal ein Lattenzaun,	There used to be a picket fence
mit Zwischenraum,	with space to gaze from
hindurchzuschaun.	hence to thence.
Ein Architekt, der dieses sah,	An architect who saw this sight
stand eines Abends plötzlich da—	approached it suddenly one night,
und nahm	removed the spaces
den Zwischenraum heraus	from the fence,
und baute draus ein großes Haus.	and built of them a residence.
Der Zaun indessen stand	The picket fence stood there
ganz dumm,	dumbfounded
mit Latten ohne was herum.	with pickets wholly unsurrounded,
Ein Anblick gräßlich und gemein.	a view so naked and obscene,
Drum zog ihn der Senat auch ein.	the Senate had to intervene.
Der Architekt jedoch entfloh	The architect absconded, though,
nach Afri- od- Ameriko.	to Afri- or Americo.

A liberal translation is needed when the author juggles words. In the following poem, readers familiar with German may appreciate the puzzlement of rendering the step from *hab acht* (actually "stand at attention") to *halb neun* (eight-thirty), into English where the author ignores the meaning and uses only the sound.

Das Gebet	*The Does' Prayer*
Die Rehlein beten zur Nacht,	The does, as the hour grows late,
hab acht!	med-it-ate;
Halb neun!	med-it-nine;
Halb zehn!	med-i-ten;
Halb elf!	med-eleven;
Halb zwölf!	med-twelve;
Zwölf!	mednight!
Die Rehlein beten zur Nacht,	The does, as the hour grows late,
hab acht!	meditate.
Sie falten die kleinen Zehlein,	They fold their little toesies,
die Rehlein.	the doesies.

Of course, there may be objections. I did not translate what was in the original. There are no perfect translations, especially in poetry. Robert Frost says "Poetry is what disappears in translation" and John Ciardi "What a translator tries for is no more than the best possible failure."

Only once have I been able to offer a perfect translation of a Morgenstern poem:

Fisches Nachtgesang	*Fish's Night Song*

```
        —                           —
      ˘   ˘                       ⌒   ⌒
     — — —                       — — —
   ˘  ˘  ˘  ˘                   ⌒  ⌒  ⌒  ⌒
     — — —                       — — —
   ˘  ˘  ˘  ˘                   ⌒  ⌒  ⌒  ⌒
     — — —                       — — —
   ˘  ˘  ˘  ˘                   ⌒  ⌒  ⌒  ⌒
     — — —                       — — —
   ˘  ˘  ˘  ˘                   ⌒  ⌒  ⌒  ⌒
     — — —                       — — —
      ˘   ˘                       ⌒   ⌒
        —                           —
```

For twelve years off and on I tinkered with those poems. In 1962 I finished the manuscript. The University of California Press published it the following year under the title *Christian Morgenstern's Galgenlieder* (later, under the revised title *Christian Morgenstern's Gallows Songs*, in paperback). It was the first book under my name only. But it noted in the acknowledgments: "My life-long pen brother Joe Fabry, with whom I have been sharing the nom de guerre of Peter Fabrizius since our student days, this time lets me gather the glory and the blame for the present effort myself, although he was a patient and helpful godfather as each new verse child was born." The book was favorably reviewed on the front page of the London *Times Literary Supplement*, in the *New York Times*, and in major American, German, and Swiss newspapers and literary journals. *Comparative Literature* commented: "The argument that Morgenstern is basically untranslatable is no longer valid."

These accolades had an unexpected side effect. Up to now I had always been uncomfortable with my adopted anglicized name, which I perceived as inappropriate and artificial; I could not identify with it. Now, when all those journals said nice things about the book, and the *Journal of English and Germanic Philology* inflated my ego by saying that "Knight's" book is "indeed a masterpiece of the translator's art," I began to warm up to that alien Knight and claimed it as my own. Since then I have identified with the name.

After the first printing, the Press adorned the jacket with a wrapper, "Surprise Best Seller!" and the *New York Times*, discussing the poetry crop of the year, included the *Galgenlieder* among its seven selections in its Christmas edition.

Best sellers are rare with university presses, and mine was one only in a limited sense. In 1961, the University of California Press had one authentic, national bestseller admired by millions. By coincidence I played a minor part in the publication of that book. One of my functions at the Press was to read newly submitted manuscripts and write an opinion before the manuscript was sent to faculty members of the editorial committee for their views. In these opinion reports I was conservative and not given to superlatives. But on one occasion, on reading Theodora Kroeber's account of the discovery, by her husband Alfred Kroeber, of the last wild Indian of America, Ishi, I used the word "sensational"—the only time I ever did. I had not known about Ishi before, and so the Press wanted to know my reaction as a reader. I was the first "outside" reader of *Ishi*.

The year 1963, when my first translation was published, was a breakthrough—more translations were to follow. The year was also a breakthrough for Joe, but in a different way.

* 15 *

Meaning is What is Meant

1963 TO THE PRESENT

JOE

In the spring of 1963, my daughter Wendy gave me Dr. Viktor Frankl's paperback *Man's Search for Meaning*. This was the third time Wendy had unintentionally brought me to a turning point. Merely by coming into this world she made me aware of responsibility. As a five-year old she raised questions that led me to the Unitarian Church. Now she presented me with a book that has given direction to these succeeding years.

Frankl had gone through the shattering experience of three years in concentration camps, and perceived the pieces to have a pattern of meaning. A victim of uncontrollable circumstances, he had mastered his fate. As I read the book, I surveyed my own life. Some inmates in the camps were plagued by the same questions that haunted me: Why did it happen? Why to me? Such questions lead to despair because there are no answers. Frankl asked a different question: What can one do now, in this desperate situation? This question did have answers; help other inmates; try to survive for one's parents' sake; plan on eventually writing a book to help suffering people. These answers focused on the future, on hope.

Frankl found freedom in a concentration camp. Not freedom *from* limitations but freedom *to* develop new attitudes. He found a meaningful attitude in a meaningless situation.

I reviewed the past years. I had banged in desperation on many locked doors—consulates, the prison cell in Brussels, Merxplas, but then I had turned my attention to those still open, often with the help of Max. And despair had turned to hope.

I read on. In the book Frankl said that meaning can be found in three ways: by doing, experiencing, suffering. Suffering? I didn't get it. I had found meaning in doing: writing—for fun, to survive, support a family, build a career. Experiencing, yes: theater performances, sunsets over the Golden Gate, friendship with Max, love from and for parents, Judith, the children. But suffering? I thought I had had my share and it seemed meaningless. Suffering, I now read, is a great teacher. I pondered this idea. My daughter Claire came to me, upset over some teenage trouble, a boy or a school problem. We had a father-daughter talk, and I felt wise and experienced. Then it struck me that I was the person I was because I had suffered; it had made me more mature, experienced, sensitive, conscious of living. Was it all worth the pain? I knew that this was not the question. I did not seek the pain to become a "better" person. The pain was unavoidable; my choice was not whether to suffer or not to suffer, but whether to be crushed by suffering or make the best of it. Here was a disturbing, yet comforting thought: without Hitler there would be no Claire. She was probably puzzled by the warm hug I gave her.

Frankl's book left many questions unanswered. I wrote to him, through his publisher, to find out where I could read more about his ideas. He answered from Vienna that he would be giving a lecture in San Francisco the following November and would be glad to talk to me.

He spoke at the Unitarian Church of San Francisco, a good omen. His ideas and Unitarianism had much in common. Both helped people approach reality from individual directions.

At that time Frankl was not well known in the United States. He had been on three lecture tours and had taught at Harvard during the summer of 1961. When I first met him in 1963, his English was not as fluent as it is now after many visits to the United States. He was glad to find someone in the Far West with whom he could speak German, especially his Viennese idiom. He was lively, enthusiastic, interested in a wide range of Americana, from breakfast cereals to the latest fashion in eyeglass frames. He was receptive to my suggestion of starting groups at the Unitarian Church of Berkeley to discuss his ideas. Only two of his books were available in English, and he promised to send me his German publications.

During the following months I received twenty books, and the more I read the more I was convinced that here were the answers many of my American friends were groping for. Frankl was a medical man, he had a prescription for health, not morality. His prescription: A meaningful life is a healthy life. Illness and suffering can be ameliorated, prevented, even cured by finding meaning. He called his method "logotherapy"—health through meaning.

I saw that many problems Americans faced in the sixties were similar to those of the German Jews in the thirties. Families were destroyed, not by Hitler but by divorce, children were yanked out of school and moved away, others came and had to adjust. Discontent, frustration, boredom were widespread. Men complained about the meaninglessness of their work, women about the meaninglessness of keeping house—they sought outside work that also was unfulfilling. Traditional values broke down, not because of Nazi persecution but in the name of progress, higher standards of living, a search for wider freedom—for students, minorities, women, children. Among my neighbors, in the church, in my Great Books group, I sensed frustration and despair leading to alcohol, drugs, and violence. On the Berkeley campus I witnessed student revolts, confrontations, tear gas.

Reading Frankl's books in 1964 I had the uncanny sense that we, Hitler's refugees, were guinea pigs in the study of how to survive chaos, uprooting, and loss of values—problems for an increasing number of people not persecuted by an outside enemy; people not forced into concentration camps, but living in traps of their own making. They felt like helpless victims, within a free and affluent society. They chased after pleasure, success, and these were not always within reach. Logotherapy said: Life does not owe us pleasures; it offers meanings. Those who expect happiness and fair breaks are bound to be frustrated. Meaning is always available, at least through attitudes taken in unavoidable suffering.

I discussed these ideas with Max. He was skeptical. He wanted a clear definition of "meaning." Here Frankl was vague, simply saying that "meaning is what is meant." I too found this circular definition unsatisfactory. But gradually it dawned on me that meaning, as understood by logotherapy, is an awareness that there is order in the universe in spite of all apparent chaos, and that each person is part of that order. I had experienced chaos, and had been comforted in the Unitarian Church by the idea of a "web of life" of which I was a part. This was a religious concept that logotherapy extended to an approach accessible also to the nonreligious. The very vagueness of the sentence "meaning is what is meant" became its strength. Meant by whom? Religious persons saw the meaning-order determined by God. Liberal persons saw it offered by the web of life. My academic friends saw it in terms of the laws of physics, chemistry, evolution; Carl Sagan saw order in the cosmos; environmentalists in nature—the ecosystem; artists in harmony. Frankl called it *logos*, Greek for "the rational principle of the universe." In the Bible passage, "in the beginning was *logos*," it is usually understood as "the word of God." Frankl rendered it as "meaning." To him, meaning is at the center of the universe, calling out to be explored, from any direction.

I had felt this urge toward exploring ever since the rug of order had been pulled out from under me. My friends, too, struggled to make sense of their lives. But meaning was not easily attained; it was like the horizon, always beckoning but receding. Important, however, was not the attainment but the pursuit.

It was, of course, frustrating that Meaning (with a capital M) was never within reach. But there is also an attainable meaning, "the meaning of the moment." Every moment offers meaning to each person in a special way. To respond to "what is meant" by the moment results in a meaningful life.

Most of these meanings are trivial—to get up in the morning, eat when hungry, drive safely. Some are deeper—to comfort a child, express love to one's spouse, help a friend. In my race for survival I had faced many moments that required a meaningful response— from ducking into a doorway to writing short stories in prison. Some responses had lasting consequences: to marry, have a child, ask for a transfer to New York, quit CBS and return to Berkeley. It was not always clear until later, and sometimes never, whether my choice had actually been "what was meant"—not taking the train to

England with Max after Hitler's takeover, leaving my parents behind, reporting to the Brussels police instead of hiding.

I tried these ideas in discussion groups, and the response convinced me that Americans were a ready audience. Frankl's German books, however, were heavy reading, full of medical and philosophical terms, long Teutonic sentences sprinkled with Greek and Latin words. He needed to write an easily understandable book that would summarize his thinking for the American reader. I offered to ghostwrite, translate, collaborate, but working with Frankl was not as simple as with Max. In fact, he was a very difficult collaborator. When I proposed a sentence that placed him in a favorable light, he wrote to say he did not want to sound self-congratulatory. When a sentence sounded critical, he was angry because he did not want to criticize himself. When I simplified his ideas he flew into a rage and was likely to throw out a whole chapter because of one paragraph. Had I not strongly believed that it was "the meaning of the moment" for me to bring his ideas to Americans I would have given up. I suffered through a year of frustrating correspondence, but through this mail dialogue I learned much about logotherapy.

In 1965 Judith and I decided it was time to visit Europe. The children were grown—Richard, the youngest, was fifteen—and we had enough savings for the trip.

I had a great desire to see Vienna again. In my effort to piece together my life, there were gaps that could be filled only by facing the memories of my youth. I knew it would be painful but I looked forward to revisiting my old hunting grounds, the Vienna theaters. Besides, I wanted to talk to Frankl directly about our book project.

To see Vienna again was a Rip van Winkle experience. The city was the same; streets, building, parks, even the stores in my old neighborhood had not changed much. But the people were all strangers. I never saw a familiar face on the streets. And there always was the thought in the back of my mind: these strangers on the street, in coffeehouses and theaters—what did they do during the Nazi period? Did they betray, beat, murder my parents? I did not want to feel that way but could not help it.

One incident helped me overcome this burden. I had written a high-school classmate that I would be in Vienna. Our stay coincided with the monthly get-together of our alumni, and he notified classmates of my coming.

The meeting was in a restaurant room. Judith was the only woman present, and we visitors from America were something of an oddity. One classmate tried to impress me with the hardships he had suffered during the war. He actually declared, "You refugees had it good, you did not have to be here during all this bombing and starving." While I weighed an answer that would not break up this short reunion, the door opened and Otto entered the room.

I had been told about his career. Otto was the success story of our class. Although a mediocre student he had become *Sektionschef* in the Ministry of Justice, a position second only to the minister. When he entered, the others jumped up to offer him their seats. He came straight to me and sat on the chair next to mine. He was impeccably dressed and groomed. After some introductory chitchat he said: "I never come to these get-togethers, but I came today to thank you."

Mystified, I asked why. "Without you," he said, "I could not have made my career."

This was even more puzzling. I could tell this was a serious matter to him. At the final written high-school exam, he explained, he could solve only one of four math problems. Two were required for passing. I was sitting in front of him and he had asked me for help. I had sneaked him the solution to one of the problems.

I had no recollection of this incident. I knew that those final high-school exams were a nightmare. Still, I did not understand. After all, they could be taken again. He shook his head. "You may not remember, but once the test is flunked, this becomes part of the record. It's a black mark."

I do not know if this was so. He obviously believed it, and he, after all, had to know because he was the man who drafted bills for the Austrian parliament.

We chatted amiably for a few minutes, then he shook my hand, thanked me once more, and left. I knew Otto had been active in a Nazi youth organization when the Nazi Party was still illegal in Austria. And now, he went out of his way, twenty-seven years later, to thank a Jewish classmate for an act of kindness. Otto's action helped me not to judge people collectively. It was a lesson about guilt and reconciliation.

And about honesty, but in reverse. I had done something that I always told my children not to do—cheat. Yet, the cheating had been the basis of Otto's career, at least he thought so. A good example that the "meaning of the moment" may fly in the face of accepted values.

Meetings with Frankl were instructive and infuriating. He took me to the Poliklinik hospital where he headed the neurological ward, and demonstrated applications of logotherapy on various patients. We discussed questions at length, my visits to his home were private seminars. The infuriating part came when we talked about the book I wanted him to write. It became clear that he did not want to do it. I had brought drafts along for a book that would be a series of dialogues. I would ask questions, he would answer. He was helpful in explaining everything, but balked when it came to putting it on paper. He wanted to load everything with footnotes, references, and qualifications. How I wished I could replace him with Max! Frankl was an individualist, unsuited for collaboration. He realized this himself, and finally, after one of our wrangling sessions, said: "You are a writer—why don't *you* write this book?"

It seemed the right thing to do. My work at the university had become routine, and I was still resentful at not being editor of *California Agriculture*. Writing articles for Pacific Features had also become stale, and I agreed with Max's challenge to write books of lasting value. A book on logotherapy would meet that qualification but it was clear to me that it would be a major break in our collaboration. We were, at that time, working on the translation of three comedies by the classic Austrian playwright Johann Nestroy, "the Austrian Aristophanes," whose word plays in Viennese slang were a linguistic challenge. As the name Peter Fabrizius had proved to be not particularly suitable in the United States, we decided to use our own names in future joint ventures. Max's translations of Christian Morgenstern's poems were published under his own name, with an acknowledgment of my assistance.

But a book on logotherapy would be entirely mine. Max challenged the concepts and forced me to think them through, but had no interest in collaborating on the book. It would be the first time I moved in a direction not common to both. But I always received his unreserved support. In all my subsequent writings on logotherapy he remained my careful editor and critic.

For the time being I followed a double course. With Max I translated Nestroy's intricate plays, approximated in English. When the book was published in 1967 the title page noted: "translated (and fondly tampered with) by Max Knight and Joseph Fabry." Thornton Wilder, one of the few Americans who understood Nestroy in the original, wrote a foreword. He had appropriated one of Nestroy's comedies as basis for *The Matchmaker*, later adapted as *Hello Dolly*. One might say that *Hello Dolly* was a grandchild of Johann Nestroy. (In the mid-1980s, the same Nestroy play was again appropriated, by Tom Stoppard for *On the Razzle*.)

During the time I worked on my logotherapy book, I accompanied Frankl on a lecture tour in the San Francisco area. One evening, after a lecture, he was approached by an official from San Quentin prison: an inmate had read Frankl's *Man's Search for Meaning* in the prison library, and it had changed his thinking. Could Frankl possibly see him? To my horror, he immediately agreed. I had to reshuffle a carefully laid-out schedule of interviews and professional meetings to make room for that visit to San Quentin.

Frankl talked to the prisoner about guilt. Guilt was not to be ignored or repressed, nor was it to be wallowed in. A person can be transformed through the experience. If it is not possible to right a wrong, it is still possible to help others in the area that produced the guilt.

For years I felt guilt that I had not saved my parents. I had done what I could, but it was not enough. I failed where others, including Max, succeeded. My emotions welled up in unexpected moments. Scenes in movies and plays where fathers see their sons after a long absence upset me. Once I attended the installation of a judge who had come from Vienna to the United States as a child, and when I shook hands with the judge's mother after the ceremony, I broke into tears. There was a scar, and opening the wound would not help. There were no hidden secrets to uncover—there were meanings to *discover*. I discovered them in the prison library listening to Frankl's talk with the inmates; I would use my guilt to

209

give others the help I did not give my parents. Logotherapy would give me that opportunity.

I concentrated on writing my book, selecting ideas from Frankl's writings and shaping them into tools for American readers. At the same time I continued working with Max on translations. In a letter to Max, Bertolt Brecht's son Stefan wrote that he had read the Morgenstern translations—would Max participate in translating some of Brecht's collected writings? Max asked me to collaborate, which appealed to me because of my interest in the theater. Ralph Manheim, the editor of the project, assigned two Brecht plays to us: *Schweyk in the Second World War* and *Turandot*.

In 1967, Judith and I visited Europe again. On this occasion we looked up Judith's cousin in Warsaw, and on the way back stopped in East Berlin to talk about *Schweyk* with Brecht's widow and literary executor, Helene Weigel. We flew in from Warsaw and called her from the East Berlin airport. She asked us to see her at once because she was leaving the next day on a tour with the Berlin Ensemble, the theater she had directed since her husband's death. It was the old Theater am Schiffbauerdamm where the *Three Penny Opera* was first performed in 1928.

Helene Weigel prepared sandwiches and sweets and served tea but she did not waste time on chitchat. She wore a heavy army coat, although we were in her apartment and it was summer. She looked like Mother Courage, a role she had created in her husband's play. From the window we could see the small cemetery where he was buried under an unhewn rock which simply said "Brecht." It was a remarkable cemetery. In a radius of fifty feet were the resting places of many of his friends and associates: the composer Hanns Eisler; the director of the first *Three Penny Opera* production, Erich Engel; writers Heinrich Mann, Johannes Becher, and Arnolt Bronnen, and nearby that of G. W. F. Hegel, the godfather of Marxism.

Next to Helene Weigel's apartment, in the same building, were the Brecht archives, the reason for my visit. They contained every scrap of paper Brecht had written on during the last seven years of his life. I was interested in going through his notes on *Schweyk* and *Turandot*. Helene Weigel arranged for me to sift through the papers. We did not have permission to stay overnight in East Berlin, and would have to go to West Berlin and return the next day.

Then she sprang a surprise. Two young writers had taken fragments of a play Brecht never finished, and combined them into *Der Brotladen* (*The Breadshop*). It was being shown that night at the Berlin Ensemble, and she had reserved two tickets. Would we want to see it, and perhaps suggest to editor Manheim that he include it in the *Collected Works*? It was an offer we could not refuse. It was drizzling and she had her chauffeur take us to the theater. She handed me fifty East German marks for incidentals because there was no way to exchange currency that late in the day. It was a thrill to see that historic theater, with its gilded rococo ornaments and red plush, converted for Brechtian realism. The play portrayed the unemployed during the thirties. The theater entrance hall was peopled with actors dressed as proletarians and the walls were papered with posters from the Depression years. The play was a crude lesson in economics, Marxist style, with rousing songs and Greek-like chorus of the unemployed. I have never seen a poorer play by Brecht in a more magnificent performance.

When we left the theater it was after 10 P.M. and we still had to go through Checkpoint Charlie to reach West Berlin. There had been no opportunity to spend money, and it was not permitted to take East German currency to the West. I put the fifty marks in an envelope and asked the head usher to return it to Frau Weigel.

This turned out to be a mistake. It took more than an hour to go through passport, baggage, and money control. We finally emerged on the West side, and there was a subway to take us downtown. The woman at the ticket counter asked me for forty West German pfennigs (about fifteen cents) for the fare. I had only American money. No good. The money exchange was at the East Berlin entrance of Checkpoint Charlie. I went back to the East Berlin policeman. Never was it more critical to speak German. He took me back and waited patiently until the woman at the exchange window made the transaction. She could not change American money directly into West German currency. I gave her a dime and a nickel which she exchanged into East German money, a transaction recorded in triplicate. Then she exchanged Eastern into Western pfennigs, again everything in triplicate. My good policeman took me back through the mass of waiting travelers, and I bought two subway tickets—an experience in bureaucracy plus politics.

We had no hotel reservations, and it was nearly midnight. We got off at a station which, according to other passengers, was in a hotel area. We had left Warsaw in the morning and it had been a long day. I left Judith and the suitcases in a coffeehouse and went room hunting. All the hotels in the neighborhood were full. I finally found a small hotel where an old, sleepy clerk said all rooms were taken but some people who had reserved a room had not arrived. I pleaded with the man to let us have it, told him about our long travels and my wife sitting on our suitcases in a coffeehouse. He looked at me and said: "Are you Jewish?"

This was my first encounter in Berlin, the capital of Nazism.

"Yes," I said.

The clerk threw his arms around me. He was a Jewish refugee from Hungary. We got the room.

*

In March, 1968, *The Pursuit of Meaning* was published. I had been a writer, editor, translator, and now I was an author. For the first time in our lives Max and I were writing in different fields. I could not even truthfully mention him in the acknowledgments, but my dedication reads: "To Judith who taught me the meaning of being a husband; to Wendy, Claire, and Richard who showed me the meaning of fatherhood; and to Max who demonstrated the meaning of friendship."

An author is considered an expert in his field, and after the reviews came out I received requests for public appearances. I did not feel like an expert, but I knew I had to respond. On radio call-in programs I received questions from people who felt their lives were empty, were unhappy in their jobs or marriage, felt trapped in situations beyond their control, had suffered losses. Here I was, called up to comfort strangers.

Again, I played the "as if" game. I acted as if I *were* the expert they expected me to be and over the years I did become a person who felt he could really make a contribution. I tried to avoid psychological jargon. I was amazed how many incidents from my own life I could use to illustrate logotherapy guidelines: move away from feeling like a helpless victim, concentrate on areas where you can master your fate and take responsibility; don't try to go through locked doors, attend to those that are open, or can be opened; don't dwell on the mess you're in, but see what you can do to get out; don't keep thinking of failure, give yourself credit for achievements. Your will power is stronger than you think—"you don't have to take every bit of nonsense from yourself."

Trite? Perhaps. Some radio technicians and newspapermen made snide remarks, but people who suffered real or imagined distress understood. I was called on a speaking tour to the East Coast. Back in Berkeley, I started groups to apply logotherapy. "Take notes," Max advised. "Soon you'll have another book."

He participated from the sidelines. We had new translation projects, but my main interest increasingly was logotherapy. We did write two articles on logotherapy for Pacific Features, but the number of our feature stories about the American West declined.

In May 1972 I retired from the University of California. Since then I have used my time primarily for lectures, groups, and further writing on logotherapy.

Among my writing projects was one in which Max was to have a new role. I was putting together a book in which logotherapists in various fields—medicine, counseling, nursing, youth problems, aging, drug addiction—discussed how they used logotherapy ideas. Max wanted to publish it. He was thinking about starting a small publishing firm after retirement. We spent a few months spinning ideas about what shape this venture might take, and what part I might play in it. In the end Max found the risks too great and abandoned the project. My book, coedited by two logotherapists in Ottawa and Boston, eventually was published in New York under the title *Logotherapy in Action*.

I have been enjoying my retirement. I had not retired *from* a job that became stale; I retired *to* a new, stimulating career. All the pieces of my life finally fell into place.

I made peace with my past and reconciled it with the present, not without pain. In Vienna it had been painful to visit the apartment I had lived in with my parents, to meet strangers in places where friends had lived, listen to schoolmates on how they managed during the Nazi era—but these were experiences I needed to go through.

Gradually, memories were replaced by current happenings. Judith and I had many touching encounters with people, especially young Germans who went out of their way to do nice things for us, as if to make up for what their parents did to our parents' generation. On lecture tours and in group sessions in Germany we made new friends. Past and present, Europe and America, writing and counseling, all came together.

I made an old dream come true and published my own magazine. I called it *Uniquest*, with the subtitle *The Search for Meaning* for subscribers in Unitarian churches nationwide—a fusion of my two main interests: logotherapy and unitarianism. Published semiannually, each issue had a leading topic—sharing groups, ecology, Schweitzer's philosophy, values of the 21st century. I found contributors among Unitarian ministers, lay people, and also well-known authors who allowed me to reprint edited versions of their articles and lectures. Among them were Schweitzer's daughter Rhena, Jonas Salk, Herbert Spiegelberg, Robert Bellah, and Maggie Kuhn. One entire issue discussing logotherapy was occasioned by the establishment of the "Frankl Library and Memorabilia" at the Graduate Theological Union in Berkeley. Dr. Robert Leslie, curator of the library, and I put on a Festival of Meaning, at which a number of Frankl followers gave lectures and seminars. The event concluded with an address by Frankl at the University of California.

The success of the Festival of Meaning demonstrated the broad appeal of Frankl's thesis. I tried to persuade Frankl to establish an institute of logotherapy in Vienna that would disseminate his philosophy and methods. He resisted, saying that an institute would water down and falsify his ideas. He wanted people to be informed about logotherapy from his own books and lectures. I argued that this was not enough. A teaching, training, and information center of logotherapy was needed. We had lively discussions, many on the Rax mountain where he did rock climbing. There he was relaxed and more open to new ideas.

One day, after a heated discussion during a long hike, Frankl stopped in mid-sentence and said: "Why don't *you* establish an institute?"

Ten years before, he had challenged me to write a book. I had done it, and it had enriched my life. But this project was different. I didn't know anything about establishing and running an institute. I did not need more work. My retirement life was full—writing, translating, editing, conducting seminars and workshops. I was approaching my seventies, was twice a grandfather; my trophy shelf had grown: my books, translations with Max, chapters on logotherapy in college texts, *The Pursuit of Meaning* in nine languages. I taught classes at University Extension; I was not ready to take on additional tasks.

But the thought appealed to me. A new departure, a challenge to do something I believed in. I invited people to come to discuss possibilities—counselors, educators, a lawyer, a businessman. We sat in our living room, spinning. We talked about bylaws, articles of incorporation, membership fees, a board of directors, and supporting all this was the enthusiasm to create something I was convinced was needed.

We discussed the function of an institute. What interested me were plans to teach and to publish. My Extension classes had shown that young people wanted guidelines to a life meaningful for *them*, not dictated by some outsider. In emptiness or doubt they reached for drugs or alcohol, engaged in indiscriminate sex, tended to violence, even suicide. I often thought that if I could start all over again I would be a teacher. Well, perhaps it was not too late.

We talked about publishing newsletters and a journal, and this whetted my appetite. Some people volunteered to take care of aspects of lesser interest to me, such as legal and financial matters. We needed a headquarters, or at least a mailing address, and a way to make it known that the Institute of Logotherapy existed.

During my talks with Frankl in Vienna I learned about a one-act play he had written in 1945, shortly after his release from concentration camp. I translated the play into English for the opening event of the institute, performed on the stage of the social hall at the Unitarian Church. Here, three of my interests merged: the Unitarian Church, logotherapy, and my love for the theater. I found a director, we held casting auditions, church volunteers built the scenery and made the costumes. I went to the Salvation Army and picked out the shabbiest clothes for the camp inmates.

We had several sellout performances in January, 1978, secured a core membership for the institute, and netted a few hundred dollars to print leaflets. We rented a room at the Unitarian Church as headquarters, and offered sharing groups for applying logotherapy.

I transformed *Uniquest* magazine into the *The International Forum for Logotherapy*. The lead article in the first issue was an interview with Frankl, "Aspects and Prospects of Logotherapy."

We have an editorial board from seventeen countries. Editing the journal has given me "meaning" over the past years. Paradox: If I had been made editor of *California Agriculture*, as I had desired, I would have been in charge of a magazine that didn't interest me. By *not* getting the position and, disappointed, turning to logotherapy, I eventually became editor of a magazine of personal significance. I turn to Max for editorial advice and help in translation. When deadlines threaten, I know I can rely on him. We still check each other's major writings.

*

Writing for Pacific Features has come to an end. Our twice a month contribution to *Aufbau* was the last assignment we gave up. I continue to write theater reviews from the San Francisco area for that paper. I am also play reviewer for *Die Buehne* (The Stage), the leading Austrian theater magazine. Although play reviewing is only a small part of my present activities, it gives me satisfaction because it goes back to my earliest interests.

The times of Peter Fabrizius short stories are long past but their spirit is alive. One example: On one of our trips to Europe, Judith and I visited Dresden in East Germany. An American woman heard about our visit and turned to us with a strange request: She had been sent from the Corning collection of Harvard University to buy the remaining samples of artificial flowers made by a Dresden professor who, at the turn of the century, used a special method of creating glass flowers using wax. These flowers were in the possession of the man's niece, an elderly ailing woman who lived in a shelled-out house. She was offered what was, for her, the astronomical sum of five thousand dollars. The American buyer made the mistake of asking for official East German permission to export the glass flowers, and was refused. She wanted to smuggle the box with the flowers out of East Germany but was afraid because now her name was known to the authorities. She heard that we were going to drive across the Czech border—would we take the flowers along? She would meet us in Marienbad, our destination. This was the stuff

Peter Fabrizius stories were made of, and it set my mind going round. If questioned at the border, I would say that these flowers were an heirloom of my wife's family and cherished by the family as a fertility charm! I was bringing them from America to a cousin in Vienna who, in her late thirties, could not have a baby. This was to explain why we carried a box of glass flowers all the way from California to Vienna. To support the story, the old lady gave us a box with a label from Montgomery Ward.

It seemed a crazy plan, and was done mainly to help out the old Dresden woman who would be able to live in comfort on the five thousand dollars for the rest of her life. I never will know whether my Peter Fabrizius story would have worked at the East German border. I never had the opportunity to tell it. We had the box in full view on the back seat of the car, and the control officer barely glanced at it. He thought the flowers were plastic and waved us through. The story, though never used, had a happy ending.

In 1980 the institute sponsored our first congress of logotherapy in San Diego. Since then we have arranged international congresses in Hartford, Connecticut; Regensburg, Germany; San Francisco; Toronto, Canada; and Buenos Aires, Argentina. Through the congresses and lecture tours I made friends in many countries. Outstanding are Dr. Elisabeth Lukas and her husband Gerhard of Munich, Germany. Lukas is the prize student of Frankl, now has her own Institute of Logotherapy in Munich, and has written several books in German; I translated two into English for our Institute of Logotherapy Press, established in 1984. Lukas gave the keynote address at our second international congress in Hartford, and she and her husband arranged the successful third congress in Regensburg, attended by more than seven hundred people. Next to Max, she is the closest collaborator I ever had, though our collaboration is mostly limited to my translating her German articles and texts.

In 1983 we established logotherapy offices in downtown Berkeley, and I have regular office hours. When I am ready to retire a second time, I shall again want to explore something new. I have crossed many frontiers; there are still some ahead.

* 16 *

Webster and the Bible

1963 TO THE PRESENT

MAX

I see the earlier years of my life in historical terms: the early happy writing years, the struggle for survival, the consolidation, and the era of my chosen profession. I think in terms of events and geographical sequences: the Continent—England—The Big Trip—Shanghai—California. I think in terms of individual years, even individual dates, milestones.

But the later years, the sixties, seventies, eighties, coalesce. These were the years when all the strands came together and, for better or worse, formed the person I am.

During those years, too, Charlotte's professional responsibilities developed from performing odd part-time jobs on the campus at the time when Anthony was born to the highest nonacademic positions attainable at the university, as administrative assistant to Professor Clark Kerr, director of the Institute of Industrial Relations and later president of the university, and to Professor Thomas Blaisdell, director of the Institute of International Relations. In later years she became interested in education and civic affairs, which led to positions in the Berkeley School District. She was widely recognized for her volunteer work in a senior health clinic, and she was a member of the City of Berkeley Commission on Aging. The cute flower-in-hair hostess of the nineteen forties grew into a well-organized, busy, mature woman.

As our children grew up, Charlotte and I took them to the green Austrian and Swiss Alps. "Look, Dad," Anthony called out when we wandered on a huge grassy expanse, "they have wall-to-wall meadows here!" And, waving his arms like the wings of a bird, and deeply inhaling: "The air is like peppermint!"

In 1966 my audience for initiation into the wonders of the Alps grew beyond the family. I proposed and scouted the first Sierra Club trip to the Alps, and in 1967, via chartered plane, led more than a hundred members to the glacial peaks of my youth. I arranged the tour with members rotating in three countries, Austria, Switzerland, Italy. They were surprised that even in the high mountains they did not have to tote sleeping bags and tents. Unlike the Rockies and the Sierra, the Alps have a large network of shelter huts, where you can stay overnight and also buy simple meals. Charlotte and the children participated in that expedition.

The response was so encouraging that the Sierra Club now arranges Alpine trips every summer. David Brower, then executive director of the Sierra Club, commissioned me to write a book about the Alps. *Return to the Alps* was published in 1970 by Friends of the Earth, which Brower founded. The photographs were by a Bavarian I met at the International Book Fair in Frankfurt, where I represented the Sierra Club and its books.

Some of what Joe calls my "religion of nature," inherited from my father, I bequeathed to our children. When Anthony was old enough, Charlotte and I took him to an international boarding school high in the Swiss mountains facing the majestic Wetterhorn. There he was in direct touch with the natural elements and with children from other nations, and so acquired a view of the United States "from the outside in." Martin followed a few years later to the same school. And—to make a big jump in time—Anthony's child, now three, is already registered to attend when she is old enough.

As the years passed, I began to feel more secure at the Press. I had found a niche where I could be myself, no longer an amateur on Manchuria, finance, and Bismarck. I recognized the value of clear presentation for communication. Time and again I was confronted with manuscripts containing valuable information in muddled, imprecise, redundant, often insecure and therefore pompous language. Increasingly I gained respect for the printed (and spoken) word. Editing matured into a general approach to living.

Joe teases me, saying I edit everything—sorting shirts in the dresser, stacking plates in the dishwasher, arranging my mineral collection in the display case. I plead guilty, and can only hope that I can tell the difference between pedantry and system. I am uncomfortable with messy writing and a messy kitchen, intolerant with messy thinking and a non sequitur answer to a question.

To Joe, order is equally important. He sees order on a more transpersonal level. To him, meaning is an order, a "web," of which we are a part. To me, order is in our minds and affects everything we do. We both trace order back to *logos*. Joe likes to quote the Bible, "In the beginning was *logos*" translated as "meaning." I translate it in the traditional sense: "In the beginning was the Word." We are both concerned with meaning—the meaning of life, and the meaning of communication. Joe quotes the Bible and I quote Webster. I believe—I am biased—that a good editor who explores and then identifies the true meaning of the word and helps authors present their information in a common-sense, natural sequence, simply and unpretentiously, is likely to be a good gardener, a good travel agent, a good job hunter; and also a good researcher in academic work. Language is the vehicle of communication. A person who thinks clearly will write clearly; a sloppy thinker will be a sloppy writer. Whoever created the harmony of the universe was a good editor. Here Joe's *logos* and my *logos* come together. In his *Pursuit of Meaning* he actually speaks of God as "a good editor."

In the beginning was the Word, and also at the end. The Austrian writer-critic Karl Kraus, who was one of the authors we translated, maintained that all evil comes from sloppy writing and speaking. Kraus could have qualified his pronouncement, but never mind, he had the guts to stick his neck out. If you want to make a point, you will make it more forcefully if you relegate qualifications to a later discussion. In my work as editor I have seen many scholars muddy their argument by making timid qualifications. The most frequent last-minute change I was obliged to make (as a result of requests from the author when the manuscript was already in page proof) was the addition of "usually" or "almost" to make a statement safe from criticism. For a scientific work, qualifications are indispensable. But in a general profession of faith, the writer should take risks and see whether he can get along without qualifications.

I have learned the wonderful precision and versatility of the English language. In England, I had to have translators; at the University Press, at first, I had to rely on the goodwill of my colleagues to teach me the rules and to correct awkwardnesses. Gradually I learned to express myself idiomatically and confidently. And finally—what irony—I could face native speakers and teach them how to use their language.

I taught my Editorial Workshop with the passion of a crusader. I preached the gospel of clear thinking/writing like a zealot. The students, many for the first time, were facing an instructor who used the taboo words "right" and "wrong." Students acquired standards and thereby confidence in themselves. I liked my subject and had excellent rapport with the students. They responded and, in turn, spread the gospel of the word. Many attained positions with publishers, universities, or government offices, and after a few years I had missionaries in many publishing houses throughout the greater San Francisco Bay Area. Some senior alumni (mostly alumnae) from the workshop, now in advanced positions, sent their junior editors to my class, a second generation of believers.

It was a joy to kindle their enthusiasm for good communication and their disdain for erosion of English. Wilson Follett, author of the standard stylebook *Modern American Usage*, cited "irregardless" as a characteristic barbarism; Webster's third edition, meekly speaks of it as merely "substandard." In our class, we did not participate in this illiterate decline. To us, "irregardless" remained a barbarism, "media" and "data" remained plurals (*regardless* of "visa" and "agenda" having become acceptable); "bimonthly" remained ambiguous, and therefore was to be avoided. We cannot prevent the insensitive use of "data" as singular, but we will not help validate it.

I fondly remember the human encounters with authors during my twenty-five years with the Press. Half of an editor's job is concerned with the manuscript, the other half with the author. An author often regards his editor as an antagonist, a meddler, a smart aleck who thinks he knows better. The editor has to win the author's confidence, convince him that both have the same goal: to produce the best possible book. Each has a different expertise: the author knows (or should know) the subject and the editor knows (or should know) how best to present it. A Nobel laureate in physics does not necessarily know how to write for easy reading. At first, many authors were suspicious, some outright hostile. I have met many "enemies" who, to my deep satisfaction, parted friends.

There was Raymond Cowles, an eminent zoologist, who made trail-blazing discoveries, spending days in a camouflaged tree house in South African preserves observing animals. He told of watching a male crowned hornbill immuring his mate in a tree hollow until only a beak-wide hole connected her prison with the outside world. Then Cowles' attention was diverted when a monitor lizard emerged inexplicably from a termite hill. At this point a white rhino entered the clearing from the edge of the forest. Back to the hornbill, the male was feeding the female through the hole while she was laying eggs in the hollow. Cowles scribbled everything in a notebook, climbed down, and typed his notes without organization into a "book." For seven years every publisher turned his manuscript down. I suggested assembling notes about birds in one chapter, amphibians in another, and so on. He balked and insisted on his presentation, apples and oranges all mixed up, loose ends on every page. "Your observations are all scattered around like the colors of a Persian rug," I said in dismay.

"But I *like* Persian rugs," he countered—which I should have foreseen.

He finally relented, resentfully, but refused to cooperate, instead letting me do all the reorganization as well as the editing. He did not talk to me until the book was published and favorably reviewed on the front page of the *New York Times* book review section. He became a friend and sealed the friendship with a Zulu headdress for our children.

Another enemy-turned-friend was J. C., a high official of the California penal system. When he handed me his manuscript about prisons, he said that editing would be a formality—he was an "anthologized author" (an article of his had been included in a symposium). When he picked up the edited manuscript and saw pages black with penciled emendations, he stalked out of the office without a word, and slammed the door. I heard nothing from him for weeks. Then, an officer from the Probation Office in Oakland called. He had received an order from headquarters in Sacramento to ask whether I could give a series of seminars to probation officers on how to write readable probation reports. Mr. J. C. would have me picked up in Berkeley and driven to Sacramento once a week. He had studied the emendations, accepted them, and now wanted his staff, addicted to governmentese, to go through the same experience.

Professor Franz Schurmann, a linguistic genius, labored for years on a manuscript, based on between-the-lines readings of Chinese, Japanese, and Russian newspapers, on ideology and organization in Communist China. The manuscript stood more than two feet high. I worked on it for a year, mostly eliminating duplications and overlappings. When the author picked up the edited manuscript, hundreds of little pieces of paper were attached to the pages, indicating duplications. If they were eliminated, the manuscript would be no more than five inches thick. When I explained, he blanched. What? Throw out more than half of what he had so laboriously assembled? He ripped off the slips and threw them in the air from which they fell like snowflakes at Christmas. Then he stormed out.

I picked up the slips, one by one. I had written the page numbers on each of them. In a few key places I had marked the explanations also on the pages themselves.

Early the next morning, in marched a pale, unshaven linguistic genius. He had spent the night checking on the (relatively few) marked places in the manuscript and had verified the duplications. Now he wanted to know where he could find the rest in his tower of a manuscript.

I gave him the slips, he took them home and revised the manuscript. When the book was published, it was a bombshell in the State Department. He invited his friends to a lavish self-prepared gourmet Mongolian dinner in the garden of his luxurious home and I was one of the guests.

Even my cherished mentor, my old teacher in Vienna and Berkeley, the always amiable Professor Hans Kelsen, scowled when I presented him with the translation of his *Pure Theory of Law*. This celebrated work on legal philosophy, *Reine Rechtslehre,* originally published in German in 1934, caused waves in law schools throughout the world. It had been translated into every conceivable language, except English because of a copyright conflict. When the conflict was finally resolved in 1966, I was allowed to do the translation.

The original was written in the cumbersome (although structurally perfect) scientific Teutonic style, the bane of every student and translator. There were no inaccuracies, careless passages, or oversights, but sentences were endless, some taking an entire page. There was no condensing—every word was important. But I divided the sentences into shorter units.

No, said Kelsen. The sentences form logical units; they can't be broken up. "But the reader will be out of breath before he gets through one of these monsters. The logic is not broken when parts follow each other. Why won't you make it easier for your students?"

"Because," Kelsen retorted, "I have learned my lesson. Reviewers opposed to the *Pure Theory of Law* will quote passages out of context, which is easier to do with broken-up sentences. Faced by the whole sentence, including the qualifications, they are at least forced to show by ellipses that they left out something."

I had no substantive answer to this argument, but he accepted an editorial suggestion: we divided the long sentences by semicolons. In this way the package between periods was held together, and the reader was allowed to breathe.

This episode was not typical of Kelsen's attitude toward reviewers. He showed an Olympian indifference to what they said. When his intellectual testament, *What is Justice?*, was published and enthusiastically discussed on many pages in one of the foremost journals, I telephoned him. No, he had not seen the review. Did he want me to send him the journal or did he want to come and pick it up?

"No-no," he said.

"No-no what? What do you want me to do?"

He wanted me to do nothing, and he would not come to pick it up. "The reviewers," he explained, "either approve of my theory or they don't—and I have heard it all. A review doesn't count."

"So what *does* count?" I asked exasperated. "Footnotes," he replied. "What counts is that other scholars cite you in their works." This was the man whom the dean of the Harvard Law School, Roscoe Pound, called "the greatest scholar in international law and jurisprudence of the century."

His attitude was no affectation. I found out that he held ten honorary doctorates, but they did not mean much to him. "Is there any honor that means something to you?" I asked.

"Yes. They named the Graduate Social Science Library on our campus after me. I was very touched by that."

I loved to pump him for episodes of his life. On one occasion Kelsen told me about his conversations with Sigmund Freud, with whom he spent a summer in Alt-Aussee. Kelsen, walking with Freud along the path by the lake, asked whether Freud thought psychoanalysis was effective as a cure. Freud, according to Kelsen, although deeply committed to human welfare, did not see himself primarily as a doctor but as a researcher who wanted to know the truth. "*Ich will wissen*," Freud told Kelsen.

On another occasion I asked Kelsen how he came to write the constitution for the Republic of Austria. It turned out he had written two constitutions. In the last days of the monarchy he tried to liberalize the Austro-Hungarian constitution by giving rights to the rebellious nationalities and thus save the throne. But although Kelsen was the legal advisor to the last emperor, Karl, he could not get the young and somewhat naive monarch to study his draft.

A high court official told Kelsen, "Give me that paper. The emperor is in Gödöllö, a famous Hungarian horse stud farm, inspecting his favorite horses. He likes to read detective stories. I'll slip the paper in the book he is now reading. *That*'ll do it."

Well, it didn't. The monarchy fell apart and Kelsen, commissioned by the new republic, had to do it all over.

Working with authors at the University of California Press was a never-ending learning process. The work sometimes extended beyond the author's death. In two instances I completed unfinished manuscripts. Professor Otto Maenchen left papers and drafts about the culture of the Huns—results of a lifetime of research; it took four years to turn those papers, with the help of a dozen scholars in different fields, into the definitive *The World of the Huns*, later also published in a German version.

And Professor Albert Ehrenzweig requested before his death that I complete his draft of a book on legal philosophy—a draft with pencil emendations, some almost illegible, some in German shorthand. The result, *Law: A Personal View*, appeared two years after his death in Holland.

These were rich and fruitful years, and I loved my work. But there was another side to the coin.

Joe and I, after many years in our positions, were frustrated by a general university ruling that reserved top job classifications to those who supervised others. This rule did not fit our situation. Our work could not be delegated and hence we could never become supervisors. But, we felt, it deserved recognition—in title and remuneration—in the form of reclassification.

I argued my case with my director but he ensconced himself behind the rule, professing that he could do nothing.

Then came an important organizational change at the Press. Freelancers were hired to replace staff editors. No one knew how to handle problems resulting from the changeover—there was no precedent. As the senior editor, I was assigned to institutionalize a new system. I introduced various mechanisms, and within a few months the system worked smoothly—in contrast to other presses that made the same change and whose woes were described in the trade journals.

I felt the time had come to make another request about reclassification.

Yes, I was told, it was true, I had performed "executive" functions, but there was the personnel manual.

In frustration I complained to Joe.

What followed was another illustration of the Peter Fabrizius football tossed back and forth. Years ago I had helped Joe to get the chair he was still occupying. Now, Joe returned the favor.

He went to *his* director and told about his own unjustified classification. Quite true, Joe argued, he was not supervising others, but this dry letter of the law made no sense in view of Joe's long-standing superior performance. Of course, he was given the same excuse as I had been, but in his quiet, irrefutable logic he argued that the supervision rule should be waived for independent editors.

He won his case. He *was* reclassified. Bureaucracies thrive on precedents. As soon as he was confirmed, my reclassification could no longer be rejected. I received the title and salary of Principal Editor of the University of California Press.

*

Now that I felt comfortable in English and was able to walk in and out of two cultures through language, translating became an increasingly fascinating game. At the Press I became a one-man department for translation projects. On one occasion I looked over a translation of Paul Klee's diaries; they were already in page proof, and I was supposed merely to give them a last quick once-over. I found *Filzhut* (felt hat) translated as filthy hat, *Lärchenwald* (larch grove) as lark-filled grove, Lieutenant a.D. (lieutenant retired, "ausser Dienst") as lieutenant Anno Domini—and so on.

Joe caught the translating bug. Gone were the times when we had to write just to keep food on the table. We were translating plays and satirical poetry or songs of the kind we loved to write for literary cabarets in Vienna. Nestroy, Kraus, Brecht fit this pattern, and even some classics. A tricky rhymed poem by Heine that begins with the lines

> *Sie saßen und tranken am Teetisch*
> *Und sprachen von Liebe gar viel.*
>
> *Die Herren, die waren ästhetisch,*
> *Die Damen von zartem Gefühl*

we turned into

> *They sat and sipped from their teacups*
> *and love they discussed without end.*
>
> *The men had esthetical hiccups,*
> *the wives a romantic bend.*

The play *The Last Days of Mankind* by Karl Kraus, a scathing indictment of the absurdity of war (the First World War), included a scene showing old emperor Francis Joseph falling asleep at his desk

and singing in his sleep, a *tour de force* only Kraus could get away
with. Kraus even satirized the personal misfortunes of the emperor,
who tragically lost wife, son, and brother, and is reputed to have
said, "Everything happens to me." We translated the first stanza of
the ditty:

> *When I was born to my mother*
> *the world was a terrible mess.*
> *I looked at all that bother*
> *and really couldn't care less.*
> *Wien was a dirndl-and-schnapps burg,*
> *and schnapps was not* my *cup of tea.*
> *Oh, why was I born a Hapsburg?*
> *Everything happens to me.*

There were five more stanzas, all ending in the line, "everything
happens to me." The last stanza:

> *I've heard that ghastly saying:*
> *old kaisers never die;*
> *they spend their time decaying*
> *and fade out by and by.*
> *I hope it's all confusion,*
> *some dreadful fantasy. (Wakes up.)*
> *But no, it's no illusion—*
> *it's really happening to me.*

Joe was not very interested in serious prose works, and limited
himself to reviewing my translations and helping with problematic
passages. Most of my own translations were by-products of work at
the University Press: the correspondence between Richard Strauss
and Stefan Zweig and Hans Kelsen's previously mentioned *Pure
Theory of Law*.

I also translated for other publishing houses, including an essay
by Goethe (incredibly never before translated) on his collection of
Italian Renaissance medals, and an anthology of classic German
poetry (for the University of Chicago Press, in preparation at this
writing). On one occasion I deviated from my cagey resistance to

translating *into* German. Ogden Nash, who felt kinship with Morgenstern, made a record, reading my *Galgenlieder* translations; I "retaliated" by translating a selection of Ogden Nash's delightful poems into German (published by Zsolnay, Vienna), and this time the reviews were more charitable than those of my Lawrence Price translation.

A special challenge was the translation of mildly bawdy fifteenth-century French love poems, found in a precious illuminated manuscript at the National Library in Florence; they were so-called *rondeaux*, twelve lines requiring a fourfold and an eightfold rhyme! My school French necessitated collaboration with a specialist in medieval French, and the translation was published by Chicago University Press (*Monuments of Renaissance Music*, in a series edited by Edward Lowinsky). Here is a sample:

> *I am not such a gallant knight*
> *to function ten, twelve times per night*
> *when with a pretty femme I lie.*
> *I do it twice or thrice, oh my,*
> *and that, I think, should be all right.*
>
> *The other day she held me tight*
> *and sweetly asked for more delight,*
> *but I just said: "My lady, why,*
> *I am not such a gallant knight, etc."*
>
> *(repeat first stanza).*
>
> *She didn't like it and took flight*
> *and left me sitting in my plight.*
> *When people blame me, I reply:*
> *"Those who don't want my love, good-by!"*
> *Then I defiantly recite:*
> *"I am not such a gallant knight, etc."*

*

While I edited and taught and Joe gained increasing recognition for his crusade in psychology, we were as close as a generation earlier. One day we talked about what we would like to be remembered by. He mentioned his writings and editings in

logotherapy, and I the *Return to the Alps*, the translation of Kelsen's
Pure Theory of Law, and my version of Christian Morgenstern's
Galgenlieder. We have different interests but Peter Fabrizius lives on.

On one of our periodic strolls in the El Cerrito cemetery,
standing on a hilly spot overlooking San Francisco Bay, we saw a
new section of the cemetery opening up.

"How about it?" Joe said.

It seemed a logical conclusion—not the surprise ending of the
old short stories but a natural finale—nothing morbid, just a
well-edited ultimate period at the end of the story.

We went to the cemetery office and signed up—two plots, one
for Joe and Judith and one for Charlotte and me, side by side. A few
days later the four of us clambered up that hill and Joe's son
Richard, a fine photographer, took our picture at the site—the first
of four projected. He is commissioned to take the second when there
are only three to be photographed, then a third, and eventually the
last. Sic transit gloria Fabrizii.

*

During the last two years before retirement I duplicated my
Press office at home. I bought the same desk exactly, the same
typewriter, the same reference works. By the time I left the Press I
had expanded my freelancing and continued as before, without a
break. Even before retirement I worked mostly at home in my
"second office," although still on the staff of the Press. That is only
as it should be for a Gemini, no?

Through my years of teaching the Editorial Workshop on
campus, many students came to know me although I did not know
all of them. "How did you hear about this course?" I once asked a
student. He seemed surprised. "Don't you know? You're an
institution around here." Being an institution is convenient. People
come to the "manuscript clinic" without my having to solicit. I have
never been out of work—work that is pleasure. What a blessing to
do something you like and be paid for it! Once a friend, visiting me
on a Sunday when I was editing a manuscript on the sundeck of our
home in the Berkeley hills, said: "This is Sunday. Why do you
work?" Editing is recreation, not work—it is like gardening or
mountain climbing; for Winston Churchill brick-wall building was

recreation, and for Kaiser Wilhelm wood chopping. Joe felt liberated when he left the university to do what he really wanted to do, start a second career. I just went right on.

Now, with my eightieth birthday within walking distance, I have developed a sense of personal history understandable for this stage. I am aware of how little the next generation knows about its elders. The sociologist Professor Reinhard Bendix, with whom I worked on his autobiography, writes that parents may talk about events of their past but will rarely give their children a comprehensive portrayal of their lives. There is no opportunity to do this— when children are small they are not interested, and when they are older they have their own interests.

This is unfortunate in a period of cataclysmic historical events. Life experiences should be recorded not only for the family but also for history. I hear about survivors of the Holocaust with searing memories which, if unrecorded, would be lost to a world that knows little more about the events in the 1940s than they learn from the grisly pictures of stacked bones.

There is ignorance about recent history and also deliberate distortion—voices claiming the Holocaust never took place. Thousands of witnesses with tattooed numbers on their arms walk the earth, but they are old and soon will be gone. What they have seen, heard, and suffered should be preserved—for their families and for posterity.

Once a woman in my class came with a manuscript. She had no writing experience but was deeply committed to putting on paper what her husband told her. He had been four years in concentration camps. She, a gentile, was devastated by what she heard and wanted him to write down what he had lived through. But he could not bring himself to do it. So she literally sat at his feet for months, made him talk, and took notes. What she accomplished was a monument to wifely devotion. She wanted me to help turn those notes into a book. Although meant as a record for the family, the result was so compelling that the book was commercially published.

This was the beginning. Since then I have done volunteer work with many octogenarians and nonagenarians who have difficulty expressing themselves but have valuable, often poignant accounts to leave to the world. I feel a commitment to assisting these people.

And I feel great satisfaction when I finally hold the completed (often self-published) manuscript in my hands. I have made many friends that way.

And so it came about that one day, Joe asked: How about us? We, too, have a story to tell. Why don't we write our own story— a *joint* autobiography?

This seemed an original and splendid idea and I loved it. A Peter Fabrizius duography!

Here it is.

Other publications by the authors

(PARTIAL LIST)

PETER FABRIZIUS

Lisa benimm dich ! (play)
Der schwarze Teufel (short stories)
Der Komet (short stories)
Siebzehn Kamele (short stories)
Wer zuletzt lacht . . . (short stories)
. . . lacht am besten (short stories)

MAX KNIGHT and JOSEPH FABRY

Willy Haas: *Bert Brecht* (translation)
Helen Mustard: *Heinrich Heine* (tr.)
Bertolt Brecht: *Schweyk in the Second World War* (tr.)
Karl Kraus: *In These Great Times*, ed. by Harry Zohn (tr.)
Johann Nestroy: *Three Comedies* (tr.)

MAX KNIGHT

The German Executive, 1850–1933
Return to the Alps
The Original Blue Danube Cookbook
Lawrence Price: *Die Aufnahme*
englischer Literatur in Deutschland (tr.)
Christian Morgenstern: *Gallows Songs* (tr.)
Hans Kelsen: *The Pure Theory of Law* (tr.)
Edward Gans: *Goethe's Italian Renaissance Medals* (tr.)
Richard Strauss/Stefan Zweig: *A Confidential Matter*
(correspondence; tr.)
Ogden Nash: *Der Kuckuck führt ein Lotterleben* (tr.)
Albert Ehrenzweig: *Law, A Personal View* (ed.)
A Florentine Chansonnier in
Monuments of Renaissance Music (tr.)

JOSEPH FABRY

The Pursuit of Meaning   Elisabeth Lukas: *Meaningful Living* (tr.)
Logotherapy in Action   *Wege zur Selbstfindung*
Swing Shift   Elisabeth Lukas: *Meaning in Suffering* (tr.)